THE PREGNANCY COOKBOOK

The Pregnancy Cookbook

Hope Ricciotti, M.D., and Vincent Connelly

W. W. Norton & Company
New York   London

Copyright © 1996 by Hope Ricciotti, M.D. and Vincent Connelly

All rights reserved.
Printed in the United States of America.
First Edition

The text of this book is composed in Berkeley Book, with the display set in Sam Sans. Composition and manufacturing by the Haddon Craftsmen, Inc.
Book design by Susan Hood.

Library of Congress Cataloging-in-Publication Data
Ricciotti, Hope.
    The pregnancy cookbook / Hope Ricciotti and Vincent Connelly.
      p.   cm.
    Includes index.
    ISBN 0-393-31386-7 (pbk.)
    1. Pregnancy—Nutritional aspects.   2. Mothers—Nutrition.
    3. Cookery.   I. Connelly, Vincent.   II. Title.
    R6559.R53   1996
    618.2´4—dc20   95-6383

W. W. Norton & Company, Inc., 500 Fifth Avenue, New York, NY 10110
W. W. Norton & Company Ltd., 10 Coptic Street, London WC1A 1PU

1 2 3 4 5 6 7 8 9 0

For Joey

CONTENTS

Appendices

PREFACE

Not long ago, I would tell my patients to "eat right" while they were pregnant. I was familiar with the concerns and problems of diet and pregnancy, having gained some insights over time by helping patients and friends through nausea, cravings, and changes in their sense of taste. I did not, however, give specific eating tips—just some generalizations like "Avoid fatty and spicy foods and things that you know upset your stomach," "Eat plenty of fiber, and drink lots of fluids if you are constipated," and "Eat bland carbohydrates if you are nauseated; delight your altered palate if you are not."

But once I became pregnant, I discovered that I had no idea what to eat, what not to eat, and even what appealed to me. The *specifics* of eating had become much more important. Could anything make this nausea go away? Which carbohydrates should I eat? Could certain foods harm my baby? Could others help my baby grow strong and healthy? How could I fill that craving for salt and sweets in a sensible way?

Luckily, I was married to a chef whose low-fat, healthy, creative cooking provided the answers to my questions. As a uniquely qualified team, we began planning meals together for our pregnancy. As an obstetrician, I provided the nutritional information that we needed for well-balanced meals that contained the necessary nutrients for a pregnant woman. Since I was also a patient, I made suggestions based upon my many new tastes, cravings, and aversions. Vince worked his magic in the kitchen, and *The Pregnancy Cookbook* was born. I ate every meal in the cookbook during the course of my pregnancy. It was such fun and so delicious that we felt we had to share it with our pregnant friends and patients.

This cookbook is for those of you who believe in moderation. You want to maintain the highest nutritional standards, but you also want to eat food that appeals to you and your family. Pregnancy is no time to become a fanatic. You simply need to get through the difficult times (we'll tell you how) and enjoy the good times by eating well and indulging in some of this book's creative and appealing recipes. Go ahead and treat yourself to an ice-cream sundae once in a while. Just stick to a good diet the rest of the time, and you and your baby will do just fine.

—*Hope Ricciotti, M.D.*

INTRODUCTION

You have just learned that you are pregnant. Your eating habits, while not terrible, could use some improvement. You have a basic knowledge of nutrition and realize the importance of a healthy, balanced diet during pregnancy. You know that caloric requirements increase. You know there is a greater need for certain nutrients, but you don't know what those nutrients are or how much of them to consume. You have heard that certain nutrients may even prevent birth defects. You may read a book to find which nutrients are important in maintaining your health and that of your developing baby, but then you wonder which foods contain these nutrients and how you can prepare them in simple, appetizing ways. And what about your family? Will they eat these foods, or is it necessary to prepare two separate meals on a regular basis? What should you eat when you are dining out?

You are not alone in your confusion. These questions and concerns have been raised by generations of pregnant women who want to do the right thing for themselves, their babies, and their family. Recent medical research has taught us what mothers have known for ages—the importance of a healthy diet in promoting a healthy pregnancy. But you do not have to consume "rabbit food" to eat well-balanced, low-fat meals. Even with fat lowered and nutrients well supplied, dining can still be a joy and cooking an art.

This book combines the latest research on nutrition in pregnancy with recipes that you can follow to term. The recipes are influenced by many cuisines—Italian, Asian, Spanish, Middle Eastern, Mexican, French, American—and will appeal to pregnant women because their cravings and desires encompass a wide spectrum of foods. These dishes use a variety of fresh ingredients in creative and sometimes offbeat ways. They emulate the eating patterns of the people of the Mediterranean, whose low-fat, high-carbohydrate diets have been extolled by members of the Harvard School of Public Health as being heart-healthy. The patterns of eating promoted here are also baby-healthy, and the recipes are tailored to meet the special nutritional requirements of pregnant and lactating women.

NUTRITION

1 A Diet for You and Your Family

There is nothing mysterious about what you eat during pregnancy. A well-balanced diet containing a variety of foods will almost automatically have the proper mix of nutrients. Eating foods in their natural, unprocessed form will ensure their wholesomeness. This style of eating is not only good for pregnancy, but is a pattern that you and your family should continue for a lifetime.

Over the years, we have learned that what constitutes a healthy diet has changed. Our mothers often encouraged us to "eat your meat"; dieters avoided carbohydrate-rich foods because such foods were "fattening"; we substituted margarine for butter because it was "healthier." Recent research has taught us that a healthy diet consists of an abundance of carbohydrates, a moderate amount of protein, and a small amount of fat. The days of the 1-pound steak for dinner are over.

And many of the basic principles of good nutrition are the same whether or not you are pregnant. The basic food groups—fruits; vegetables; bread, rice, pasta, and cereal; milk, yogurt, and cheese; and meat, poultry, fish, eggs, nuts, and legumes—are identical; you should eat from all of them. (See page 41.)

A DIET FOR THE 1990S

Carbohydrates, protein, and fat are the basic components of your diet. The required ratios are essentially the same whether you are pregnant or not. The only difference is that pregnant women should take in about 10 more grams of protein per day—the amount of protein in 1 ounce of chicken. Therefore, you *and* your family can together enjoy all the dishes in the book, allowing this pattern of eating as a family to continue for a lifetime. In other words, your pregnancy can launch a healthy style of eating for your entire family.

For all individuals, at least half of your calories should come from carbohydrates, less than 30 percent of your calories should come from fat, and your protein sources should come from lean meats or vegetables. This means that your meals should be based upon foods like pasta, potatoes, grains, and fresh vegetables, with meat or other protein sources serving more as a garnish. (The Chinese, among others, have known this for centuries.)

Carbohydrates

Most of the calories in your diet should come from carbohydrates. No specific number of grams of carbohydrate are recommended because the amount of carbohydrate in the diet depends on caloric needs, which are highly variable. This may come as a surprise to you since many think of pregnancy as a time when protein should constitute the bulk of the diet. But it is carbohydrates that should make up most of your diet, both in pregnancy and throughout your life.

Carbohydrates come in two forms: simple carbohydrates, which are found in fruits as well as table sugar and candy, and complex carbohydrates, which are found in potatoes, vegetables, beans, and whole grains. Although both forms of carbohydrate are usable as fuel, complex carbohydrates are usually preferable. The body does not handle large quantities of simple carbohydrates well. They are quickly digested and passed immediately into the bloodstream, where they place great demands on the regulatory system. In addition, foods high in complex carbohydrates are also rich in important vitamins, minerals, and fiber. Fruits, although they contain simple sugars, are also a nutrient-

and fiber-packed source of carbohydrates. Other simple-carbohydrate foods such as candy and cookies are full of "empty" calories since they generally contain few nutrients.

Restricting carbohydrates can be very dangerous, especially during pregnancy. Glucose, the breakdown product of carbohydrates, is the primary fuel used by the baby's developing nervous system. If your fat reserves are broken down for energy because you do not eat enough carbohydrates or because you skip meals, acids called ketones are formed. And there is some evidence that ketones may be harmful to the baby's developing nervous system.

Protein

Protein is required for your increase in blood volume, the health of your breasts and uterus, and building your baby's body. The protein recommendation during pregnancy is 60 grams per day—approximately 10 grams more than a nonpregnant woman requires. This is not a big increase: 10 grams of protein are found in 1 ounce of chicken or ⅓ cup of yogurt. The average pregnant female in the United States eats much more protein than is needed—on average, from 75 to 110 grams per day.[1] Vegetarians will need more than 10 grams additional protein since extra protein is needed if it all comes from vegetable sources. Most vegetable proteins do not supply all eight essential amino acids, but different plant foods may be consumed in combination in order to become complete proteins. Combining vegetable proteins in this manner is biologically the same as eating protein from meat but requires you to eat slightly more protein.

While you will have no problem filling your protein requirement during pregnancy, you should try to obtain protein from low-fat sources. Many people mistakenly believe that protein comes only from animal foods and dairy products, which may also contain undesirable amounts of fat and cholesterol. Yet foods such as grains and vegetables also contain protein. Consuming several generous servings of these plant foods each day can help you meet a substantial portion of your protein requirement without increasing your intake of fat or cholesterol. Vegetable sources of protein provide the core ingredient for many of the interesting and delicious recipes in this book.

SOME ANIMAL SOURCES OF PROTEIN

Cheese
Eggs
Fish and shellfish
Lean meat
Milk
Organ meats
Poultry
Yogurt

SOME VEGETABLE SOURCES OF PROTEIN

Black beans
Bulgur
Chickpeas
Lentils
Pinto beans
Quinoa
Rice
Split peas
Tofu
White beans

Fat

When you are pregnant, your body stores fat in order to build up energy reserves to support the unborn baby as it grows and to enable you to breast-feed your baby adequately once it's born. In addition, a certain amount of fat is needed in the diet to help produce hormones and utilize the fat-soluble vitamins A, D, E, and K (see page 27). Thus, pregnancy is not a time when you must minimize fat intake, although many pregnant women consume far more fat than is necessary. As always, your (and your family's) diet should promote healthy habits for a lifetime of eating.

Most health organizations recommend a diet that provides no more than 30 percent of calories from fat for adults, and the lastest FDA guidelines recommend keeping the percentage of calories from fat at 30 percent or lower. However, there are no published studies that indicate whether this standard applies to pregnant women. Recent evidence from Columbia University suggests that maternal fat gain does not benefit fetal growth—in other words, weight gain above the recommended amount will not increase the weight of the newborn. Rather, the mother will end up with a larger weight gain postpartum, which may not be healthy. Thus, keep your fat intake to a reasonable level during pregnancy by following the FDA guidelines, which will probably stand you and your baby in good stead.

Do not, on the other hand, eat an extremely low-fat diet since this may accelerate the breakdown of your body's stored fat into ketones (see page 5). It is fine to have an occasional ice-cream cone, rich dessert, or even sinfully fatty meal during pregnancy. Just don't make it a habit, or you'll gain too much weight.

Eating enough fat, though, is generally no problem for Americans, who often obtain more than 50 percent of their daily calories from fat. In order to keep your intake of fat to 30 percent of your daily calories, you will need to choose low-fat protein sources such as vegetable protein, cut back on fried foods, eat more carbohydrates, and generally be aware of the fat content of the foods you eat. Note that all the recipes in this book derive 30 percent or fewer calories from fat.

There is a relationship among the fat content of the diet, the blood

PRINCIPAL FOODS CONTRIBUTING FAT TO THE DIET

Avocados

Cheese

Egg yolks

Meat

Nuts

Olives

Poultry skin

Salad dressing (especially mayonnaise)

Vegetable oil

Visible meat fat

Whole milk

SOME FAT SOURCES

Fats to try to avoid

Saturated fat	Hydrogenated fat	Cholesterol
Butter	Coconut oil	Beef
Cheese	Margarine	Egg yolk
Meat	Palm oil	Liver
Whole milk	Shortening	

Better sources of fat

Unsaturated fat	Omega-3 fatty acids
Canola oil	Anchovy
Corn oil	Bluefish
Safflower oil	Salmon
Sunflower oil	Swordfish

Note: Olive oil is primarily monounsaturated, which may have a cholesterol-reducing effect.

cholesterol level, and coronary artery disease. Cholesterol, which is not a fat but a member of a chemical family called lipids, is very important in the body, forming the basic structure of many hormones, bile salts (which emulsify fat in the intestine), and cell membranes. It is uniquely found in animal products, organ meats and egg yolk being especially rich sources. Although cholesterol comes from our diet, it is also synthesized in the liver. This synthesis happens independent of dietary intake (even though it appears to be raised by the ingestion of saturated fats). To a degree, one's cholesterol level is inherited, but diet can strongly affect it. Cholesterol can be deposited on the walls of our blood vessels and lead to circulatory problems. A high blood-cholesterol level (220 milligrams or more) is a well-established risk factor for heart disease.

Fats are not soluble in water and, therefore, must receive special treatment during digestion for the body to handle them. In order to be distributed to the rest of the body from the stomach, fats are carried as complexes with blood proteins for their journey in the blood to the liver or to adipose tissue (the storage form of fat in the body). These lipid-protein complexes, called lipoproteins, come in a few varieties: high-density lipoproteins (HDLs) and low-density lipoproteins (LDLs). Recent research has found that the levels of these substances may affect the risk of heart disease. High levels of HDLs, which carry cholesterol to the liver, are associated with a lower risk of heart disease, whereas high levels of LDLs are associated with a higher risk of heart disease.

The concentrations of cholesterol and lipoproteins found in the blood increase appreciably during pregnancy. These increases are thought to be from the stimulating effect of estrogen and progesterone on the liver synthesis of these substances and is independent of diet. Thus, cholesterol, HDLs, and LDLs are all elevated during pregnancy. After delivery, however, the concentrations of these substances decrease to their prepregnancy levels, and there is no known effect of these elevated levels during pregnancy and any disease states.

In addition to an increased chance of getting heart disease, the risk of colon cancer in both sexes and breast cancer in women is greater in those who eat a high-fat diet. Thus, people in those countries with high dietary intakes of saturated fats (like the United States) have an increased incidence of coronary artery disease and cancer; people in those countries with lower dietary intakes of saturated fat (like Japan) have reduced incidences of these diseases. On the other hand, ingesting the fats from fish (especially fatty fish like salmon and bluefish) is associated with a reduced incidence of coronary disease. These fats, known as omega-3 fatty acids, act as natural blood thinners, thus lessening the risk of heart disease and thrombotic stroke. Too much omega-3 fatty acids may lead to bleeding problems because of these same anticoagulant properties, such as hemorrhagic stroke.

Fat is classified as saturated and unsaturated. Saturated means that chemical bonds are saturated by hydrogen (unsaturated fats have fewer of these bonds occupied by hydrogen). Animal fats, particularly those found in red meat and dairy products, are predominantly saturated, whereas vegetable fats are predominantly unsaturated. The small differences in hydrogen content result in large differences in the physical state of fat. Unsaturated fats are mostly liquid at room temperature (such as oils). To increase the solidity of unsaturated fats (so that they can be used as a spread, for example), some of the unsaturated bonds have hydrogen added in a chemical process known as hydrogenation. This changes the physical state of fat from liquid to solid by changing some unsaturated bonds to saturated. Margarine is an example of a fat that has been hydrogenated in order to convert it from a liquid to a solid. In a similar process, the position of the hydrogen bond is changed from its natural position (known as *cis*) to an unnatural position (known as *trans*). This process of partial hydrogenation, resulting in straight molecules that pack together more solidly, also converting liquid fat to solid fat, was commercialized to create vegetable shortening and solid vegetable oils.

Products containing trans fatty acids, especially margarine, have been heavily promoted as being healthier than foodstuffs containing saturated fats. It was thought that they did not raise blood cholesterol in the same manner that saturated fats did. However, such claims were never substantiated. Concerns have arisen because consumption of these partially hydrogenated vegetable fats has tracked closely in time with the epidemic of coronary disease in the United States and elsewhere.[2] Recently, substantial new data on the health effects of trans fatty acids have become available. Trans fatty acids raise LDLs to a similar degree as saturated fats; they also decrease HDLs. Both of these factors increase the risk of heart disease.[3]

A high-fat diet also makes you gain weight faster and easier than a high-carbohydrate diet. And the weight gain from a fat-rich diet is far greater than that from a carbohydrate-rich diet with the same number of calories.[4] In addition, since fat is generally appetizing and readily satisfies hunger, too much fat in your diet may suppress your appetite before you have ingested sufficient carbohydrates and other important nutrients. And in pregnancy, almost every calorie should supply you with important nutrients.

Again, aim to keep the calories from dietary fat at 30 percent, and try to consume your fat in the form of unsaturated fat and omega-3 fatty acids.

EATING FOR A LIFETIME TOGETHER

Your pregnancy can serve to alter positively your and your family's eating habits. All of the recipes in this book are healthy—that is, they are high in carbohydrates and low in fats, which will leave you feeling full and satisfied while keeping your family's weight under control. Best of all, the meals are delicious and simple to prepare. Eating well is a joy and something that you can all do together during your pregnancy since eating to build a healthy baby will also build a healthy family.

NOTES

1. Subcommittee on the Tenth Edition of the RDAs, Food and Nutrition Board, Commission of Life Sciences, and National Research Council, *Recommended Dietary Allowances,* 10th ed. (Washington, D.C.: National Academy Press, 1989).

2. W. C. Willett and A. Ascherio, "Trans Fatty Acids: Are the Effects Only Marginal?" *American Journal of Public Health* 84 (1994): 722–724.

3. W. C. Willett, M. J. Stampfer, J. E. Manson, *et al.,* "Intake of Trans Fatty Acids and Risk of Coronary Heart Disease among Women," *The Lancet* 341 (1993): 581–585.

4. E. Danforth, "Diet and Obesity," *American Journal of Clinical Nutrition* 41 (1985): 1132–1145.

2 PREPARING FOR PREGNANCY

You want to get pregnant. You are already ahead of the game in that you are reading this book and thinking about what is good for you and your baby before conception. Many women do not even realize that they are pregnant until their period is late, by which time the fetus can be four weeks along, with its many major organ systems already formed. Planning can have a big impact on the health of your baby. This includes working out a nutritious, well-balanced diet, which can also make your pregnancy more comfortable and enjoyable. And you will look great, too!

DIETARY CONCERNS

Now is the time to take a dietary inventory and make healthy adjustments. Your diet should consist of fresh fruit, vegetables, whole grains, and lean meats or other low-fat sources of protein. You should try to obtain at least 50 percent of your calories from carbohydrates and less than 30 percent of your calories from fat. Avoid saturated fats, and try to consume foods in their natural, unprocessed forms. These recommendations will serve you well not only during pregnancy, but will help you and your family develop good eating habits that will last a lifetime.

The recipes in this book follow these basic guidelines and are designed to appeal to all members of your family. These dishes are proof positive that healthy, low-fat eating can be exciting, delicious, and simple.

Weight Status

There is no issue that attracts more attention during pregnancy than weight. Your self-image and self-esteem take a beating during pregnancy regardless of how beautiful people say you look while you are pregnant. No amount of healthy glow overcomes the disconcerting feeling that accompanies catching a glimpse of yourself sideways in the mirror!

But take heart. The weight gain truly is only temporary, the average residual weight gain after pregnancy amounting to 2 pounds. By following the recommendations and recipes in this book, you may even find yourself down a few pounds several months after you have given birth, especially if you breast-feed, since breast-feeding burns many calories.

Make time preconceptionally to take an objective look at your weight. The weight/height table on page 13 will give you an idea of what a normal weight range is for your height, depending upon your frame size. Remember, you do not need to be model-perfect to support a healthy pregnancy. You may even be surprised to learn that overweight women—unless they are extremely overweight—have fewer weight-related pregnancy problems than do underweight women.

If you do wish to adjust your weight, however, pregnancy is not the time to do it. If you are overweight and wish to get down to standard weight, you should start your diet several months before conception. Your practitioner can help you find a low-fat diet right for you. Once you become pregnant, you will gain back some of the weight you lost, but it will be weight that helps build the baby, the placenta, and the extra maternal stores required to support a healthy pregnancy. Much of the weight will be gone after delivery, and the rest can come off postpartum, especially if you breast-feed (breast-feeding burns 500 calories a day). By following the recipes in this book to achieve a controlled weight gain during pregnancy and weight loss postpartum, you may be pleased with your figure as soon as 6 weeks after delivery. (See the

WEIGHTS/HEIGHTS FOR NONPREGNANT WOMEN

Height	Standard weight	Underweight	Overweight	Obese
4'9"	105–126	104	127–137	138
4'10"	107–130	106	131–141	142
4'11"	109–132	108	133–143	144
5'0"	111–134	110	135–145	146
5'1"	114–137	113	138–149	150
5'2"	116–141	115	142–153	154
5'3"	119–144	118	145–156	157
5'4"	122–147	121	148–160	161
5'5"	124–150	123	151–163	164
5'6"	127–154	126	155–167	168
5'7"	130–157	129	158–171	172
5'8"	132–160	131	161–174	175
5'9"	135–164	134	165–178	179
5'10"	141–170	140	171–185	186
5'11"	142–172	141	173–187	188
6'0"	143–174	142	175–189	190
6'1"	146–177	145	178–192	193

Source: Metropolitan Life tables

exercise section on pages 33–38 for help in reaching these goals.)

If you are underweight, you would be much better off gaining weight before you become pregnant than trying to gain weight quickly during your pregnancy. Underweight women who have trouble conceiving because they do not ovulate regularly may find that if they gain weight, they will ovulate more frequently, thus increasing the odds of becoming pregnant each month.

If you enter pregnancy underweight, your nutritional needs will compete with the baby's for nourishment. If you do not get enough calories and nutrients from your diet during your pregnancy, your baby's growth will be limited. Underweight women are at risk of having babies that are small for their gestational age, which may result in a child with health problems at birth or developmental problems later in life. To reduce this risk, women who begin their pregnancy underweight will need to gain extra weight during the pregnancy. Your doctor or practitioner can help you determine your prepregnancy ideal body weight based upon your height and bone structure.

Achieving these weight goals before conception will aid in increasing the weight of your future baby, which may prevent problems associated with low-birth-weight infants. And it may make your pregnancy more comfortable since you will not need to gain as much weight during the pregnancy in order to provide for the nutritional needs of your baby.

Iron Status

Your practitioner may wish to check your hemoglobin and hematocrit, which are blood tests used to measure your red-blood-cell mass. Anemia, or low red-blood-cell count, can leave you feeling tired and run down. It also can cause problems in pregnancy because the red blood cells deliver oxygen to your baby. Once you become pregnant, your body will be manufacturing extra red blood cells to support the baby and prepare you for blood loss during delivery. Since iron is required for this process, you will need extra iron at this time.

Pregnancies complicated by anemia can result in small-for-gestational-age babies, which may lead to problems associated with low-birth-weight infants. In addition, if you start your pregnancy with a low red-blood-cell count, your blood loss at delivery will leave you even more anemic postpartum. And with a new baby to take care of, the last thing you need is to feel tired and run down.

The most common cause of anemia in women is iron deficiency, but low folic acid or B_{12} deficiency may also cause anemia. Iron deficiency usually results from blood loss, and healthy women who menstruate monthly are at risk for this condition because of the regular loss involved. Others at risk for iron deficiency are those who may not obtain enough iron in their diet, such as vegetarians.

If you have iron-deficiency anemia and it was detected preconceptionally, now is the time to start building up your iron stores and increasing your red-blood-cell count. Your practitioner will most likely prescribe an iron supplement. In addition, you can enrich your diet with meals that are high in iron. Iron is contained in such foods as meat, green leafy vegetables, beans and legumes, and dried fruit. (See the list on page 24 for specific sources of iron.) And cooking your foods in cast-iron pots and pans will add to the iron content of a meal.

You can take measures to increase your body's absorption of iron from your diet and from your iron supplement by accompanying your high-iron diet or your supplement with foods and beverages rich in vitamin C. There are also foods and beverages that you must avoid—including all drinks containing caffeine, tea (phytic acid), and chocolate—since they decrease the absorption of iron.

It is a good idea to increase your iron stores preconceptionally since you will not need as much iron supplementation during pregnancy. For once you become pregnant, you may find iron supplements difficult to tolerate in the first trimester. Also, iron will aggravate constipation, a common condition among women in their second and third trimesters. And you will be more comfortable and energetic with a higher hematocrit, and your baby will probably be healthier.

Folic Acid

There is some evidence that low nutritional intake of the vitamin folic acid (also known as folate and folacin) may increase your baby's chances of having a neural-tube defect (the brain and spine develop from the neural tube, and defects can cause paralysis and mental retardation). Trials using folic-acid supplementation during preconception (twenty-eight days before through twenty-eight days after the last menstrual period) have been found to reduce the incidence of neural-tube defects.[1] Since neural-tube closure is complete four weeks following conception, folic-acid supplementation that starts after that time is not likely to be of value.

Presently, the U.S. Public Health Service recommends that all women in the United States who might possibly become pregnant consume 0.4 milligrams of folic acid per day to lower the incidence of neural-tube defects.[2] The American College of Obstetricians and Gynecologists has not yet made a routine recommendation of preconceptional folic-acid supplementation because it feels that adequate study has not yet been carried out. Therefore, taking folic-acid supplements is not agreed upon by all groups, but there are strong indications it may be helpful. One month before trying to conceive, discuss this with your medical practitioner.

Prenatal vitamins contain at least 0.4 milligrams of folic acid, but regular multivitamins usually contain only 0.3 milligrams or less. However, the 0.4-milligram level of folic acid can be reached without fortification or supplementation simply by following a good diet.[3] Pregnant teens, women carrying more than one baby, and other women in high-risk groups for folic-acid deficiency should supplement their diets with the vitamin.

Good sources of folic acid are green leafy vegetables, legumes, nuts, and fruits. Note that more folic acid is destroyed by microwave cooking than by any other cooking method. Also, this vitamin is lost whenever high temperatures or large amounts of water are used in cooking. And some medications, including anticonvulsants, as well as alcohol and cigarettes may interfere with folic-acid utilization. See pages 97–109 for dishes high in this nutrient.

OTHER LIFESTYLE CONCERNS

Exercise

If you do not already have a regular exercise routine, several months preconceptionally is the time to start one. Other than regular walking, your practitioner will probably not want you to begin a new regimen once you become pregnant.

In order to achieve cardiovascular fitness, you need to raise your heart rate (140 beats per minute minus your age) for 22 to 25 minutes three to four times a week. It is important to realize that this moderate, regular exercise plan is much more beneficial than occasional, vigorous exercise. In fact, weekend jogging may even be detrimental because you do not maintain your fitness level during the week, which puts a strain on your system. Walking, swimming, jogging, or bicycling are all excellent ways to raise your heart rate, thus promoting cardiovascular fitness.

Once you establish such a routine, there is no reason why you can-

**SOME SOURCES
OF FOLIC ACID**

Asparagus
Broccoli
Chicken
Collard greens
Corn
Egg yolks
Fish
Fruits
Kale
Lean beef
Legumes
Nuts
Potatoes
Spinach
Squash
Swiss chard
Tomatoes
Turnip greens

not continue this regimen during pregnancy. There are just a few simple rules that you should follow in order to keep you and your baby safe while you exercise during pregnancy (see pages 33–38). Remember to keep your practitioner informed about your exercise routine. Use your common sense. Do not exercise to exhaustion (you should be able to talk comfortably). If you feel pain, stop what you are doing. Do not engage in activities such as skiing or skating in which you could fall and traumatize your abdomen. Use moderation in all that you do. Regular exercise during your pregnancy will increase your energy level, enhance your self-image, prepare you for labor, and speed your recovery postpartum.

Hot Tubs

You should keep from getting overheated around the time of conception and during pregnancy. An increase in your core body temperature above 102.5°F (39.2° Celsius) has been associated with increases in congenital anomalies in babies. These observations have been reported in conjunction with elevations in maternal temperature due to hot-tub use.[4] This is why women are advised not to use hot tubs while trying to become pregnant and during pregnancy.

Smoking

Any benefit you gain from following a healthy diet and lifestyle will be negated if you smoke. Smoking is associated with low-birth-weight babies, increased risk of miscarriage, increased risk of death in utero, increased incidence of sudden infant death syndrome, and respiratory problems in children taking in secondary smoke. Smokers have higher rates of many cancers and cardiovascular diseases. If you smoke, you owe it to yourself and your future baby to quit. It is the best thing you can do for your health and your baby's health.

Alcohol

Alcohol, a known teratogen (a substance that causes abnormal fetal development), is responsible for fetal alcohol syndrome, which is characterized by mental retardation, facial anomalies, low birth weight, and behavioral problems, including attention deficit disorder and hyperactivity. Heavy drinking is a major risk to the health of the fetus, and reduction, even in midpregnancy, can be of benefit. An occasional drink during pregnancy carries no known risk, but no level of drinking is known to be safe.

Drugs

Do not use recreational drugs if you are trying to get pregnant. Check with your practitioner if you are taking any over-the-counter drugs, including cold and headache medications, or prescription drugs. Your fetus can be very susceptible to adverse effects from these drugs during the first few days after conception. Since you will probably not know if you are pregnant for several weeks after conception, you must take the same precautions you would if you knew you were pregnant.

NOTES
  1. M. M. Werler, S. Shapiro, and A. A. Mitchell, "Periconceptional Folic Acid Exposure and Risk of Occurrent Neural Tube Defects," *Journal of the American Med-*

ical Association 269 (1993): 1257–1261; Medical Research Council Vitamin Study Research Group, "Prevention of Neural Tube Defects: Results of the Medical Research Council Vitamin Study," *The Lancet* 338 (1991): 131–137.

2. D. Rush, "Periconceptional Folate and Neural Tube Defect," *American Journal of Clinical Nutrition* 59 (1994): 511S–515S.

3. Subcommittee on Nutritional Status and Weight Gain during Lactation *et al., Nutrition during Lactation* (Washington, D.C.: National Academy Press, 1991).

4. A. Milunsky, M. Ulcickas, K. J. Rothman, W. Willett, S. S. Jick, and H. Jick, "Maternal Heat Exposure and Neural Tube Defects," *Journal of the American Medical Association* 268 (1992): 882–885.

3 NUTRITION IN PREGNANCY

Your practitioner has advised you to eat a nutritious and well-balanced diet during your pregnancy. What does this mean? Are there foods you should eat more of? Foods you should avoid? Should you supplement your diet with vitamin pills? The following background on nutrition in pregnancy may help clarify some of these issues.

RECOMMENDED DIETARY ALLOWANCES

The Food and Nutrition Board of the National Academy of Sciences has published the Recommended Dietary Allowances (RDAs) periodically since 1943. The tenth and most recent listing was published in 1989. RDAs are based on a combination of estimates and clinical research data. The values, which are neither means nor averages, are adjusted near the top of the normal range in order to encompass the needs of most people. Therefore, many individuals eat a diet that is nutritionally adequate but that may not meet the RDAs.

Dietary allowances for most substances increase during pregnancy. According to the 1989 recommendations, during gestation

- the RDAs for iron, folic acid, and vitamin D double
- the RDAs for calcium and phosphorus increase by one-half

- the RDAs for pyridoxine and thiamine increase by about one-third
- the RDAs for protein, zinc, and riboflavin increase by about one-fourth
- the RDAs for all other nutrients except vitamin A increase by less than one-fifth
- there is no increase in the RDA for vitamin A since it is adequately stored in the body

VITAMINS AND MINERALS

Supplementation

All nutrients required during pregnancy, with the exception of iron, are supplied by a well-balanced diet. The National Academy of Sciences currently recommends that 30 milligrams of ferrous-iron supplements be prescribed for pregnant women daily because the iron content of the typical American diet and the iron stores of many women are not sufficient to provide the increased iron required during pregnancy.

The 30-milligram iron supplement is contained in approximately 150 milligrams of ferrous sulfate, 300 milligrams of ferrous gluconate, or 100 milligrams of ferrous fumarate. Your practitioner may prescribe any one of these forms of iron to supplement your diet. Some women tolerate some form of iron supplement better than others, so if one kind upsets your system, try a different one, with your practitioner's approval. Some kinds come combined with a stool softener (usually docusate sodium) to counteract the constipating effect that iron has on the digestive system.

You can enhance your body's absorption of iron from your diet and from your iron supplement. You may take your iron with foods containing vitamin C. Do not, however, take your iron supplement with coffee or other caffeinated beverages since this will inhibit the nutrient's absorption. Also, you may take your supplement between meals on an empty stomach, but many women find that iron on an empty stomach is a sure bet for an upset stomach. Finally, you may cook your meals in cast-iron cookware since a significant amount of this iron finds its way into your food and is absorbed. The best way to maximize your iron absorption and minimize side effects such as stomach upset and constipation is to eat a high-fiber diet, stay well hydrated, and take your iron supplement with meals while drinking a beverage high in vitamin C such as orange or cranberry juice. (See the following section for more information on iron.)

There is no need to take any vitamin supplement other than iron during pregnancy. The Subcommittee on Dietary Intake and Nutrient Supplement during Pregnancy of the National Academy of Sciences maintains that healthy American women should be encouraged to get the vitamins they need from their diet rather than from supplements. The subcommittee points out that there is a much greater risk of overdose from supplements than from foods.[1] For example, exposure to levels of 25,000 IUs (international units) of vitamin A has been associated with birth defects. But there is no evidence that vitamin A in normal doses, such as in prenatal vitamins, is dangerous. Individuals should discuss with their practitioner what is best for their particular situation. Vitamins are often given to pregnant women by medical practitioners, and many women feel shortchanged if the vitamins are not prescribed. If they make you feel more energetic, by all means take the vitamins. But during the first trimester, when nausea abounds, take comfort in knowing that you are not doing your baby harm by not taking prenatal vitamins.

There are women who do have special nutritional needs. For example, some vegetarians need supplementary vitamin B_{12} and zinc. Additional folic acid is appropriate for women with twin pregnancies, on seizure medication, or with certain blood disorders such as sickle-cell anemia. Supplemental vitamin D is beneficial for women not adequately exposed to sunlight who eat no dairy products. Adolescents and smokers may also benefit from a prenatal vitamin supplement.

Supplementing vitamins other than iron and a prenatal multivitamin is not only unnecessary, it can be dangerous. For example, taking megadoses of vitamin A may cause birth defects. Vitamin-A intake in the range of 25,000 IUs or more daily can result in defects of the fetal bone, urinary tract, and central nervous system.[2] Before taking any vitamin supplements, ask your practitioner.

Iron

Your need for iron begins during the preconception period and continues to term. Iron is necessary during pregnancy for forming red blood cells in both you and your baby.

Because monthly menstruation depletes the body of iron, most women enter pregnancy with less-than-optimal iron stores, or iron-deficiency anemia, a condition characterized by an inadequate number of red blood cells and, thus, an inadequate supply of oxygen to you. This can leave you feeling chronically tired and run down.

During pregnancy, your red-blood-cell volume undergoes a rapid expansion so that your body can deliver enough oxygen to your baby. This expansion of your blood volume is nature's way of preparing you for the large blood loss that occurs at delivery (on average, ½ liter for a vaginal delivery and 1 liter for a cesarean delivery). In addition, increased iron is needed for your baby's blood formation and growth.

For this expansion of your red-blood-cell volume to occur, you need to consume extra iron. You should begin adding iron to your diet in the first trimester (if not before) and continue this high-iron diet throughout your pregnancy. You should also take any iron supplements prescribed by your practitioner.

Iron in foods takes two forms: heme iron, found in meat, poultry, and fish, and nonheme iron, found in plant foods. Heme is an iron-carrying substance only found in humans and animals, and is produced in the red blood cells. Nonheme iron, on the other hand, is found in plant foods.

Heme iron is absorbed far better than nonheme iron. Iron absorption is inhibited by substances containing caffeine and phytic acid (which is found in tea), and is enhanced by foods rich in vitamin C. For example, drinking orange juice while you eat a piece of chicken boosts your absorption of the iron in the chicken. Conversely, drinking coffee or tea with that same piece of chicken would inhibit your absorption of the iron. If you are a vegetarian, combining tomatoes, which contain a lot of vitamin C, with dark-green leafy vegetables, which are high in iron, will boost your absorption of the iron from the

SOME SOURCES OF IRON

Apricots
Beef
Black beans
Blackstrap molasses
Broccoli
Chicken
Chickpeas
Clams
Collard greens
Egg yolks
Enriched breads and cereals
Kale
Kidney beans
Navy beans
Pinto beans
Prunes
Pumpkinseeds
Shrimp
Spinach
Swiss chard
Tofu
Tuna
Turkey
Wheat germ
Whole grains

vegetables. Many of the recipes in this book that are high in iron take advantage of these principles.

Iron-containing foods include lean meats, poultry, fish, eggs, legumes, green leafy vegetables, enriched breads and cereals, and dried fruits. However, it is very difficult to get enough iron from your diet alone, and a 30-milligram iron supplement taken during pregnancy is recommended. For women who begin their pregnancy anemic or for those who become anemic during pregnancy, iron supplementation above 30 milligrams may be prescribed by your practitioner.

Constipation is a problem in women taking iron supplements, so keep your diet high in fiber and stay well hydrated in order to keep your bowel movements regular.

Folic Acid

Your increased need for folic acid (also known as folate and folacin) begins in the first trimester, doubling during pregnancy. Folic acid is necessary for red-blood-cell formation in both you and the baby. It is also involved in the general growth of your baby. You may have begun taking folic-acid supplements preconceptionally to prevent neural-tube defects (see Chapter 2).

Folate-deficiency anemia, which can be detected by a blood test, can leave you feeling tired and run down in much the same way the more common iron-deficiency anemia can. In your baby, folate deficiency preconceptionally has been linked with neural-tube defects (spina bifida).

The increased requirements for folic acid can be met by a good diet without fortification or supplementation. However, pregnant teens, women carrying more than one baby, and other women in high-risk groups for folate deficiency should take folic-acid supplements.

Folic acid is found in large quantities in green leafy vegetables, meat and poultry, fish, legumes, nuts, and fruits (see page 16). It is more readily destroyed by microwave cooking than by other cooking method and is lost whenever high temperatures or large amounts of water are used in cooking. Substances that may interfere with the processing of folic acid in the body include anticonvulsants, alcohol, and cigarettes.

Calcium

Calcium requirements increase by 50 percent during pregnancy—to 1,200 milligrams daily. Calcium is required to sustain life processes in your body such as heartbeat, cellular function, and muscle contractions. In your baby, calcium is used to build teeth and bones, processes that begin in the first trimester and continue to term. Calcium reserves are in your bones, and if you do not consume enough dietary calcium, it will be drawn from your bones to maintain adequate blood levels. This can lead to osteoporosis later in life in some women.

There is new evidence that calcium may prevent preeclampsia (toxemia), a condition that develops during pregnancy which is characterized by high blood pressure, swelling, and abnormal amounts of protein in the urine. The causes of this syndrome are not clear since the data pertaining to it are still at the experimental stage. Therefore, routine supplements of calcium at this time are not recommended.

It is very difficult to meet calcium requirements without consuming dairy products. Individuals who do not consume milk or milk products may require calcium supplementation. Those who do consume dairy products can easily meet this requirement by following a well-balanced diet. It is important to watch which dairy products you eat since many of them, in addition to being good sources of calcium, are, unfortunately, very high in fat. For high-calcium alternatives to milk products, emphasize greens from the cole family: kale, collards, broccoli, and bok choy.

Some substances can hinder the absorption of calcium, including oxalic acid (found in spinach and Swiss chard) and phytic acid (found in the outer layers of whole grains). Both of these form insoluble compounds with calcium, binding it in such a way that it cannot be absorbed from the intestine.

Phosphorus

The need for phosphorus increases by 50 percent during pregnancy. Phosphorus is required as a constituent of the genetic materials DNA and RNA, and is a component of the phospholipids that make up cell membranes. Like calcium, it is stored in bones and may be drawn

SOME SOURCES OF CALCIUM

- Blackstrap molasses
- Bok choy
- Broccoli
- Buttermilk
- Collard greens
- Fortified juices
- Frozen yogurt
- Ice cream
- Kale
- Legumes
- Low-fat cheeses
- Low-fat or skim milk
- Mangoes
- Sesame seeds
- Tofu
- Turnip greens
- Whole grains
- Yogurt

from there to serve these functions. Milk and whole grains are good sources.

Vitamin D

Vitamin D is needed for maintenance of normal levels of calcium and phosphorus in your body. The RDA for vitamin D doubles during gestation. Low levels of this vitamin may predispose you to osteoporosis later in life. Severe deficiencies have been associated with seizures and rickets in newborns.[3]

Vitamin D is found in vitamin D–fortified milk (approximately 98 percent of milk sold in the United States is fortified with vitamin D), liver, egg yolks, and cereals fortified with vitamin D. Vitamin D is also formed in the skin when the skin is exposed to sunlight.

SOME SOURCES OF VITAMIN D

Egg yolks
Fish-liver oil
Fortified milk
Sunlight

Pyridoxine (Vitamin B$_6$)

The RDA for pyridoxine increases by one-third during pregnancy. This vitamin helps your body to produce energy by playing a role in the breakdown of glycogen to glucose and the conversion of one amino acid to another, and is important for the development (neuron differentiation) of your baby's brain and nervous system. Pyridoxine has been given as a supplement to women who are suffering from severe nausea and vomiting caused by pregnancy. As always, before taking any medication during your pregnancy, discuss it with your practitioner.

Pyridoxine is widely found in unprocessed foods such as wheat germ, whole-grain cereals and bread, bananas, beans, nuts, poultry, fish, and carrots.

SOME SOURCES OF PYRIDOXINE

Bananas
Beans
Carrots
Fish
Nuts
Poultry
Wheat germ
Whole-grain cereals and bread

Thiamine (Vitamin B$_1$)

The RDA for thiamine increases by one-third during pregnancy. This vitamin promotes the breakdown of carbohydrates, thus providing energy for your body and supplying carbohydrates for your baby's brain development. It is necessary for both maternal and fetal growth. Deficiency can cause loss of appetite, fatigue, constipation, backache, and insomnia. If maternal deficiency is severe, the baby may be born with

~-~-~-~-~-~-~

Enriched cereals

Enriched or whole-grain
       bread

Fish

Lean pork

Legumes

Nuts and seeds

Wheat germ

Yeast

congenital beriberi (a syndrome of heart failure and mental confusion that may progress to coma).

Generally, most pregnant women easily meet their needs for thiamine. Thiamine deficiency is found most commonly in alcoholics and patients who require dialysis for kidney failure. The best source of thiamine is lean pork, but it is found in many other sources, including legumes, enriched or whole-grain breads and cereals, nuts and seeds, lean meat, and fish. While the best sources of thiamine are in meat, vegetarians who eat plenty of whole grains and enriched breads and cereals can get adequate thiamine.

Zinc

The RDA for zinc increases by one-fourth during pregnancy. Zinc is important for digestion, metabolism, respiration, wound healing, and maintenance of skin and hair. During pregnancy, zinc plays an important role in the formation of the baby's developing organs, skeleton, and internal systems like nerves and circulation. This nutrient is thought to be essential for successful reproduction.

Some preliminary data indicate that dietary deficiencies of zinc may be linked with premature delivery and low-birth-weight infants. In a recent study, low dietary-zinc intake was associated with twice the incidence of low-birth-weight infants and an increased risk of preterm delivery.[4] In addition, supplementation with zinc has been shown to improve pregnancy outcomes. You should not, however, take additional zinc supplements routinely.

SOME SOURCES
OF ZINC

~-~-~-~-~-~-~

Beans

Cereals and whole grains

Fish and shellfish

Lean meat and poultry

Milk

Nuts

Wheat germ

Yogurt

Like iron, zinc is better absorbed from animal than from vegetable sources. Vegetarians, therefore, need to pay close attention to their diet to ensure adequate zinc.

The best source of zinc is shellfish, especially oysters. The belief in the aphrodisiacal qualities of oysters comes from their high content of zinc since zinc is vital in reproduction. However, during pregnancy you should only eat cooked oysters because raw mollusks, particularly oysters, often carry the bacteria *Vibrio vulnificus*. These bacteria can cause a rapid, life-threatening infection for some, especially those with liver disease, diabetes, immune deficiencies, or gastrointestinal disorders associated with decreased gastric acidity.

Other sources of zinc include lean meats, yogurt, beans, cereals, and milk.

Riboflavin (Vitamin B$_2$)

The RDA for riboflavin increases by one-fourth during pregnancy. Riboflavin is essential to produce energy from the breakdown of carbohydrates, fat, and protein in the diet. It promotes good vision and healthy skin. Riboflavin deficiency in the mother may cause a cracked and sore mouth as well as dermatitis.

Riboflavin is found in dairy products and meat. Most pregnant women easily meet this requirement, but vegetarians who do not eat dairy products should eat more green leafy vegetables, whole grains, beans, nuts, and seeds in order to obtain adequate amounts of this nutrient.

SOME SOURCES OF RIBOFLAVIN

Chicken
Green leafy vegetables
Lean beef
Legumes
Low-fat cheese
Nuts and seeds
Skim or low-fat milk
Whole grains
Yeast
Yogurt

OTHER NUTRITIONAL NEEDS

Salt

More sodium is needed during pregnancy and lactation than at any other time of life, but virtually all women meet this need with their normal intake of salt. Salt is necessary to regulate fluid balance in cells and blood. During pregnancy, your blood volume expands by 50 percent, and this increase requires salt. In the past, pregnant women were told to restrict salt to prevent edema (swelling) and preeclampsia, but this has not been found to be helpful. In fact, cutting back on salt can be harmful to you and your baby.

Edema, or swelling, during pregnancy, is a normal problem, especially as you approach your due date. It most often occurs in your lower body, especially feet and calves. If swelling suddenly becomes severe, especially in your hands and face, you may be developing preeclampsia, and you should see your practitioner to be evaluated and to get your blood pressure checked.

Your salt intake, however, will not affect your risk of developing preeclampsia, and it will not affect the amount of swelling you develop. *Note well:* taking diuretics is not advised and may be dangerous—both to you and your baby.

There is, therefore, no need to restrict salt intake during pregnancy. Pregnant women should salt food to taste. Most of the recipes in this book contain a modest amount of salt for flavor, which you may adjust.

Fluids

During pregnancy and lactation, water intake is vital. You will find that you will become quite thirsty as your pregnancy progresses. It is your body's way of saying you need to drink more. This extra fluid goes toward increasing your blood volume, amniotic fluid, and the water containing the baby's cells and blood.

You should drink between 6 to 8 glasses of liquid each day. It can be water, milk, juice, or carbonated beverages. In order to drink this much, you must plan for it. Have 2 glasses of fluid with each meal and 1 at some other time during the day, and your requirement will be met. You may want to avoid drinking at bedtime since this will probably cause you to get up during the night to urinate (which you may already be doing because of that baby bouncing on your bladder like a trampoline).

You should not count caffeinated beverages—coffee or tea, for instance—as part of your daily allotment. The caffeine in these drinks acts as a diuretic, and you will urinate more in response to them. This makes their net effect on your fluid intake approximately zero.

Soda and diet soda are both fine during pregnancy. Aspartame (brand name: NutraSweet), the most common diet sweetener on the market today, has been found in numerous studies to be safe for pregnant women. One of the breakdown products of aspartame is phenylalanine, which must be strictly limited in the diet of children with PKU (phenylketonuria) to prevent mental retardation. However, aspartame does not raise the blood phenylalanine levels in the fetus to the range generally associated with mental retardation. So even if your newborn is found to have PKU (a rare inherited metabolic disease), the aspartame you consumed during your pregnancy would not have been the culprit. Since it is always best to practice moderation, you may wish to limit your diet soda and soda intake to 12 ounces a day. Taking in too many calories from simple sugars is a bad idea because you will not be obtaining enough of the nutrients you need.

You can gauge your hydration by examining the color of your urine. If it is dark amber, you are probably dehydrated and should take in more fluid. If it is clear to light yellow, you are well hydrated and your fluid intake is adequate.

Keeping hydrated will also aid in preventing constipation. The colon absorbs more water during pregnancy, making your stools harder. The more water you take in, the softer the stool and the lesser the likelihood of getting hemorrhoids.

NOTES

1. Subcommittee on Nutritional Status and Weight Gain during Pregnancy *et al., Nutrition during Pregnancy* (Washington, D.C.: National Academy Press, 1990).

2. American College of Obstetricians and Gynecologists, *Vitamin A Supplementation during Pregnancy,* Committee Opinion 112 (Washington, D.C.: American College of Obstetricians and Gynecologists, 1992).

3. D. V. Edidin, "Resurgence of Nutritional Rickets Associated with Breast-Feeding and Special Dietary Practices," *Pediatrics* 6 (1980): 232–235.

4. T. D. Scholl, M. L. Hediger, and J. I. Schall, "Low Zinc Intake during Pregnancy: Its Association with Preterm and Very Preterm Delivery," *American Journal of Epidemiology* 137 (1993): 1115–1124.

4 Exercise in Pregnancy

THE BENEFITS OF EXERCISE

Exercise may have been an integral part of your lifestyle before you became pregnant. In the absence of obstetric or health problems, you can continue to engage in a moderate level of physical activity to maintain cardiorespiratory and muscular fitness throughout your pregnancy and the postpartum period. Be sure to check with your practitioner before you begin any exercise program. You will find that the more active you are during your pregnancy, the better you will feel and look. Both you and your baby will enjoy good health together, just as you will throughout life after pregnancy.

Pregnancy causes profound changes in your physiology. Your blood volume, cardiac output, and resting pulse are all increased. Your blood pressure is lower. You breathe harder even at rest. All of these changes make exercise a bit harder, but not impossible, during pregnancy.

The benefits of regular exercise during pregnancy—better self-esteem and physical well-being—are worth the effort. You will find that with regular exercise, you will be more comfortable and have less aches and pains during your pregnancy. Your weight gain will be well controlled and in the right places: while your breasts and your abdomen will expand in a healthy way, the rest of your body will remain toned and supple. You will feel less tired. Finally, you will recover more quickly postpartum and regain your prepregnancy shape faster.

Pregnancy is not the time to begin a new exercise regimen. If you did not exercise regularly prior to becoming pregnant, start a regular walking regimen. Walking is one of the best exercises for both you and your baby. Instead of taking the car to the grocery store for that one item you forgot, why not walk there? If you can, walk to work, and save the environment while you exercise your body. You can make walking a family affair by including your partner and your children in your jaunts since their health is as important as your own and your future baby's. In this manner, your walking routine can become part of your daily activities, taking little extra time from your busy lifestyle.

Because of the increased resting oxygen requirements and the increased work of breathing brought about by the physical effects of the enlarged uterus on the diaphragm, there is less oxygen available for the performance of aerobic exercise during pregnancy. Thus, your exercise performance will not be as high as it was before your pregnancy.[1] You will find that you become exhausted and short of breath sooner than before you were pregnant. Therefore, it is important to use good sense when exercising, toning down your usual routines if you find them too arduous and stopping them well before exhaustion sets in. You should be exercising in a comfortable way, not pushing yourself to the brink of collapse. Moderation is the key. If you are uncertain about your level of activity, ask your practitioner.

A COMMON-SENSE APPROACH TO EXERCISE

Since your center of gravity will be shifted because of the enlargement of the uterus and breasts that occurs during normal pregnancy, your balance may be affected, which must be kept in mind when you are performing activities in which balance is important. Activities such as ballet dancing or aerobics may be continued, but take precautions to prevent injury from falls.

Certain types of exercise should be avoided during pregnancy. Any activity that has the potential for causing trauma to your abdomen—skiing, ice skating, rollerblading, contact sports—should not be undertaken at this time.

Theoretically, an increase in certain hormones during pregnancy corresponds to an increase in the laxity of your joints, which could predispose you to injury when you exercise. The hormone relaxin is produced by the placenta to loosen your joints and make more room in the pelvis to accommodate your baby during delivery. This has caused some to worry that pregnant women may be more prone to injury during weight-bearing exercise. There are, however, no objective data to support this contention. Exercise that could cause joint injury, such as running, may be continued, but moderation is the key. And minimizing impact by running on a treadmill may decrease any potential risk as well as being more comfortable for you.

You should try to keep from getting overheated during exercise in pregnancy. An increase in your core body temperature above 102.5°F (39.2° Celsius) has been associated with increases in congenital anomalies in babies. These observations, however, have not been reported in association with exercise, but rather elevations in maternal temperature related to hot-tub use.[2] This is why pregnant women are advised not to use hot tubs during pregnancy. Also, avoid exercising in extreme heat, wear appropriate clothing, and stay well hydrated.

Approximately 300 extra calories per day are required to meet the needs of pregnancy. This caloric requirement is increased further in those pregnant women who exercise regularly. Since pregnant women use up carbohydrates at a fast rate, it is important to take in adequate carbohydrates if you are exercising regularly during pregnancy. You can modify your diet to include carbohydrate-rich meals much the way distance runners do since your needs are very similar.

Several studies have suggested a decrease in birth weight in babies of women who exercise intensely throughout pregnancy.[3] This reduction in birth weight averaged 300 to 350 grams and appeared to reflect primarily a decrease in fat in the newborn. There were no other deleterious short- or long-term effects of decreased fetal weight found in these babies. Thus, exercising regularly during your pregnancy may cause your baby to be ½ pound or less smaller but has not been found to cause any problems in the baby.

There are no data in humans that indicate that pregnant women should limit exercise intensity and lower target heart rates because of potentially adverse effects on the pregnancy. Without such information, it is prudent to moderate your activities. In the past, the American College of Obstetricians and Gynecologists had recommended that women not raise their heart rate above 140 beats per minute. This restriction has now been removed. Instead, their most recent recommendations stress common sense and moderation.

These recommendations are intended for women who do not have additional risk factors for adverse maternal or fetal outcome. A number of medical or obstetric conditions may lead your obstetrician or practitioner to recommend modifications of these principles. Discuss any exercise regimen with your practitioner before you begin to be sure that your routine does not need to be modified based upon your individual needs.

I exercised very moderately in all three trimesters of my pregnancy. I continued my routine right up to the day before my delivery. My routine was to jog on a treadmill three times a week for a minimum of 22 minutes to glean some cardiovascular benefits, but I did not push myself to go longer if I was exhausted. If I felt well, I would jog for as long as 45 minutes. In addition, I continued with my ballet, going through a 45-minute rigorous bar (under the watchful eye of Mme. "Enough, Dr. Hope") once a week throughout the pregnancy. I found that after exercising, even if I was tired when I began, I would feel energetic and infused with a sense of well-being following the exercise session. Sometimes I really had to push myself to begin the exercise routine, but once I got going I almost always felt well. I jogged on the treadmill because, as my abdomen became larger, the decreased impact of treadmill running was more comfortable than running outside. In addition, I avoided problems with icy as well as extremely hot conditions in my climate-controlled setting. I am convinced that this routine enabled me to have a very fast labor. By one week postpartum, I was back in my same exercise routine and feeling light as a feather, although I must admit that

ACOG RECOMMENDATIONS FOR EXERCISE DURING PREGNANCY AND POSTPARTUM

1. During pregnancy, women can continue to exercise and derive health benefits even from mild-to-moderate exercise routines. Regular exercise (at least three times per week) is preferable to intermittent activity.
2. Women should avoid exercise in the supine (lying on your back) position after the first trimester. Such a position is associated with decreased cardiac output in most pregnant women. Prolonged periods of motionless standing should also be avoided.
3. Women should be aware of the decreased oxygen available for aerobic exercise during pregnancy. They should be encouraged to modify the intensity of their exercise according to maternal symptoms. Pregnant women should stop exercising when fatigued and not exercise to exhaustion. Weightbearing exercises may under some circumstances be continued at intensities similar to those prior to pregnancy throughout pregnancy. Non-weight-bearing exercises such as cycling or swimming will minimize the risk of injury and facilitate the continuation of exercise during pregnancy.
4. Morphologic changes in pregnancy should serve as a relative contraindication to types of exercise in which loss of balance could be detrimental to maternal or fetal well-being, especially in the third trimester. Further, any type of exercise involving the potential for even mild abdominal trauma should be avoided.
5. Pregnancy requires an additional 300 calories per day in order to maintain metabolic homeostasis. Thus, women who exercise during pregnancy should be particularly careful to ensure an adequate diet.
6. Pregnant women who exercise in the first trimester should augment heat dissipation by ensuring adequate hydration, appropriate clothing, and optimal environmental surroundings during exercise.
7. Many of the physiologic and morphologic changes of pregnancy persist 4–6 weeks postpartum. Thus, prepregnancy exercise routines should be resumed gradually based on a woman's physical capability.

Source: American College of Obstetricians and Gynecologists, "Exercise during Pregnancy and the Postpartum Period," American College of Obstetricians and Gynecologists Technical Bulletin 189 (Washington, D.C.: American College of Obstetricians and Gynecologists, 1994).

back at dance class without Joey I did feel lonely. By four weeks post-partum, you would never have known I was pregnant. I never felt run down. People were constantly stopping me on the street when I had Joey with me and could not believe from looking at me that I had delivered him just a short while ago. "Good genetics," they would tell me.

"Good living," I would reply. "Good eating and regular activity."

NOTES

1. R. Artal, R. Wiswell, Y. Romem, and F. Dorey, "Pulmonary Responses to Exercise in Pregnancy," *American Journal of Obstetrics and Gynecology* 154 (1986): 378–383.

2. A. Milunsky, M. Ulcickas, K. J. Rothman, W. Willett, S. S. Jick, and H. Jick, "Maternal Heat Exposure and Neural Tube Defects," *Journal of the American Medical Association* 268 (1992): 882–885.

3. J. F. Clapp III and E. L. Capeless, "Neonatal Morphometrics after Endurance Exercise during Pregnancy," *American Journal of Obstetrics and Gynecology* 163 (1990): 1805–1811.

5 First Trimester

THE FIRST FEW WEEKS

The little dot in your home pregnancy test has changed color, and you realize that you are pregnant. From the 200 million sperm that were deposited, one reached the egg and fertilization occurred. You are filled with joy and excitement. But anxiety also sets in as you think about all that lies ahead. You want to do everything in your power to enhance the development of this baby.

A pregnancy test can turn positive as early as one to two weeks after ovulation, which is approximately the time you would expect your period. At this point, the embryo is one to two weeks old and consists of a mass of cells, some of which will develop into the fetus and others of which will develop into the placenta.

Some women begin to feel "pregnant" even at this early stage. Your breasts may become tender, you may be nauseated, and you may feel tired. All this is normal and reflects the huge changes your body is going through. It is important to take care of yourself by getting plenty of rest and eating a well-balanced diet since this will ensure the optimal chance for a healthy pregnancy and baby.

As soon as you know that you are pregnant, you should register for prenatal care. Whether you choose an obstetrician or a midwife is up to you. The important thing is to receive prenatal care from the start.

One of the purposes of prenatal care is to make sure, through counseling, that women receive adequate nutrition for pregnancy. Much is known about the dietary allowances for most substances needed during pregnancy (see Chapter 3). However, many obstetricians and health-care providers know little about the specific foods that constitute a healthy diet during pregnancy. Even less information is available about combining these specific foods in ways that are palatable to pregnant women, whose tastes for different foods may change drastically during the course of a pregnancy.

During the first weeks of your pregnancy, there are few outward signs that you are pregnant. Inside, however, tremendous changes are taking place.

By two weeks after conception, the future baby's blood circulation has begun, and the formation of the nervous system is starting. By four weeks, the heart, eyes, and ears are forming. And by week 5, there is a recognizable fetus. At this time, your pregnancy is most sensitive to the environment, including your diet. You want to take the best possible care of yourself, by eating well and getting plenty of rest, in order to maximize your baby's potential.

We have devised some recipes specifically for the first trimester, found in Chapter 12, that will help you do this. They are designed to appeal to your newly altered palate and are high in carbohydrates and packed with the necessary nutrients for this early point in pregnancy.

The Food Pyramid

Now that you are pregnant, continue to eat a well-balanced diet by selecting foods from the food pyramid. The food pyramid was created to replace the older four basic food groups and teaches about nutrient adequacy while guarding against nutrient excesses. You should eat 6 to 11 servings from the bread, cereal, rice, and pasta group; 3 to 5 servings from the vegetable group; 2 to 4 servings from the fruit group; 2 to 3 servings from the milk, yogurt, and cheese group; 2 to 3 servings from the meat, poultry, fish, beans, eggs, and nuts group. Use fats, oils, and sweets sparingly. The pyramid illustrates the dietary guidelines both for pregnancy and general health: eat a variety of foods; choose a diet low in fat, saturated fat, and cholesterol; emphasize vegetables, fruits, and grain products; use sugar only in moderation.

Calories

Many think of pregnancy as a time when you can eat as much as you want and anything you want without worrying about weight gain or fat content. Nothing could be further from the truth. In fact, the increase in calories that pregnant women generally require is only 15 percent compared to nonpregnant women—that is, usually between 300 to 500 calories per day, depending on the mother's weight and activity.

This increase in calories is far from a license to eat whatever you wish. With only this modest increase in calories, pregnant women need to increase their intake of certain nutrients from 25 to 200 percent. Packing all this extra nutrition into only 300 calories is difficult. While eating empty calories such as sweets and ice cream is okay for a treat, you should be consuming primarily those foods that satisfy your extra nutritional needs, not just your cravings. If you eat too many treats, you

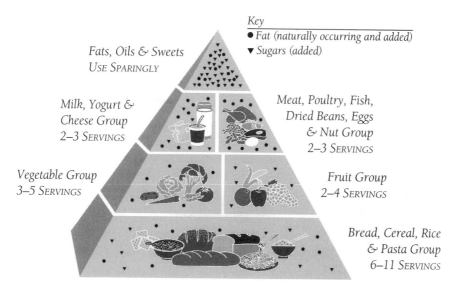

Key
● *Fat (naturally occurring and added)*
▼ *Sugars (added)*

Fats, Oils & Sweets
Use Sparingly

Milk, Yogurt & Cheese Group
2–3 Servings

Meat, Poultry, Fish, Dried Beans, Eggs & Nut Group
2–3 Servings

Vegetable Group
3–5 Servings

Fruit Group
2–4 Servings

Bread, Cereal, Rice & Pasta Group
6–11 Servings

Source: The Food Guide Pyramid, Home and Garden Bulletin No. 252 (Washington, D. C.: U.S. Department of Agriculture, Human Nutrition Information Service, 1992).

will be left with a tremendous weight gain to get rid of once the pregnancy is over. With careful attention paid to the content of each and every calorie, you can gain the required amount of weight for a healthy pregnancy and still fulfill your nutritional requirements without gaining a tremendous amount of weight. There is even room for treats, and with the recipes in this book, each meal can be nutritious and delicious.

Weight gain is an individual matter. The bottom line is that instead of counting calories, make every calorie you eat count. Eat a variety of foods, especially fruits and vegetables. Try to limit fats and cholesterol. As long as your baby is growing adequately (your practitioner will measure your belly at each prenatal visit after 20 weeks to determine this), your diet is supplying the needed nutrients to your baby.

Weight Gain

There is a positive correlation between how much weight you gain during pregnancy and the weight of your newborn. Independent of your weight gain during pregnancy, there is also a positive relationship between your prepregnant weight and the weight of your newborn.[1] The total weight gain recommended during pregnancy is 25 to 35 pounds for women of normal weight. Underweight women may gain up to 40 pounds, and overweight women can limit weight gain to 15 pounds.

RECOMMENDED TOTAL WEIGHT GAIN DURING PREGNANCY

For normal-weight women	25–35 pounds
For underweight women	40 pounds
For overweight women	15 pounds

During the first trimester, the required weight gain is small—usually 3 to 6 pounds—and 6 to 12 pounds (½ to 1 pound per week) should be gained in the last two trimesters of pregnancy. These gains are only rough guides; many women's weight-gain patterns deviate considerably from these, yet these women do just fine in their pregnancy. Your practitioner can tell you if your weight-gain pattern is healthy for you and your baby if you find yourself deviating from these ranges.

WEIGHT GAIN DURING PREGNANCY (BY TRIMESTER)

First trimester	3–6 pounds
Second trimester	6–12 pounds
Third trimester	6–12 pounds

Not all of this gain in weight is accounted for by the baby. Most comes from changes your body made to accommodate and support the pregnancy and lactation. About 2 to 3 pounds are from increased fluid retention, 3 to 4 pounds from increased blood volume, 1 to 2 pounds from breast enlargement, 2 to 3 pounds from enlargement of the uterus, and 2 to 3 pounds from amniotic fluid. At term, the baby may weigh approximately 6 to 8 pounds and the placenta 1 to 2 pounds. A 4- to 6-pound increase in maternal stores of fat and protein are important for lactation.

COMPONENTS OF WEIGHT GAIN IN TERM PREGNANCY

Fluid retention	2–3 pounds
Increased blood volume	3–4 pounds
Breast enlargement	1–2 pounds
Uterus enlargement	2–3 pounds
Amniotic fluid	2–3 pounds
Baby	6–8 pounds
Placenta	1–2 pounds
Fat stores	4–6 pounds

During the first trimester, an average woman should add 100 calories per day to her caloric intake, increasing to 400 calories by the third trimester. This does not translate into a very large amount of extra food since just one banana provides 100 calories. Therefore, although the first trimester is a time you must pay careful attention to the nutrient content of your food, you should increase your caloric intake very little. The way to do this in a healthy manner is to limit your fat intake.

Underweight

Low prepregnant weight and inadequate weight gain during pregnancy contribute significantly to the problem of low-birth-weight infants.[2] Low birth weight is defined as weighing in the bottom tenth in relation to the length of gestation. Some infants who fall below this cutoff are at increased risk for health problems in the immediate postpartum period and for developmental problems later in life. Therefore, it is vital to the development of your baby that you gain enough weight during pregnancy.

In the recent past, physicians advised pregnant women to restrict their food intake so that they would not gain too much weight, mistakenly believing that this helped make labor easier. Since then, it has been demonstrated that not gaining enough weight poses greater risks than gaining too much. If you do not gain 10 pounds by midpregnancy, you must carefully evaluate your nutritional intake.

Inadequate weight gain seems to be most problematic in women who were underweight before pregnancy. Underweight mothers must gain more weight during pregnancy to produce infants of normal weight. It is generally advised that a very thin woman try to achieve a desirable weight before conception so that she and her child do not compete for nutrients during pregnancy. To do this, you may follow the recipes that appear on pages 153–63. Although the recipes are relatively high in calories compared to other recipes in this book, they are still low in fat, but contain larger portions and utilize more calorie-dense ingredients.

Overweight

Women who begin their pregnancy overweight need not gain as much weight during the pregnancy. However, you should never try to loose weight during pregnancy. Total weight gain in those who are overweight can be modified downward to approximately 15 pounds. Less weight gain than this has been associated with lack of increase in blood volume and with risk of low-birth-weight infants (weighing in the bottom tenth in relation to the length of gestation).[3] In addition, weight loss during pregnancy contributes to the production of ketones, which are by-products of the breakdown of fat. Ketones have been associated in some studies with a decrease in subsequent mental and motor scores as well as IQ scores in infants.[4] There is some controversy about this issue since the sporadic occurrence of ketones is found in almost all normal pregnancies. Still, we must assume for now that dieting may be harmful to the fetus. Pregnancy is not the time for weight loss.

The recipes that appear on pages 164–71 are low in fat and calories yet still contain all the nutrients for a well-balanced pregnancy diet. They are intended for women who start their pregnancy overweight and want to minimize weight gain, especially in the first trimester. Your first-trimester weight gain can safely be kept to 3 pounds, with 6-pound gains in each of the next two trimesters, for a total weight gain of 15 pounds. Again, individual weight gain can vary. The important thing is that your baby gain weight adequately.

Twins

As with singleton infants, the birth weight of twins is directly affected by both maternal prepregnant weight and total weight gain during pregnancy. The incidence of low-birth-weight twins decreases as both maternal prepregnant weight and total weight gain during pregnancy increase.[5] Mothers carrying twins should try to gain 35 to 45 pounds. Remember that you must make twice as much baby, two placentas, and more amniotic fluid. You will need extra iron and folic acid to support your twin pregnancy, and your practitioner will likely prescribe supplements for both.

WEEKS 6 THROUGH 12

By now, you are well into your first trimester. Your baby's heart has formed and can be seen as a blinking light on ultrasound. Your baby has developed fingers and toes and all of the basic organs for life. There is active fetal movement going on that can be seen on ultrasound examination of your fetus, but you cannot as yet feel any of these movements.

Your own body is undergoing some profound changes despite your outwardly unchanged appearance. While others may not see your body changing, you probably do. You may notice larger breasts and a slight bulge in your lower abdomen. Your blood volume has already increased about 20 percent, your blood pressure has decreased, and your heart rate has increased.

You should aim to gain between 3 and 6 pounds by the end of the first trimester. Much of the weight gained during this period goes toward preparing your body to carry the pregnancy—increased blood volume, extra fat stores, breast and uterus enlargement. The fetus is still quite small, about the size of your thumb, so very little of the weight you have put on is here.

You need extra iron and folic acid as early as this point, and your diet should reflect this need. These nutrients go toward increasing your blood volume and manufacturing red blood cells in your baby.

Nausea and Vomiting

Women vary greatly in their feelings of well-being during the first trimester. Some women feel energized and wonderful. Others suffer greatly from nausea, vomiting, and fatigue.

Nausea and vomiting—"morning sickness"—is present in up to 70 percent of pregnancies.[6] *Morning sickness* is a misnomer; it actually should be called *all-day sickness*. Although distressing, morning sickness rarely poses health problems for the mother. In a few individuals, though, it can cause serious dehydration and electrolyte imbalances, a condition known as hyperemesis gravidarum. In severe cases, hyperemesis may require hospitalization for fluid and electrolyte restoration. In most women, the nausea and vomiting stop by the end of the first trimester and are gone in almost all women by around week 16. There are, however, a few unlucky women who have persistent nausea and vomiting until delivery.

The cause of this most troublesome problem has remained elusive. Relaxation of the smooth muscle of the stomach because of the high levels of the hormone progesterone probably plays a role. There is some evidence that elevated levels of human chorionic gonadotropin (HCG), the hormone measured in pregnancy tests, may be involved. However, the correlation between high levels of this hormone and the degree of nausea and vomiting is not perfect, so some other factor must be involved. In the past, hyperemesis was thought by the medical establishment to be a psychological disorder, and patients were "treated" by placing them in a dark hospital room with only a towel to clean up their own vomit. While there may be an anxiety or psychological component to this problem in some individuals, it clearly is only a small part of the cause of hyperemesis gravidarum.

Treatment for the nausea and vomiting of pregnancy involves changing the diet to one that is better tolerated. Taking many small meals helps some women since, paradoxically, it seems to relieve the nausea to have the stomach partially filled. Carbohydrates like potatoes, bread, and pasta, served as bland as possible with a minimum of fat and protein, also seem to sit better with many women. In the worst cases, only liquids can be tolerated. In these situations, the goal is simply to stay hydrated and take in calorie- and nutrient-containing beverages like juices instead of plain water or tea, if possible. Speak with your doctor about managing your nutritional intake if you suffer from hyperemesis gravidarum.

Despite the frightening idea of starving your baby in the first trimester, the obstetrical outcome of babies of mothers with even severe hyperemesis are no different than of babies of mothers without this problem.[7] Apparently, nature protects the fetus from many insults. You can feel reassured that your baby will be just fine and can focus on getting yourself through this trying time by staying well hydrated.

We have devised recipes that are high in carbohydrates, relatively bland, and have a minimum of added fat and protein, which may sit better in your nauseated stomach. See pages 112–25.

Fatigue

I felt more tired during the first trimester than at any other point in my pregnancy. The best remedy for fatigue is good, old-fashioned sleep. Sleep late whenever you can; nap during the day, if possible; early to bed. Easier said than done!

In addition, you will find that eating right will energize you. Stay away from high-fat, empty-calorie meals. Many of the recipes in Chap-

SAMPLE FIRST-TRIMESTER MENU

Breakfast
Cantaloupe-banana shake (p. 115)
Dry toast

Lunch
White bean and roasted butternut squash soup (p. 118)
Crackers
Milk (if you can tolerate it)

Dinner
Chicken soup with kale and orzo (p. 119)
Herbed basmati rice with tomatoes (p. 122)
Sparkling water

Snack
Cranberry-corn muffins (p. 112)
Milk (if you can tolerate it)

ter 12 will give you an energy boost in the first trimester and throughout the pregnancy since they provide all of the extra vitamins and nutrients required for pregnancy and comply with the recommendations for a high-carbohydrate, low-fat diet.

The first trimester is a time of tremendous physical changes for the mother. If you treat yourself right during this time, you will reap the rewards of a healthier and happier pregnancy. Take the time needed to eat well and enjoy your meals. Make the necessary adjustments in your diet to support your newly pregnant state. Exercise in moderation, and get plenty of rest. You and your future baby deserve it.

NOTES
1. N. J. Eastman and E. Jackson, "Weight Relationships in Pregnancy, I: The Bearing of Maternal Weight Gain and Pre-Pregnancy Weight on Birth Weight in Full Term Pregnancies," *Obstetrical and Gynecological Survey* 23 (1968): 1003–1025.

2. J. C. Kleinman, *Maternal Weight Gain during Pregnancy: Determinants and Consequences,* NCHS Working Paper No. 33 (Hyattsville, Md.: National Center for Health Statistics, Public Health Service, U.S. Department of Health and Human Services, 1990).

3. A. Gormician, F. Valentine, and E. Satter, "Relationship of Maternal Weight Gain, Prepregnancy Weight, and Infant Birthweight," *Journal of the American Dietetic Association* 77 (1980): 662–667.

4. J. A. Churchill, and H. W. Berendes, "Intelligence of Children Whose Mothers Had Acetonuria during Pregnancy," in *Perinatal Factors Affecting Human Development,* Scientific Publication 185 (Washington, D.C.: Pan American Health Organization, 1969), pp. 30–35.

5. J. E. Brown, and P. T. Schloesser, "Prepregnancy Weight Status, Prenatal Weight Gain, and the Outcome of Term Twin Gestations," *American Journal of Obstetrics and Gynecology* 162 (1990): 182–186.

6. A. Jarnfelt-Samsioe, G. Samsioe, and G.-M. Veliner, "Nausea and Vomiting of Pregnancy: A Contribution to Its Epidemiology," *Gynecologic and Obstetrical Investigations* 16 (1993): 221.

7. F. D. Tierson, C. L. Olsen, and E. B. Hook, "Nausea and Vomiting of Pregnancy and Association with Pregnancy Outcome," *American Journal of Obstetrics and Gynecology* 155 (1986): 1017–1022.

6 SECOND TRIMESTER

The second trimester generally spells relief from many of the problems of the first trimester. Your appetite is back, your nausea is gone, and your energy level is high. Take time to enjoy being pregnant by indulging your altered palate with the dishes that are offered in Chapter 13.

WEEKS 12 THROUGH 17

Breathe easy. You have passed the 12-week mark. By the end of the first trimester, all of your baby's basic parts are in place, and the rest of the pregnancy is spent in maturing and developing these parts. The risk of miscarriage is largely past after this point, and the susceptibility to environmental toxins has greatly decreased.

Many women find the second trimester to be the most enjoyable part of pregnancy. Much of the nausea and fatigue of the first trimester disappears (except for a few unlucky women in whom it may continue for a few weeks or even months). The fetus is still small enough so that you are not uncomfortable from the extra weight of the baby. Your energy returns, and you may feel more like exercising or walking.

Your Baby

Between 12 and 14 weeks, your baby's heartbeat will be detectable in the office with the help of Doppler ultrasound. Hearing your baby's heartbeat is a very exciting moment, one during which many women first really realize that this miracle of pregnancy may result in a baby being born. Your practitioner will check your baby's heartbeat at every visit now, and you will find that you never tire of hearing it. It is normally approximately twice as fast as your own heartbeat—anywhere from 120 to 180 heartbeats per minute—so do not be alarmed when you hear it racing away. Folklore says that you can tell the sex of your baby by the sound of the heartbeat (unfortunately not true).

Your baby is approximately 9 to 14 centimeters (3 to 6 inches) long and weighs between 60 to 200 grams (¼ to ½ pound). Your baby's fingers and toes are becoming well defined, and tooth buds are appearing. The bones are forming and growing, and the head is beginning to expand rapidly as the brain develops. You will need to increase your intake of carbohydrates, folic acid, and calcium since your baby needs these nutrients in increasing amounts.

The external genitalia of your baby have now developed, and the sex of your baby can be determined about this time by ultrasound examination. Occasionally, however, babies position themselves in such a way that we cannot see between their legs with the ultrasound. So prepare yourself to be disappointed if you are trying to find out the sex of your baby during your ultrasound examination.

Your Body and Its Requirements

Your body continues to undergo profound changes, and now many of them are visible externally. You will begin to show as your uterus grows out of the pelvis. You will notice your lower abdomen swelling and your clothes becoming tight. Your breasts enlarge, and your skin may darken a bit. You can no longer keep your pregnancy a secret.

Your body continues its internal physiological adaptation to pregnancy as well. Your blood pressure is lower and your heartbeat faster. You may find yourself becoming winded more easily when you walk or exercise. Your blood volume increases by approximately 30 percent at this point. To achieve this, you need extra iron in your diet.

Increased Appetite and Cravings

Your appetite will begin to increase as your body demands the extra calories and nutrients you and your baby need. You may find yourself craving some unusual foods. Some women crave fresh fruit, red meat, sweets, salty foods, or spicy foods. Some of your favorite foods may no longer taste good to you. Your sense of smell may now be very acute.

Cravings are perhaps your body's way of signaling your nutritional needs at this point. You can fulfill many of these cravings in healthy, satisfying ways. For some ideas, see the recipes in Chapter 13, including Broiled Swordfish with Mango-Kiwi Salsa (page 185), Roasted New Potatoes with Red Bell Peppers, Thyme, and Fennel (page 183), Linguine with Monkfish, Pecans, Thyme, and Raspberry Vinegar (page 192), Paella with Salt Cod (page 194), and Cashew and Black Bean Chili (page 196). Although these recipes are designed to appeal to some of the cravings that begin now, they provide all the nutrients you need in the second trimester.

Fuel

Glucose, produced when carbohydrates are metabolized, is the primary fuel for your developing baby. It is transported directly from your bloodstream to the placenta, where it passes through to the fetus. Since your baby is constantly drawing glucose from your blood, you are now very susceptible to hypoglycemia (low blood sugar). (Because of the mother's constant diversion of glucose to the baby, pregnancy is sometimes known as a state of "accelerated starvation.") Therefore, to maintain your own glucose level, it is important for you not to skip meals.

If you do not eat every few hours, you will find yourself getting dizzy (a symptom of hypoglycemia); you might even faint if you wait too long to eat. This can be very dangerous to your health. Likewise, your baby needs a constant supply of glucose in order to grow and develop to full potential.

Skipping breakfast is a particularly bad idea because of the extended amount of time that you and your baby went without fuel. You do not have to sit down to an elaborate breakfast to provide adequate fuel. If you take a few bites of toast or crackers and a drink of juice, you will be providing the glucose you and your baby need. Throughout the day, snacking on crackers, bagels, or bread with juice provides excellent nutrition anytime you do not have time for full meals. Actually, frequent snacking is a healthy way to eat. It provides a constant level of fuel for you and your baby, which avoids large swings in your hormonal response from the fasting state to the fed state. These large swings can put a strain on your system.

Continued Need for Iron and Calcium

Nutritionally, it is important to keep up your iron intake: your blood volume is still expanding, and extra iron is required to manufacture red blood cells. Your baby is manufacturing red blood cells as well, so your iron intake helps your baby, too. Keeping your intake of iron high now will prevent anemia (low red-blood-cell count) postpartum, which could leave you feeling tired and drained at a time you can ill afford to feel that way. Many of the recipes in Chapter 13 are rich in iron.

Extra calcium is required throughout pregnancy, and the second trimester is no exception. Calcium is used to build bones and teeth in your baby and is required for muscle contraction and normal heart function in both you and your baby. There is also new evidence to indicate that women with dietary calcium deficiencies may be more likely to develop preeclampsia (toxemia) during pregnancy.

Dairy products are excellent sources of calcium but may also be high in fat; try to choose low-fat varieties. You may be surprised to find that many vegetables, including broccoli and dark-green leafy vegetables (see the list on page 26), are high in calcium. Also available in the market are calcium-fortified fruit juices, which are a nourishing, low-fat way to obtain this nutrient. In addition, calcium-carbonate–based antacid tablets are another safe way to supply your body with extra calcium. As always, ask your practitioner before taking any medication in pregnancy.

WEEKS 18 THROUGH 24

Fetal Movement

At approximately 18 to 22 weeks, you will begin to feel your baby move. This is known as quickening. Initially, it feels like flutters or gas, but eventually it will become quite strong and even uncomfortable. At first, the movement will be irregular, but eventually your baby will settle into a pattern that you will recognize as normal for you. Many babies are more active at night and may even keep you awake. Pregnant women who have already had a baby tend to feel movement earlier, whereas first-time moms tend to notice the movement slightly later. Feeling your baby move is a special event, a moment that reminds you of what is most important in life.

Weight Gain

You should aim to gain between 6 to 12 pounds by the end of the second trimester. Your baby is much larger now, weighing in at about 1 pound by 24 weeks. Your amniotic-fluid volume has increased, as has the size of your placenta. Your blood volume is now increased by 40 percent, and you should begin to accumulate some extra body fat. All of this accounts for the weight you gain during this trimester.

Constipation, Iron, and Fiber

You may notice that your bowels are not moving as regularly as they did before you became pregnant. This is due to a combination of factors in the second trimester. The hormone progesterone is being produced in very large quantities by the placenta. Progesterone is very important in maintaining your pregnancy. It does, however, have some side effects, one of which is the slowing of the motility of your intestine, resulting in constipation. There is also increased water absorption from the colon, resulting in harder stools. Finally, the iron supplement that you may be taking is also constipating.

The need for iron and the problem of constipation can be solved by eating a diet rich in foods containing iron as well as fiber. Many of the recipes in Chapter 13 use these ingredients, which will keep your bowels regular. As always, these dishes also contain the extra vitamins and nutrients your body requires during pregnancy. Be sure to continue drinking plenty of water with every meal, which will also help keep your stools soft. And don't forget to take advantage of the tricks mentioned on pages 15 and 24 to maximize iron absorption.

Frequent Urination

If you find yourself constantly running to the bathroom, don't worry. Frequent urination is a normal sign of pregnancy. You may be urinating several more times during the day, and may even need to get up once or twice during the night to go to the bathroom. Drinking less fluid will not help this and may be dangerous. Continue to drink your 6 to 8 glasses a day, and just make extra trips to the bathroom part of your usual routine.

Swelling

Swelling, or edema, can start as early as the second trimester. It is a normal symptom of pregnancy and is caused by fluid shifts due to the many hormonal changes going on in your body. Avoiding salt will not decrease the amount of swelling you have, nor will limiting fluids. Both of these practices should be avoided. You may salt your food to taste in pregnancy, and you should always drink 6 to 8 glasses of fluid a day. If you find yourself craving salty food, it is fine to indulge. Just be cautious of overdoing the salt or you will become accustomed to very salty food and find it difficult to cut back once you are no longer pregnant.

Heartburn

At about this time, many women begin to feel heartburn. In the second trimester, heartburn results from a relaxation of the sphincter muscle between the lower portion of the esophagus and the stomach. Normally, this sphincter muscle keeps the acid and stomach contents away from the esophagus. In pregnancy, the hormone progesterone causes this muscle to relax, which, in turn, allows the stomach acid to come in contact with the esophagus, which results in heartburn. In addition, as you progress further along in gestation, especially in the third trimester, the growing uterus pushes up on the stomach, compounding this problem.

Your diet can diminish heartburn. Eating many small meals instead of a few large ones will help stop food and stomach acid from refluxing into the esophagus. Keeping a small amount of food in your stomach will aid in neutralizing stomach acid, and by not overeating at each meal you will have less reflux. In addition, many pregnant women find

SAMPLE SECOND-TRIMESTER MENU

Breakfast

Blueberry-corn pancakes (p. 176)

Juice

Coffee

Lunch

Cannellini bean hummus (p. 179) on pita bread

Fruit

Frozen yogurt

Dinner

Tomato-bread salad (p. 182)

Pan-seared monkfish with corn-avocado relish (p. 184)

Baked potato

Snack

Chocolate-almond biscotti (p. 292)

Decaffeinated coffee or tea

that fatty and spicy foods exacerbate the problem. You will also notice that certain foods help your heartburn and others make it worse. You will have to experiment to see which foods are best for you since every pregnant woman is different.

We have devised several dishes for women who find their heartburn particularly bad. The recipes for Irish Soda Bread (page 175), Blueberry-Corn Pancakes (page 176), Potato Gnocchi with Butter and Parmesan (page 204), and Classic Risotto (page 205) are low-fat and relatively bland and may relieve or prevent heartburn.

The second trimester is a time of pleasant changes for both you and your baby. You have become noticeably pregnant, and your baby now looks human. By eating well during this time, you are paving the way for good health for both you and your baby in the potentially difficult months that lie ahead. Your diet can help you stay more comfortable now by preventing some of the common problems of the second trimester, including constipation and heartburn.

7 THIRD TRIMESTER

You can now see light at the end of the tunnel. Your due date is near enough so that it seems like a reality. For a while, it probably felt as if you would be pregnant forever. Although you will soon get to see this child that you have worked so hard to keep healthy, do not stop the good habits you have started. It is as important as ever to eat well and care for yourself and your baby in the third trimester.

WEEKS 25 THROUGH 38

Your Baby's Development

Your baby will grow during this final trimester from approximately 1 pound to its final weight—normally, 6 to 8 pounds. Your baby's development, though far from complete, has reached what the medical establishment calls "viable." This means that your baby now has the potential to survive outside your uterus (womb). Of course, it would be greatly preferable for the baby to continue to mature inside for a while since its maturing now consists largely of further lung development and brain growth.

For the baby's brain to keep growing, you should continue to eat plenty of carbohydrates so that your baby can get a constant supply of glucose, which is produced when carbohydrates are metabolized. Your baby continues to manufacture red blood cells, a process that requires both iron and folic acid, which should come from the maternal diet, as should calcium, which is needed to help the baby's bones become larger and stronger.

Your Body

You will notice your abdomen growing rapidly at this stage. Pregnancy can become quite uncomfortable as the baby takes up more and more room inside you during the third trimester. Your ribs can get sore from the constant kicking, your lower back may ache from carrying the extra weight, and you may have difficulty sleeping.

At each prenatal visit, your practitioner will measure your growing abdomen, which is an indication of your baby's growth. Your fundal height—the measurement from your pubic bone to the top of your uterus—corresponds in centimeters to the number of weeks gestation you have completed. Thus, if you are 30 weeks pregnant, your fundal height should be approximately 30 centimeters. Any significant deviation from these norms may mean that your baby is either large or small, and your practitioner may decide to perform an ultrasound evaluation to estimate the weight of your baby more precisely.

Weight Gain

You should aim to gain between 6 and 12 pounds during this trimester, at an average rate of ½ to 1 pound per week. During some weeks you will gain no weight, while during other weeks you may gain several pounds. The recommendations are only rough guidelines. As long as your baby is growing—and this is determined by measuring your abdomen at your prenatal visits or by ultrasound if there is any question—your weight gain is adequate. Don't become obsessed with the scale. All that really matters is that your baby get adequate nutrition, as evidenced by normal growth.

Breasts and Lactation

Your nipples will grow darker and larger. Your breasts are fully capable of producing milk at this point, and you may even notice some leakage of fluid from your nipples, although not every woman has leakage. This fluid, called colostrum, is the food your baby will receive just before your milk comes in after giving birth and is packed with disease-fighting antibodies. It is important to continue taking in extra calcium, especially if you plan to breast-feed.

Swelling (Edema)

Your feet and calves may swell as your body retains fluid. Keep your feet up as much as possible, and always keep them elevated when you are sitting, if swelling is a problem for you. When you lie down, lie on your side to encourage the circulation in your body, which can help minimize the problem of swelling. But do not be discouraged if you cannot prevent or get rid of it. If you notice a rapid onset of swelling, especially in your hands and face, let your practitioner know immediately since this could be one of the signs of preeclampsia. Your practitioner will be checking your blood pressure at every visit to screen for this problem.

Despite the extra fluid in your body, you should continue to drink 6 to 8 glasses of fluid per day. You may continue to salt your food to taste since minimizing salt intake will not help to decrease the swelling.

Decreased Appetite

You may lose your appetite during the third trimester as the growing uterus takes up more room inside you, pushing up on your stomach. Large meals may make you uncomfortable since there is only so much room inside for your baby and your food. Try eating many small meals instead of three large ones, if you find you get uncomfortably full halfway through your meals. Several of the recipes in Chapter 14 are for dishes that will not make you feel uncomfortably full, yet contain the nutrition you need during this important time.

Your Dietary Needs: Iron, Calcium, Fiber, and Zinc

At the start of the third trimester, your practitioner may recheck your hematocrit to be sure that you have not become anemic from iron deficiency. Women who are anemic during pregnancy tend to remain so postpartum. If you have developed iron-deficiency anemia, now is the time to address this problem. You will need to take in extra iron—in the form of food and supplements. Chapter 14 offers many iron-rich dishes that also contain the proper balance of nutrients to maximize the absorption of iron. If you take your iron supplement after eating these dishes, you will maximize your absorption of iron from it as well.

You should continue to eat foods rich in calcium for several reasons. First, your body is preparing to lactate. Second, meeting your daily requirement of calcium may be important in preventing osteoporosis (thin, porous bones) later in life. Third, your baby needs calcium as its bones become larger and stronger. Finally, as mentioned in Chapter 5, calcium may be important in preventing preeclampsia.

The third trimester can be terrible for constipation and hemorrhoids. The hormone progesterone continues to be present in very high quantities, slowing down the motility of your intestines, resulting in constipation. In addition, in the third trimester the uterus has become very large and obstructs the colon, making the problem of constipation even worse. All of this can lead to hemorrhoids.

Hemorrhoids are varicose veins of the rectum. They are a result of increased pressure in the venous blood system of the rectum. Because straining during bowel movements makes hemorrhoids worse, avoidance of constipation is important. Again, dietary modification to increase stool bulk will usually do the trick (many of the recipes in Chapter 14 are very high in fiber), as will staying well hydrated. Prolonged sitting should also be avoided since this causes blood to pool in the area and dilate the veins further. Hemorrhoids will often regress after delivery but usually will not disappear.

The early third trimester can be a time when premature labor strikes, so be aware of your body and be sure to report to your practitioner any regular contractions or menstrual-like cramps. It is possible that a diet rich in zinc may prevent several types of premature labor. Some preliminary data indicate that dietary deficiencies of zinc may be linked with premature delivery and low-birth-weight infants.

The richest sources of zinc include fish and shellfish (see page 28 for a more complete listing). Some delicious dishes rich in zinc are found in Chapters 14 and 15, including Gravid Granola (page 220),

Shrimp, Scallop, and Squid Risotto (page 247), and Mussels with Ginger, Tamari, and Herbs (page 273).

WEEKS 38 THROUGH 42

Your delivery could be days away. Labor is not called labor for nothing—it is very hard work, both emotionally and physically. You have spent the last nine months preparing for it and for a healthy baby. Now is the time to put the finishing touches on all this preparation.

Sleep

Get plenty of rest. You do not want to begin the childbirth process sleep-deprived. Remember that after labor, the work of raising a child begins, and you should be as rested as possible when you and your baby start this new life together. However, at the end of pregnancy, many women find it difficult to sleep because they are uncomfortable. At this point, you should not lay on your back since your uterus, which is now quite big, will then compress the large blood vessels that are returning blood from your lower extremities to the heart. This impedance of blood flow will make you uncomfortable and short of breath, and is not good for the baby. Try lying on your side. In addition, a hot shower or bath can work wonders to sooth and relax aching muscles and allow you to sleep. Finally, get your partner to give you a deep muscle massage—your shoulders, lower back, and feet.

Certain foods can also help you sleep. A high-carbohydrate meal often leads to feelings of sleepiness. Foods that contain tryptophan, an amino acid found in milk, can help lull you to sleep. Try a glass of milk before bedtime or one of the bedtime snacks found in Chapter 14.

Carbohydrate Loading

Endurance athletes, especially marathon runners, have been carbohydrate loading since the 1960s, when Scandinavian researchers studying runners showed that muscle glycogen (the storage form of carbohydrates) can be increased by a high-carbohydrate diet eaten 7 days prior to a big race. This extra stored glycogen may then be used as fuel for the muscles during a long race, resulting in improved performance.

Labor may be considered similar to running a marathon. Some labors last as long as 24 to 48 hours. Your body will benefit from increased stores of muscle and liver glycogen during this arduous time. You can begin to carbohydrate load 1 to 2 weeks before your due date by increasing the carbohydrate content in your diet. Normally, you should derive at least 50 percent of your calories from carbohydrates. Try to increase your intake by eating pasta, potatoes, rice, bread, and cereals during this period. Several of the recipes in Chapter 14 are for dishes that contain large amounts of carbohydrates.

8 POSTPARTUM

Congratulations! You are now the mother of a beautiful new baby. During your pregnancy, you probably anticipated labor and delivery as a huge event, but it pales in comparison with the new life you have just delivered and are responsible for. Whether you had a vaginal delivery or a cesarean section, it is now critically important that you take good care of yourself as well as your baby. Eating right and getting as much rest as possible will only enhance your enjoyment of and ability to care for the newest member of the family.

POSTPARTUM CHANGES

Postpartum is the period during which the many changes your body went through preparing for childbirth now reverse. These changes began immediately after the delivery of your placenta. Your body will not be back to "normal" for at least 6 weeks.

Postpartum Blues

Around day 3 after giving birth, you may start to feel moody, anxious, or depressed. Most women go through emotional changes after childbirth. In fact, 50 percent of women get the postpartum blues. There are huge changes going on in your body postpartum, your hormone levels dropping rapidly immediately after delivery. Most experts agree that hormonal changes are in part responsible for the postpartum blues. The moodiness usually lasts only a day or two.

But there are many other factors besides hormonal ones that contribute to your emotional state. First of all, you just went through an arduous birth process, one that can leave you physically exhausted, even bruised and battered. Your sleep has very likely been frequently interrupted and not very deep, given that you are now fully responsible for a new life. You may feel overwhelmed by this new responsibility. Maybe you are even a little disappointed in your birth experience or in your baby. In addition, you were on center stage for much of the pregnancy, and now you have been pushed aside by your baby. This is all quite normal, so don't feel guilty. It is important to verbalize your feelings, not keep them inside. Speak to your partner about them since your partner may share many of the same feelings.

Of all the factors involved, one of the greatest contributors to the blues is being overtired and poorly nourished. Try starting your day with a good breakfast since this meal—the most important one of the day—will reset your metabolism and provide strength and equilibrium. Your morning meal need not be elaborate in order to be nutritious. Try the Whole-Grain, Yogurt, and Berry Pancakes (page 261) or Buckwheat-Raisin-Pecan Bread (prepared and frozen before the baby was born, page 264), or simply toast a bagel or other bread and enjoy it with fresh fruit. Avoid foods containing chocolate, which can add to your emotional imbalance (in the same manner that it can worsen premenstrual syndrome).

Cesarean Delivery

If you had a cesarean birth, you underwent major abdominal surgery. You will need to take extra care of yourself to ensure proper recovery while you take care of your baby. This can be done, but it requires lots of help from family and friends. Accept all the help you can get.

There is some evidence that zinc is involved in wound healing. Zinc is found in fish and shellfish (see page 28 for a more complete listing), so try to include more of these foods in your diet.

Meals in the Hospital

The food you are given in the hospital may not appeal to you and may not supply the necessary nutrients your depleted body now requires. After a long and arduous labor, your muscles and liver require replenishing amounts of carbohydrates. So the postpartem steak that many hospitals offer is not the best meal to eat.

Try preparing Carons Restaurant's Raisin-Bran Muffins (page 263) ahead of time and freezing them. You can then have them brought to the hospital during your stay and can nibble on these nourishing, carbohydrate-rich snacks while you care for your baby and entertain family and friends. You or your partner can also prepare and freeze ahead of time such dishes as Autumn Lentil Soup (page 268), Creole Red Beans and Brown Rice (page 285), and Eggplant-Mozzarella Grinders with Tomato-Spinach Sauce (page 281) and then heat them in the hospital's microwave. Home cooking will have never tasted so good!

Posthospital Decrease in Appetite

Some mothers detect a temporary loss of appetite the first couple of weeks after delivery. If you find that you do not have much desire to eat, try some particularly flavorful dishes to stimulate your appetite. (Several of the recipes in Chapter 15 fit the bill.) Continue to eat meals on schedule since this regularity will help you regain some equilibrium in your daily activities.

Hair Loss

You may notice that your hair is falling out. This generalized loss of hair (telogen effluvium) is caused by hormonal changes following childbirth.

Normally, your hair does not grow continually, but rather in a cycles, with alternating phases of activity and inactivity. Postpartum, your hair follicles have shifted simultaneously into a resting phase, resulting in hair loss. This postpartum hair loss is seldom severe—you will not go bald. It lasts for approximately 3 to 6 months. Changing your diet will not affect it.

Frequent Urination

In the first few days after your delivery, you will urinate frequently and in large amounts. Your body is getting rid of much of the excess fluid that you may have noticed as swelling in your feet and ankles. Occasionally, the swelling gets worse during the first day or two postpartum; but it then goes away rapidly as your body transfers the extra fluid back to your bloodstream, which you then eliminate by urination. Do a lot of walking in the halls while you are in the hospital since this will help to mobilize the excess fluid and will keep your circulation going, thus preventing blood clots.

Contractions

If this is not your first baby, you will have some painful contractions of your uterus, especially during breast-feeding, as your uterus expels its inner lining and begins to shrink back to its former small size. You will also have a bloody vaginal flow, or lochia, which will continue for up to 2 weeks.

Sore Bottom

If you had a vaginal delivery, your vagina, perineum, urethra, and rectum may be extremely sore. You may have tears or an episiotomy that required stitches to repair. Many women find their perineum so painful that medication is needed to control the pain. Pain medications containing a narcotic can be constipating, so drink plenty of fluids and eat a fiber-rich diet to prevent this problem.

Constipation

During the first few days after delivery, constipation often worsens. This is compounded by the fact that your hemorrhoids, if you have them, may have swelled from all that bearing down you did during your delivery. In addition, pain medications, as mentioned above, are often constipating. With all this soreness, the first bowel movement can be a terrifying experience. But do not despair—anticipation is often the worst part, and your stitches will not pop.

To minimize constipation, keep yourself well hydrated by drinking at least 6 to 8 glasses of fluid a day. And try some of the high-fiber dishes found in Chapter 15.

Anemia

You will have lost between ½ liter and 1 liter of blood during the delivery of your baby—possibly more, if bleeding was excessive. Your body was prepared for most of this loss because you manufactured extra red blood cells during the course of your pregnancy. Since your practitioner may recheck your hematocrit postpartum, you will know if you must change your diet to increase your red-blood-cell count, if it is low.

To boost your blood count, you will need to take in extra dietary iron, or your practitioner may have you continue your iron supplement, if your blood loss was large. This will keep you from becoming anemic postpartum, a time when you can ill afford to be run down since you are caring for your newborn. See the list of sources for iron on page 24, or try some of the iron-rich dishes found in Chapter 15. Also see the list of iron-rich dishes in the appendix.

At your six-week checkup, your practitioner will test your blood again to be sure that you are not anemic. Prior to that time, if you find yourself feeling continually tired despite adequate rest or if you appear very pale, discuss this with your doctor since your blood count may still be low.

BREAST-FEEDING

The physiology of pregnancy prepares your body to lactate and breast-feed. Optimal milk production requires a total diet of at least 1,800 calories per day. The energy sources for this are your fat stores and diet (about an additional 500 calories per day, which is 200 more calories per day than you needed during pregnancy). Caloric intake above your total energy needs will not increase milk production. Breast-feeding mothers who consume less than 1,500 calories per day will find themselves exhausted and may be unable to produce enough milk to nourish the baby.

Milk Composition and Your Diet

The major components of breast milk are water, fat, protein, carbohydrates, and minerals. Most of the calories in human milk are derived from fat and reflect the fat content of the mother's diet. Even if your diet is less than what is recommended, human milk consistently supplies enough carbohydrates, fat, protein, and most minerals to meet an infant's needs. The vitamin composition of the milk, however, is more directly related to what the mother eats.[1]

You will find that you are thirsty when you are breast-feeding. Drinking water, juice, and milk to satisfy thirst is acceptable for breast-milk production.[2] You should continue to consume between 6 to 8 glasses of liquid a day.

Breast-feeding means an ongoing responsibility toward maintaining a well-balanced and varied diet. A diet for the breast-feeding woman is similar to the well-balanced diet you consumed during your pregnancy. Neither iron nor vitamin and mineral supplements are routinely required.

Weight Loss

Milk production is largely independent of nutritional intake during the first few months of breast-feeding partly because the extra fat you accumulated during your pregnancy is now available as a ready supply of calories. When your diet is inadequate, however, your milk production usually continues at *your* expense, leading to fatigue, listlessness, and rapid weight loss. It is, therefore, important to maintain an adequate diet so that you can enjoy your baby without tremendous fatigue.

After the rapid weight loss in the first postpartum month, you may lose weight at a rate of 2 pounds (0.9 kilogram) a month without affecting milk volume. If you began your pregnancy overweight, an acceptable weight loss is 4 pounds (1.8 kilograms) a month. Regular exercise is appropriate, but purposeful weight-reduction diets and rapid weight loss are not advisable. At one year after delivery, an average residual weight gain of 2 pounds (0.9 kilogram) has been found.[3]

If you are trying to loose some extra postpartum pounds, the low-fat recipes in Chapter 15 may help. They still contain all the needed nutrients for successful breast-feeding and speedy recovery.

Alcohol

Many substances are secreted from your blood into the milk you produce, alcohol included. In general, alcohol is not recommended for nursing mothers, but small amounts probably do not affect your baby. Consuming an occasional glass of beer or wine is not believed to be harmful. Excessive amounts of alcohol, however, may result in lethargy in your baby and a decrease in the milk let-down reflex (ejection of milk from the sacs where milk is made).[4] Too much alcohol can also impair your judgment and dull your instincts, which you can ill afford with a new infant to care for. In the long term, excessive consumption of alcohol can cause liver disease and increase your risk for many different types of cancer.

Caffeine

Caffeine is passed through your breast milk to your baby. You should limit your coffee and tea intake to no more than 2 cups a day. Caffeine intake equivalent to more than 3 cups of coffee a day may result in an irritable, wide-awake, colicky infant. Caffeine has been shown to decrease the baby's absorption of iron, which can result in iron-deficiency anemia.

Smoking

Smoking is a maternal health hazard, increasing your risk of many kinds of cancer, heart disease, and respiratory disease. It can also reduce your milk volume. It may cause respiratory problems in your infant, including bronchitis, pneumonia, and asthma, and has been associated with an increased risk of crib death (sudden infant death syndrome).

If this is not enough, the hazards of passive smoking include an increased risk of lung cancer and respiratory problems in the recipient (your baby). Now is the time to quit—for both of you.

YOUR NEW NUTRITIONAL NEEDS

Carbohydrates

You should continue to take in the majority of your calories—more than 50 percent—from carbohydrates in the same manner you did while you were pregnant. In fact, you should continue to eat in this fashion for the rest of your life. Meals based upon pasta, potatoes, rice, and other grains, with plenty of fresh fruit and vegetables and a minimum of meat are healthy, filling, and energizing. See Chapter 15 for some ideas.

Protein

You need slightly more protein in your diet now than you did while you were pregnant—65 grams daily instead of 60 grams. This requirement is easily met, especially if you are drinking milk (skim or low-fat is best) for extra calcium.

Fat

The amount of fat you consume in your diet will be reflected in the fat content of your milk. The amount of cholesterol you consume, however, will not affect the cholesterol content of your milk. Therefore, continue to get 30 percent of your daily calories from fat, but minimize cholesterol in your diet. If you do this, you will protect your health by lowering your cholesterol, while providing ample fat calories for your baby.

Vitamins and Minerals

Your baby depends on your diet to provide the essential vitamins through your breast milk. Most vitamins are needed in larger amounts during lactation than during pregnancy. The requirement for vitamin C increases from 70 milligrams per day during pregnancy (60 milligrams are needed for nonpregnant women) to 95 milligrams per day during lactation. It is not difficult to meet this requirement: 70 milligrams are found in 1 orange, 30 milligrams in 1 tomato.

Lactating mothers tend to be most commonly deficient in dietary calcium and zinc. Many of the dishes in Chapter 15 are rich in these nutrients. It is best to obtain the vitamins you need by eating a varied diet rather than from supplements. However, a lactating woman on a strict vegetarian diet (no eggs or animal and dairy foods) requires vitamin B_{12}, zinc, and vitamin D supplements.[5]

Iron

The amount of iron in breast milk is low and is not affected by your diet. There is generally enough iron stores in your baby from your pregnancy to last several months, so most babies do not need any supplements. However, if you are anemic postpartum, as will be determined by your postpartem hematocrit, you should increase the iron content of your diet to build up your own red-blood-cell count.

Your period will be very light or absent while you are breast-feeding; thus, you will loose very little blood during these months, and your body will be able to get its red-blood-cell count back to normal. Your iron stores are usually replenished if you just eat a well-balanced diet—no need for iron supplementation.

Calcium

The calcium level of your breast milk is constant regardless of your diet. However, if you routinely do not meet your need for calcium from your diet, this nutrient will be drawn from the reservoir in your bones to supply your baby, possibly making you more susceptible later in life to osteoporosis. This is a special concern for younger women who breast-feed since the calcium content of bones increases until age twenty-five, after which time you can no longer increase it.

The daily requirement for calcium for lactating women is 1,600 milligrams, even higher than the 1,200 milligrams required for pregnant women. To give you an idea of what this means, there are 300 milligrams of calcium in an 8-ounce glass of milk, 1 cup of yogurt, 1 ounce of Swiss cheese, or 2 cups of broccoli.

Many nutritionists recommend that a nursing mother drink 5 glasses of milk a day. But there is no need to drink milk if you do not like it or cannot tolerate it. Although milk is an excellent source of calcium and protein, other foods can be substituted to meet these needs.

I did not drink any milk during my pregnancy since I dislike it. I do love yogurt and ice cream, however, so I took in much of my calcium in this manner. For those who do not eat dairy products at all, there are some alternative dietary sources of calcium.

Surprisingly, many vegetables are high in calcium. A diet based on green leafy vegetables and legumes can provide sufficient calcium during pregnancy and postpartum. Four ounces of tofu processed with calcium sulfate has 250 to 765 milligrams of calcium. A cup of cooked collard greens or turnip greens has over 350 milligrams of calcium. Many legumes, including pinto beans, black beans, and soybeans, have at least 100 milligrams of calcium in a ½-cup serving. In addition, available today are calcium-fortified orange, apple, and grapefruit juices, which contain a form of calcium that is very well absorbed. Also available is milk that is doubly fortified with calcium. Several of the dishes in Chapter 15 are rich in alternative sources of calcium for nursing mothers who do not eat dairy products.

GETTING BACK TO "NORMAL"

Quick-to-Prepare Meals

In addition to the tremendous physical changes your body is undergoing, you are also spending a great deal of time and energy caring for your baby. You should rest as much as you possibly can—sleep whenever your baby sleeps. Your diet should be varied and well balanced. Since this may be difficult because there is so little time for cooking, you should consider those recipes in the postpartum section for dishes that are nutritious yet can be prepared in minutes.

You and Your Partner

The two of you have been enjoying your baby, and the topic of nearly every conversation is the baby. Now you should focus on your relationship together. Drop your baby off at a trusted friend's or relative's house for a few hours, and, to renew romance, prepare and dine on one of the dishes found in Chapter 15.

NOTES

1. Subcommittee on Nutritional Status and Weight Gain during Lactation *et al., Nutrition during Lactation* (Washington, D.C.: National Academy Press, 1991).

2. Institute of Medicine, Food and Nutrition Board, Committee on Nutritional Status during Pregnancy and Lactation, Subcommittee on Nutrition during Lactation, *ibid.*

3. Institute of Medicine, Food and Nutrition Board, Committee on Nutritional Status during Pregnancy and Lactation, Subcommittee on Dietary Intake and Nutrient Supplements during Pregnancy and Subcommittee on Nutritional Status and Weight Gain during Pregnancy, in *Nutrition during Pregnancy,* I: *Weight Gain* (Washington, D.C.: National Academy Press, 1990).

4. *Ibid.*

5. Institute of Medicine, Food and Nutrition Board, Committee on Nutritional Status during Pregnancy and Lactation, Subcommittee on Nutrition during Lactation, *op. cit.*

9 Snacks, Foods on the Go, and Eating Out

You need to be practical when you are pregnant. You will not always have the time or energy to cook full meals, especially if you work or have other children. You may enjoy eating out, and wish to continue to go to restaurants. This chapter provides ideas for nutritious snacks, foods on the go, and tips for eating out.

SNACKS

Snacks are an important and inevitable part of a pregnant woman's diet. In fact, you may need to snack while you are pregnant because you are hungry between meals. And, if you do not have time for full meals or are uncomfortable eating large meals, snacks can provide the extra calories and protein, vitamins, and minerals you need during pregnancy, if the levels of fat and sugar are kept to a reasonable level. Thus, consuming three meals and several snacks a day is an acceptable and healthy way of eating during pregnancy.

Snacks are often referred to disparagingly—as "empty" calories, devoid of any valuable nutrients. But no food by itself is entirely useless since it does provide the calories you and your baby require. While eating foods that are high in sugar and fat are not the best way to obtain your nutrients on a regular basis, occasionally they are the most accessible source of energy. For example, if you are feeling light-headed from hypoglycemia (low blood sugar) because it has been several hours since you last ate and the only available food is a brownie or candy bar from the snack machine, it is okay to eat this. It is not "junk" under these circumstances: the sweet snack is providing nourishment. On the other hand, if you are filling up on sweets just before eating your meals and are, therefore, not eating your Spinach Fettuccine with "Wild" Mushroom Sauce (page 147), then your snacking is probably not healthy.

If you snack to obtain your nutrients, choose snacks that provide nutrition. Fresh and dried fruit are an excellent source of fiber and vitamins. Nuts and seeds are rich in protein and fiber, but be cautious of overdoing it since nuts and seeds are also high in fat. Trail mix can be a nutritious snack, but choose one that contains mostly dried fruits since nuts are high in fat. Granola can be an excellent snack if you choose a low-fat or nonfat variety (see the recipe for Gravid Granola on page 220). Bread is a terrific snack. And bagels are quick, delicious, and widely available. But beware of spreading too much high-fat stuff on top, like peanut butter or cream cheese. Instead, use a small amount of spread, or use nothing at all and eat two bagels. Crackers are a con-

SNACKS

Fresh friut	Dried fruit	Seeds, nuts, and grains	Breads	Cookies	Dairy products
Apples	Apples	Almonds	Bagels	Fig bars	Cottage cheese
Bananas	Apricots	Cashews	Graham	Hermits	Frozen yogurt
Grapefruit	Banana chips	Granola	crackers	with dried	Low-fat cheese
Grapes	Dates	Peanuts	Low-fat	fruit and	Low-fat ice
Melon	Figs	Pecans	crackers	nuts	cream
Nectarines	Pineapple	Pretzels	Matzoh	Oatmeal	Yogurt
Oranges	Prunes	Pumpkinseeds	Melba toast	cookies	
Peaches	Raisins	Sunflower seeds	Whole-grain	Peanut-	
Pears		Trail mix	bread	butter	
Pineapple		Walnuts		cookies	
Plums					

venient snack, but many of them are very high in fat. Try the nonfat or low-fat varieties. (Read the label carefully to be sure they really are low in fat; they may be lower than traditional crackers, but not low enough.) When choosing cookies, try to pick the ones that have some nutritional value—for example, those that contain nuts, dried fruit, or whole grains are acceptable. Snacking on dairy products can be a great way to get the extra calcium you need during pregnancy. Again, choose nonfat or low-fat varieties. Some of the low-fat ice creams and frozen yogurts available today are so creamy and delicious you will not even notice the missing fat.

FOODS ON THE GO

The meals that you eat while you are away from home or that you bring to work do not need to be elaborate to be nutritious. Invest in some plastic containers with lids, and last night's leftovers from dinner will make a terrific lunch today. Be sure to refrigerate these meals adequately to prevent bacteria contamination (see pages 89–92). Since many of the dishes in this book make terrific lunches when reheated in the microwave, simply make a little extra and put the leftovers in your plastic containers to take with you to work the next day.

With a little planning, you can stock your refrigerator and cupboard with the components you need to pack meals on the go. See the "Shopping List" of ingredients for nutritious dishes you can eat if you do not have time to cook or if you would like to pack a brown-bag meal to carry with you. All breads may be kept in the freezer. Buy less ripe fruit if you do not plan to use it immediately. Plan ahead when you shop.

The following combinations of the ingredients found in the "Shopping List" constitute healthy meals for the pregnant woman that fit in with her busy lifestyle:

- *Turkey and Swiss cheese on whole-grain bread with mustard, lettuce, and tomato; fresh fruit.* The turkey provides protein and iron, the cheese calcium, and the whole-grain bread complex carbohydrates. Using mustard instead of mayonnaise keeps the fat low.
- *Low-fat cheese (2 ounces), bagel, and grapes.* There are many low-

SHOPPING LIST

Breads and grains	Protein sources	Fruits and vegetables	Extras
Bagels	Canned salmon	Alfalfa sprouts	Balsamic vinegar
English muffins	Canned tuna	Avocados	Honey
Low-fat crackers	Cheese wedges	Baking potatoes	Jams
Pita	Eggs	Bananas	Mustard
Pretzels	Hummus	Cucumbers	Olive oil
Sliced bread	Low-fat cottage cheese	Olives	Red-wine vinegar
	Low-fat cream cheese	Seasonal fruit	
	Peanut butter	Tomatoes	
	Sliced roast beef		
	Sliced turkey		

fat varieties of cheese now available, including Swiss, goat, and part-skim mozzarella. You may not be able to taste the difference between these and the higher-fat varieties.

- *Hummus on pita with lettuce, tomato, and sprouts.* If you not have time to make your own hummus (see the recipe for Cannellini Bean Hummus, page 179), there are many excellent ones available commercially. Hummus can be low in fat and rich in protein, carbohydrates, and fiber.
- *Microwaved potato with low-fat cottage cheese.* You can cook a potato in a microwave in minutes. Serve it with cottage cheese instead of butter, and you have added protein and calcium to your carbohydrate-rich potato—a perfect pregnancy dish.
- *Cantaloupe filled with cottage cheese; pretzels.* Calcium and protein are supplied by the cottage cheese. Accompany this with pretzels for some carbohydrates. Delicious and convenient, too.
- *Lean roast beef (not rare) with lettuce and tomato on whole-grain bread; fresh fruit.* Roast beef is an excellent source of iron, and the vitamin C in the tomato helps you absorb it better. Use whole-grain bread for extra fiber, and hold the mayonnaise to keep the fat content down.
- *Low-fat cream cheese (Neufchâtel), tomato, and cucumber sandwich.*

Low-fat cream cheese is convenient to have on hand and is a good source of protein and calcium. Make this sandwich on whole-grain bread to boost the fiber content.

- *Tomato, feta, olives, and olive oil in pita.* Feta is a delicious source of protein and calcium, and the salty taste may be just what you are craving. Go easy on the olives since they are surprisingly high in fat.
- *Peanut butter, banana, and honey on a toasted bagel.* This old favorite is nutritious and delicious, and the ingredients are in most pantries.

EATING OUT

Eating out can be a relaxing social affair. With a little effort, it can also provide you with the nutrients you need in pregnancy—and without much fat. Your meals can be delicious since healthy eating does not mean you have to give up everything you love.

When ordering in a restaurant, choose foods such as legumes, grains, vegetables, and fruits. Avoid dishes that focus on heavy batters or sauces—for example, choose broiled or poached fish rather than batter-dipped, fried fish. Instead of meals based upon meat, choose meals based upon starches such as pasta, rice, or potatoes. If you do order meat, choose a lean cut that has been trimmed and prepared in a low-fat manner (broiled, roasted, or grilled, not fried).

Pay attention to fats that may be hidden in the dishes you order. Do not be afraid to ask your waiter about how things are prepared. Today, many chefs welcome requests for low-fat treatments of various dishes. You may also ask for all dressings and sauces on the side so that you can control how much is added to your portion.

Certain phrases on the menu should clue you in that a dish contains a great deal of fat: "buttery," "in butter sauce," "pan-fried," "crispy," "fried," "creamed," "in cream sauce," "hollandaise," "au gratin," "escalloped." These types of preparations are sure to contain more fat than you will want to consume.

The following suggestions may also help you when you eat out:

- You do not have to eat everything that is on your plate.
- Trim all visible fat off meat, and remove the skin from poultry.
- Limit the portion size of cooked meat, fish, or poultry to 4 ounces.
- Help yourself to plenty of bread, but forgo the butter.
- Limit your intake of salad dressings since they are mostly fat.

Italian

Italian food is always a good choice. Try to choose meals based on vegetables and pasta or risotto. Order meat, chicken, and fish that is roasted, baked, or broiled, not fried. Beware of dishes that contain large amounts of cheese. Choose the traditional "red sauce" over a "white sauce," which may be much higher in fat.

Chinese

Chinese food can be tricky. Stay away from deep-fried items like egg rolls and pot stickers. Choose vegetarian items (you never can be sure how much of the meat is really fat). Dishes based upon noodles, such as lo mein or rice noodles, are excellent choices, as are many of the main-course soups. Enjoy plenty of steamed rice with all entrées.

Pizza

I consider pizza a staple in my diet. It is widely available and inexpensive. But you must watch out for fat-laden toppings. Again, sticking to vegetarian toppings is a safe bet. Stay away from pepperoni, sausage, and hamburger since they add too much fat. If you would like meat on your pizza, chicken or lean sliced beef are good lower-fat choices.

Indian

Indian food tends to be low in saturated fat and cholesterol. Many of the dishes use a yogurt-based curry. Tandoori chicken and fish, which are roasted in a clay oven, get their flavor from spices rather than oil. Vegetables and legumes are an important part of Indian cooking. Beware of some bean dishes since they may be high in fat. Again, eat plenty of rice with each meal.

Mexican

Mexican food does not necessarily deserve the bad reputation it has received. But avoid refried beans—they are cooked in lard—and don't eat the cheese and sour-cream garnishes. Enjoy rice and beans, fajitas, and tortillas that are baked.

Steak House

Eating a broiled steak is fine on occasion—it is a good source of iron. Just trim the fat, and be sure the steak is cooked medium-well to well-done. Do not add butter to your baked potato, and avoid French fries. And watch out for the dressings at the salad bar—they may have more fat than your entire meal contains.

Vegetarian

You should not assume that all vegetarian cooking is low in fat. Be cautious of meals based upon cheese or nuts since these ingredients are very high in fat. Stick to selections in which the main ingredients are beans and grains.

Middle Eastern

Hummus and falafel are based upon ground chickpeas, which are an excellent low-fat source of protein. Falafel, however, is deep-fried. (The sauces for falafel, though, may be yogurt-based, which is fine.) And hummus often contains a large amount of tahini (sesame-seed paste), which can add considerable fat to the dish. Couscous and bulgur are great high-carbohydrate accompaniments to many Middle Eastern dishes. If you would like to eat meat, shish kebab is a good choice since it is grilled and much of the fat drips into the fire.

French

Classic French cuisine, based upon sauces made with egg yolks and butter, is very rich. While this is fine for a treat, do not make a habit of eating this high-fat, high-cholesterol style of cuisine. For example, hollandaise is made with egg yolks, butter, and lemon juice; béchamel is made with milk, butter, and flour; béarnaise sauce is a variant of hollandaise. All are poor choices. A wine-based sauce such as a bordelaise is a better choice. Don't be afraid of wine-based sauces since they are simmered long enough for the alcohol to evaporate, leaving behind only the flavor.

Fine Dining

A good rule for dining in upscale restaurants is to keep it simple. Choose meals that are based upon wholesome ingredients such as grains and vegetables, with flavorings from the foods themselves rather than from sauces. And choose items rich in carbohydrates, with meat playing a supporting role.

Fast Food

Be very wary when ordering in fast-food chains. The meals are often filled with hidden fat and empty calories. If you want a hamburger, choose one that is flame-broiled (some of the fat drips off this way), and eat it without mayonnaise, sauce, or cheese (ketchup or mustard is fine). Grilled chicken sandwiches are a good choice, but, again, stay away from toppings. Baked potatoes with salt, pepper, and a drizzle of olive oil or butter you add yourself in small amounts are fine, but potatoes that are already prepared with fat and sour cream are poor choices. Salads should be consumed with a small amount of oil and vinegar, not the creamy prepared dressings since these are unhealthy. Avoid deep-fried items such as French fries, onion rings, and fish fillets. In general, choose items from the "light" menu.

Japanese

Japanese noodle soups are an excellent choice—they are usually light and filled with fresh vegetables. Stay away from tempura, which is fried. Avoid sushi and sashimi that contain raw fish; the vegetarian varieties and those containing cooked fish are fine. Sushi rice is carbohydrate-rich, and the seaweed wrappings (nori) are a rich source of calcium.

Deli

Sandwiches from a deli can be delicious and healthy, but you must follow a few basic rules. Lean turkey and well-cooked roast beef are good choices, but avoid corned beef and pastrami since these are loaded with fat, salt, and additives. For condiments, choose mustard instead of mayonnaise. Rotisserie chicken is fine, especially if you remove the skin. Avoid egg salad, tuna salad, chicken salad, potato salad, macaroni salad, and coleslaw; these are all prepared with mayonnaise, which adds a great deal of fat to the diet. Beware of marinated salads such as bean salad and pasta salad that contain oil-based dressings. Instead, opt for grilled vegetables, fruit salads, and fresh fruit for side dishes.

10 PREGNANCY-PROOFING YOUR KITCHEN

To ensure a safe pregnancy, there are a few simple precautions that you should take when you prepare your meals. Several microorganisms can cause devastating infections in you and your baby. By following the information below, you can prevent this from happening.

KITCHEN SANITATION

A clean, sanitized kitchen is not only important when cooking food, but is critical in preventing bacteria from growing and spreading. Even if your kitchen looks clean, there is still a chance that bacteria are present. For instance, did you only wipe the wooden cutting board with a damp towel last night before putting it away? Did you simply rinse the wooden spoon that you used to stir the sauce before using it again? I have occasionally been so pressed for time that I have resorted to these "quick cleans." The cutting board and spoon may look clean, but they are ideal breeding grounds for bacteria, so extra attention needs to be paid to their cleaning. There are several critical procedures that must be followed to ensure that your kitchen is a safe place to prepare and serve food.

Hands

Wash your hands frequently with warm, soapy water, and dry them on paper towels. This is especially important after handling meat, poultry, or fish. In addition, if you have any exposed cuts or sores on your hands, cover them.

Dishtowels and Aprons

Keep dishtowels and aprons clean by changing them frequently. Moist towels and aprons can harbor bacteria and enhance their ability to multiply.

Wooden Kitchen Equipment

Wooden spoons, cutting boards, spatulas, and bowls are porous and can contain bacteria in places that even hot, soapy water cannot reach. Wash these utensils frequently in the dishwasher, or discard them when they become cracked or chipped. Never prepare raw poultry, fish, or meat on a wooden surface. The grooves that a knife makes in the wood will harbor bacteria and increase the likelihood of cross contamination, which occurs when bacteria from the raw poultry, fish, or meat contaminate other items—such as vegetables—that have been prepared on the same cutting board and then eaten raw. I recommend stocking your kitchen with two or three plastic cutting boards, using one exclusively for the preparation of raw poultry, seafood, and meat, to eliminate this problem. Use a separate board for fruit and vegetable preparation. Wash each board after every use in hot, soapy water or, preferably, in the dishwasher.

Knives and Other Food-Preparation Tools

Knives, spoons, spatulas, and other utensils used during cooking should be washed in hot, soapy water and immediately dried. Again, this is never more important than when preparing raw poultry, fish, and meat.

FOOD PREPARATION

A clean, sanitized kitchen is only one part of successful, safe food preparation. You also need to understand how to deal safely with a variety of food products.

Produce

In a perfect world, all produce would be certified organic and we would not have to be concerned with pesticides and other chemical contaminants. But this isn't a perfect world, and the harmful chemicals on produce are a reality. Chemicals can reach the baby either through the placenta or breast. Since no one really knows the effect of these substances on a growing baby, it is best to try to minimize their presence.

Three procedures should be followed to decrease any likelihood of chemical contamination from fresh produce. First, wash, scrub (when appropriate), and rinse all produce before using them. Next, vary the produce you consume. This is not only an excellent way of ingesting a variety of nutrients, but also a way of decreasing the accumulation of any one chemical in your body since different plants are sprayed with different pesticides. Last, peel all waxed produce such as cucumbers. Even though you will be discarding fiber and nutrients, you will also be discarding the wax, which not only destroys the flavor and texture of food, but is unhealthy. Most importantly, purchase certified organic products whenever possible. Your health and the health of your baby are worth the greater expense.

Meat and Poultry

Toxoplasmosis. Toxoplasma gondii is a protozoan parasite that can infect any warm-blooded animal. When pregnant women are infected with *T. gondii,* the developing fetus may be in danger. The organism is found in cats, raw or undercooked meat, and the soil. Infection occurs when contact is made with the feces of infected cats—for instance, when the cat's litter is changed. Therefore, pregnant women must assign this chore to someone else. The organism is also found in raw or undercooked meat. So do not eat any raw or rare meat, but make sure it is cooked well—170°F. You must also take care to prevent cross contamination when preparing food. For example, if you are handling raw meat, wash utensils, kitchen surfaces, and your hands thoroughly after you're done. Do not use the meat cutting board to prepare raw vegetables afterward unless you first wash the board thoroughly with hot, soapy water. Since *T. gondii* is also found in the soil, you can become infected if you garden without gloves. Wear them.

Infection in the mother is often asymptomatic. But when symptoms are present, they include swollen lymph glands (especially in the back of the neck), sore throat, aches, and general malaise. These are non-specific and, thus, may be caused by any number of viruses and illnesses. If you have these symptoms, contact your practitioner and let her or him decide if further investigation is warranted.

Approximately 60 percent of those pregnant women who become infected by this parasite will transmit the organism to their fetus. In the fetus, infection may cause severe problems, including mental retardation, ophthalmologic problems, and miscarriage. Transmission during the first trimester causes the most severe damage but is uncommon; transmission during the second and third trimesters is more common but causes less severe damage to the more developed baby.

If you are diagnosed with acute toxoplasmosis during your pregnancy, there are drug therapies available to you that reduce the risk of damage to your fetus by as much as 50 percent. However, prevention is the best medicine.

Salmonellosis. The most common type of food poisoning is caused by *Salmonellae,* bacteria found in meat, poultry, and eggs and egg products. In pregnant women, it can cause severe gastroenteritis (which, in turn, causes diarrhea, fever, and sometimes vomiting). It will not damage a developing baby, but the diarrhea can be debilitating to the mother, causing dehydration that requires intravenous rehydration. The first symptoms usually appear 6 to 48 hours after eating the contaminated food. Symptoms include abdominal cramps, nausea, fever, headache, vomiting, diarrhea, and/or chills.

Again, simple precautions in food preparation, including hand washing and not allowing food to stand at room temperature (it should be either cooked or refrigerated), will minimize this infection. In addition, be wary of foods that may contain raw eggs: Caesar salad, eggnog, hollandaise and its variations. Restaurants often prepare salad dressings with raw eggs to emulsify the ingredients. Ask your server specific questions about the salad-dressing ingredients. *Salmonellae* are killed by cooking foods in temperatures of 140°F for at least 10 minutes, so soft-boiled or runny eggs may present some risk.

Staphylococcal food poisoning. Staphylocccocal food poisoning is caused by bacteria that multiply rapidly in dairy products, processed meats, fish, mayonnaise, and other foods that have been improperly refrigerated. It, too, can cause severe gastroenteritis in pregnant women but does not harm the fetus. Its onset tends to be very rapid, from 30 minutes to 8 hours after consuming the contaminated food. Unlike salmonella poisoning, the toxin made by the bacteria is not killed by heating it, so prevention is key. Contamination arises when foods are left too long at room temperature: brown-bag lunches left unrefrigerated; meats on display in inadequately cooled cases; foods from warming tables. Try not to consume these types of prepared foods.

Escherichia coli (E. coli). Chopped meat infected with these bacteria has caused several small epidemics in this country. One epidemic was linked to a fast-food chain. The diarrhea associated with *E. coli* may be bloody, and there may even be life-threatening complications from the infection. There is no evidence that *E. coli* will have any direct harmful effects on your baby. Be sure to cook your food well and to wash your hands thoroughly to prevent this potentially serious infection.

Botulism. Botulism, caused by the bacillus *Clostridium botulinum,* is an extremely dangerous and sometimes fatal form of food poisoning; it is also very rare. Botulism spores are widely found in the environment and are highly heat-resistant, but are not dangerous when they are exposed to oxygen. The spores can germinate, however, in a low-oxygen, low-acid environment. This type of environment is most commonly found in improperly processed home-canned foods. Commercially prepared canned goods are rarely contaminated because of strict processing guidelines. When eaten, active botulism spores can release a toxin that affects the nervous system and can cause paralysis and even death. Infant botulism can be caused by feeding honey to children under 1 year of age since the dormant spores may be present in honey and can germinate in the intestines of young children. These same spores pose no danger for older children or adults. Avoid eating home-canned foods during your pregnancy.

Seafood

Pregnant and breast-feeding women should avoid eating any fish that swim or spawn in polluted fresh water. Many lakes, rivers, and streams have become a dumping ground for industry waste, the resulting chemical pollution being passed on to the fish. Fish that swim in polluted waters probably contain high levels of PCBs, which can be dangerous to a mother and her baby. If you do not know their source to be non-polluted, the fish to avoid include striped bass, whitefish, and trout. Salmon and catfish should also be avoided if they have not been farm-raised (most on the market today are farm-raised).

All saltwater seafood is safe to eat, assuming that it is well cooked. Raw fish, on the other hand, can contain parasites that are only destroyed by cooking. In addition, I suggest removing the dark spots on swordfish and tuna since toxins tend to accumulate in these areas.

Shellfish should not be eaten raw while you are pregnant. It is possible to become infected with hepatitis A by consuming raw shellfish contaminated by the virus. This virus may sometimes cause severe nausea and vomiting. Although it will not damage your developing baby, you could become severely ill from this infection. In addition, oysters often carry *Vibrio vulnificus,* which can cause a rapid, life-threatening infection for some, especially those with liver disease. It is fine to eat cooked shellfish.

In the kitchen, follow the same procedures when preparing seafood as you do with meat and poultry. The best advice I can offer is to purchase seafood from a reputable fishmonger, one who knows when and where his or her products were harvested. Seafood should be prepared as quickly after purchase as possible. Store all seafood in the refrigerator or on ice. Heat spoils seafood very rapidly.

IMPORTANT INFORMATION ABOUT FOOD SAFETY

- Never use foods from bulging cans. A bulging can is a sign that the food in the can is contaminated with bacteria.
- Never refreeze food that has been thawed. Thawed food needs to be cooked. It can, however, be refrozen in its cooked state.
- Defrost all frozen food in the microwave or the refrigerator. Don't defrost food at room temperature.
- Keep all food covered and protected. Besides the bacteria that may already be present in food, exposed products are susceptible to bacteria from outside sources.
- Treat all leftovers with great care. It is best to use them within 48 hours.
- Cool foods as quickly as possible before refrigerating them. For example, the best method to cool hot soup is to pour it into a container, place the container in a sink full of ice water, and stir the soup until it is cooled. The container can then be tightly covered and the soup safely refrigerated.
- Arrange food loosely in the refrigerator. This will allow the cold air to circulate adequately and keep everything cold.
- Avoid alternate heating and cooling of food. This is a common practice in many restaurants. You may want to avoid eating food from steam tables. Once leftovers have been reheated, they must be consumed or discarded.
- *When in doubt, throw it out.* If food is discolored or has an unpleasant odor, it is probably rancid. Don't take a chance.
- Most importantly, *keep hot food hot and cold food cold.* Bacteria thrive on the same things we do: warmth and food. They grow most rapidly at body temperature. It is critical to cook food to a temperature of over 140°F as quickly as possible and to cool food to a temperature of below 40°F just as rapidly. Avoid exposing food to the dangerous 60°F-to-100°F zone for any length of time

RECIPES

11 PRECONCEPTION

Tomato and Corn Salad · Grilled Marinated Vegetables · Sugar Snap Peas with Mint and Butter · Spicy Asparagus with Red Bell Pepper and Herbs · Broiled Spinach, Mushroom, and Goat Cheese Sandwiches · Stuffed Acorn Squash · Radiatore al Forno with Leafy Greens, White Beans, and Three Cheeses · Calamari and Spinach Casalinga · Swiss Chard Stuffed with Gnocchi

Tomato and Corn Salad

This simple tomato salad contains fresh, uncooked corn and a splash of raspberry vinegar. Prepare it when tomatoes and corn are abundant, inexpensive, and wonderfully sweet. Both the tomatoes and corn are rich sources of folic acid.

PREPARATION: 10 minutes
CHILLING: 1 hour
YIELD: 4 side-dish servings

3 to 4 large tomatoes, diced (approximately 4 cups)
3 ears fresh corn, kernels removed
2 tablespoons extra-virgin olive oil
1 teaspoon raspberry vinegar
⅓ cup cilantro, finely chopped
   Salt to taste
   Pepper to taste

Combine the tomatoes, corn kernels, olive oil, vinegar, and cilantro in a large, nonmetal bowl, and toss them well. Season the ingredients with the salt and pepper. Tightly cover the salad, and refrigerate it for 1 hour before serving it.

Grilled Marinated Vegetables

Serve these vegetables with grilled meat, poultry, or fish. They will add folic acid to your meal. They can also be layered in crusty bread with fresh mozzarella, tomatoes, and basil pesto to make a great sandwich. **Tip:** *If you prefer, you may substitute 2 tablespoons of fresh oregano or 1 tablespoon of fresh rosemary for the thyme.*

PREPARATION: 15 minutes
MARINATING: 1 hour
COOKING: 15 minutes
YIELD: 4 side-dish servings

¼ cup balsamic vinegar
2 cloves garlic
2 tablespoons fresh thyme

½ cup fresh basil, snipped
¼ cup extra-virgin olive oil
   Pepper to taste
3 purple eggplants, sliced vertically into ⅓-inch-thick pieces
4 leeks, trimmed, thoroughly washed, and sliced in half lengthwise
2 zucchinis, sliced vertically into ⅓-inch-thick pieces
3 red bell peppers, cored, seeded, and cut into 2-inch pieces

1. Combine the vinegar, garlic, thyme, basil, olive oil, and pepper in a large nonmetal mixing bowl, and whisk the ingredients well.
2. Rinse the eggplants, and pat them dry. Combine them with the leeks, zucchinis, and red bell peppers in a large, shallow, nonmetal dish. Pour the marinade over the vegetables. Tightly cover the dish, and refrigerate the vegetables for 1 hour.
3. Light a charcoal fire, or heat the broiler. Drain the marinade from the vegetables. Place the vegetables on the prepared grill or in the broiler, and cook them until they are tender, turning them often.

HARDWOOD
~~~~~~~~~~~

We used to grill with charcoal briquets, which is terribly unhealthful. There is an alternative: hardwood charcoal. It improves the flavor of your grilled food and is much better for the environment and your body. Hardwood charcoal is the pure residue of burned and seasoned hardwood. It is free of additives, burns hotter and more evenly than briquets, and doesn't require lighter fluid.

Sugar Snap Peas with Mint and Butter

This dish is the essence of summer. Sugar snap peas, like corn, are best eaten immediately after they have been picked. The longer they sit before eating, the more starchy and less sweet they will be. In addition to folic acid, they are a good source of fiber.

PREPARATION: 5 minutes
COOKING: 3 minutes
YIELD: 4 side-dish servings

1 tablespoon unsalted butter
½ cup fresh mint, finely chopped
1½ pounds sugar snap peas, strings removed
   Salt to taste
   Pepper to taste

1. Melt the butter over low heat in a large skillet. Add the mint, and mix the ingredients well. Set the skillet aside.
2. Bring a large pot of lightly salted water to a boil. Add the peas, and blanch them until they are bright green and tender-crisp. Quickly drain the peas.
3. Add the peas to the melted butter and mint, and toss the ingredients well. Season the peas with the salt and pepper, and serve the dish immediately.

Spicy Asparagus with Red Bell Pepper and Herbs

PREPARATION: 10 minutes
COOKING: 10 minutes
YIELD: 4 side-dish servings

CHILIES

Chilies not only provide heat and flavor to a dish, but are also nutritious and contain medicinal properties as well. They are high in vitamins A and C, and, when consumed in moderation, can increase the flow of gastric juices and aid the digestive process.

Asparagus, which is rich in folic acid, is the first indication of the arrival of the summer harvest. When choosing fresh asparagus, select those that are deep green and crisp with tightly closed buds. I prefer pencil-sized stalks, but many people prefer the thicker ones. **Tips:** *Be extremely cautious when working with fresh chilies. They contain oils that can burn your skin. Many people wear plastic gloves or coat their hands in vegetable oil (it acts as a barrier between your skin and the pepper oils) when cutting chilies. If your skin begins to burn, wash the affected area immediately under cool running water. Never touch your face or eyes when working with chilies, and always thoroughly wash your knife and cutting board when you are finished. Since much of the heat in chilies is concentrated in the seeds and ribs, removing them will lessen the intensity of the peppers. Soaking fresh chilies in cold water for 45 minutes will also decrease their fire. If you are fortunate enough to have access to purple or white asparagus, use them or a combination of all of them. The color contrast will be eye-catching.*

1 tablespoon olive oil

2 cloves garlic, peeled and finely chopped

1 medium red bell pepper, cored, seeded, and diced

1 jalapeño, seeded and finely chopped

4 scallions, trimmed and thinly sliced, white and green parts
   separated

   Salt to taste

2 tablespoons fresh basil, snipped

2 tablespoons fresh mint, snipped

2 pounds fresh asparagus, tough ends snapped off and discarded,
   stalks loosely tied together with kitchen string

1 tablespoon unsalted butter

   Pepper to taste

1. Bring a large pot of lightly salted water to a boil.
2. Meanwhile, heat the olive oil in a Dutch oven over medium heat. Add the garlic, and sauté it until it is soft and fragrant. Add the red bell pepper, jalapeño, the white part of the scallions, and a dash of salt. Sauté the ingredients until the red bell pepper begins to soften.
3. Add the basil, mint, and the green part of the scallions. Remove the pot from the heat.
4. Drop the asparagus into the boiling water, and blanch them until they are bright green and tender-crisp. Quickly drain them, and add them to the sauté.
5. Add the butter, and season the asparagus with additional salt and some pepper.

Therefore, if you can tolerate it and feel like eating something hot and spicy during pregnancy, go ahead.

All chilies are hot, but in varying degrees. Identifying chilies is confusing. Not only are there hundreds of them, but some have more than one name. The habañero from Mexico, also known as the Scotch bonnet in Jamaica, is the hottest. These tiny neon-orange, red, or green lantern-shaped firebombs are many times hotter than the jalapeño, which is hot but manageable. Jalapeños, deep-green, finger-shaped peppers, are available fresh or pickled in brine. Serranos, milder than jalapeños, are either red or pale green, taper to a point, and are widely available fresh.

Broiled Spinach, Mushroom, and Goat Cheese Sandwiches

These sandwiches are rich in folic acid. Enjoy them during the preconception period.

4 tablespoons pine nuts
1 tablespoon olive oil
4 cloves garlic, peeled and finely chopped
12 ounces cultivated white mushrooms, sliced
    Salt to taste
12 ounces spinach, chopped, washed, and drained
    Pepper to taste
4 sesame bagels, each cut in half
4 ounces goat cheese, divided

PREPARATION: 10 minutes
COOKING: 20 minutes
YIELD: 4 main-course servings

1. Heat the broiler.
2. Heat the pine nuts in a small skillet over very low heat. Toast them, tossing them often, until they are golden. Set the pine nuts aside.
3. Heat the olive oil in a Dutch oven over medium heat. Add the garlic, and sauté it, stirring it constantly, until it is soft and fragrant.
4. Add the mushrooms and a pinch of salt. Sauté the mushrooms and garlic, stirring them often, until the mushrooms are soft and all of their liquid has evaporated.
5. Add the spinach, and sauté it, stirring it constantly, until it has wilted.
6. Remove the pot from the heat, and stir in the pine nuts. Season the vegetables to taste with the pepper.
7. Lightly toast the bagels, then place them on a baking sheet.
8. Evenly distribute the vegetable–pine nut mixture over the bagel halves. Place ½ ounce of goat cheese on each half bagel. Broil the sandwiches until the cheese is melted.

Stuffed Acorn Squash

*This dish is as visually appealing as it is delicious. Many of the ingredients, including the squash, wild rice, apples, pumpkinseeds, and pecans, contain folic acid, making it a very rich source of this vitamin for the preconception period. But since it is also high in fiber and carbohydrates, you may enjoy it throughout your pregnancy as well. And it makes a great Thanksgiving dish for vegetarians. **Tips:** This recipe can be prepared a day in advance. Twenty minutes before it is to be served, sprinkle each squash half with the cheese, and bake. Butternut or buttercup squash can be substituted for the acorn squash, brown rice for the wild rice, and dried cranberries for the raisins.*

PREPARATION: 15 minutes
COOKING: 1 hour
YIELD: 6 main-course or side-dish servings

3 medium acorn squash, halved and seeded
1 cup raisins
1 cup plus 2½ cups water
  Salt
1¼ cups wild rice, thoroughly rinsed
1 tablespoon butter
1 Spanish onion, peeled and diced
1 rib celery, diced
2 Cortland apples, cored and diced
⅓ cup roasted pumpkinseeds (available at many supermarkets and
  ethnic groceries)
½ cups pecan pieces, lightly toasted
  Pepper to taste
6 ounces Cheddar, grated

1. Heat the oven to 400°F.
2. Place the squash, skin side up on a lightly buttered baking tray. Bake the squash until they are tender, approximately 40 minutes. Remove the squash from the oven, and set them aside. Do not turn off the oven.
3. While the squash are baking, bring the 1 cup of water to a boil, and pour it over the raisins. Allow the raisins to plump for 15 minutes. Drain the raisins, reserving the soaking water.

4. In a medium-sized pot, combine the raisin water and the remaining 2½ cups of water. Bring the water to a boil, and lightly salt it. Add the wild rice, and stir it. Return the water to a boil, and reduce the heat to a simmer. Cover the pot, and simmer the rice until it is tender, approximately 40 minutes. Set the rice aside.

5. While the squash and rice are cooking, heat the butter in a large skillet over medium heat. Add the onion and a pinch of salt. Sauté the onion, stirring it often, for 5 minutes. Add the celery, and sauté it 3 minutes longer. Add the apples, and cook them until they begin to soften.

6. Combine the reserved raisins, cooked rice, onion mixture, pumpkinseeds, and pecans in a large bowl. Mix the ingredients well, and season the mixture with the salt and pepper. Fill the cavity of each squash half with the rice mixture, and sprinkle the stuffed squash with the cheese.

7. Return the squash to the oven, and bake them until the cheese has melted, approximately 10 minutes.

Radiatore al Forno with Leafy Greens, White Beans, and Three Cheeses

PREPARATION: 1 hour
BAKING: 25 minutes
YIELD: 6 main-course servings

This dish contains not only an abundance of folic acid, but has, in addition, many of the critical nutrients, in moderate quantities, needed for a healthy pregnancy: calcium, potassium, iron, vitamins C and E, fiber, protein, and carbohydrates. Therefore, even though the dish is especially recommended for women who are preparing for conception, it may be enjoyed throughout the pregnancy as well. Prepare it during early summer, when the greens are in season and early tomatoes are available. Radiatore is a corkscrew-shaped pasta that is ideal for this dish since it will act like a sponge and absorb the wonderful vegetable juices. Al forno is Italian for "baked." **Tips:** *You may substitute other types of folate-rich cooking greens for those in the recipe,* *including broccoli rabe, red Swiss chard, mustard greens, dandelion greens, and escarole. If canned beans are used, skip step 1. To prepare the various greens in this recipe for cooking, fill a sink with cold water after chopping the greens. Place the kale in the water along with two colanders. Place the chard stems and turnip greens in one colander and the chard leaves in the other. After the stems and turnip greens are added to the pot, place the spinach in the colander and into the sink. This technique makes it easy to add the greens to the pot at the appropriate intervals without hindering your rhythm.*

½ cup dried white beans, picked over, rinsed, soaked for 8 hours,
    and drained, *or* 1 cup canned white beans, rinsed

2 tablespoons plus 6 teaspoons extra-virgin olive oil

6 cloves garlic, peeled and finely chopped

1 pound radiatore

½ pound kale, roughly chopped, washed, and drained
    Salt to taste

½ pound green Swiss chard, stems and leaves separated and
    roughly chopped, washed, and drained

⅓ pound turnip greens, roughly chopped, washed, and drained

½ pound spinach, roughly chopped, washed, and drained

4 medium tomatoes, peeled, seeded, and chopped
    Pepper to taste

3 ounces fontina *or* Cheddar, grated

6 ounces mozzarella, grated

3 ounces goat cheese, crumbled

TO PEEL, SEED, AND CHOP TOMATOES

Bring a pot of water to a boil. Cut an X on the bottom of each tomato, and carefully place each in boiling water for 30 seconds. Allow the tomatoes to cool. Slip off their skins, remove their core, cut them in half, and gently squeeze them to remove the seeds.

1. Place the dried beans in a medium-sized pot, and cover them with water. Bring the water to a boil, reduce the heat, and simmer the beans until they are tender, approximately 1 hour. Drain the beans, and set them aside.

2. Bring a large pot of lightly salted water to a boil.

3. Heat the oven to 400°F.

4. Heat the 2 tablespoons of olive oil in a large Dutch oven over medium heat. Add the garlic, and sauté it until it is soft and fragrant.

5. Add the pasta to the boiling water.

6. Add the kale and a pinch of salt to the Dutch oven, and steam the kale for 7 minutes. The water that clings to the leaves should be sufficient to steam the vegetables.

7. Add the Swiss chard stems and turnip greens to the Dutch oven. Raise the heat to high, and sauté the greens for 2 minutes, stirring them constantly.

8. Add the chard leaves to the Dutch oven. Cover the pot, and steam the vegetables, stirring them often, until they are tender, approximately 3 minutes. Add the spinach. Stir in the chopped tomatoes.

9. Drain the pasta. Add it to the cooked greens and tomatoes. Stir in the cooked beans. Gently cook the ingredients together for 2 minutes, stirring them often. Season the ingredients with the salt and pepper. Stir in the fontina or Cheddar and half of the mozzarella.

10. Transfer the ingredients to a large casserole. Scatter the remaining mozzarella and the goat cheese over the top.

11. Bake the casserole for approximately 10 minutes or until the top is golden. Divide the casserole into 6 portions, and drizzle 1 teaspoon of the olive oil over each portion.

Calamari and Spinach Casalinga

PREPARATION: 10 minutes
COOKING: 20 minutes
YIELD: 4 main-course servings

We had this dish at Casalinga, a wonderful trattoria in Florence. Calamari and spinach may seem like a strange combination, but it works. The spinach provides a rich source of folic acid, and iron. **Tips:** *In most recipes, spinach is only cooked until it wilts. In this dish, however, a long, slow cooking is necessary to release the rich flavor of the anchovies and spinach. Monkfish filets or sea scallops can be substituted for the squid. If you use monkfish, cut the fish into 3-ounce pieces, and sear them in 1 to 2 tablespoons of olive oil 10 minutes before the spinach is done. Add the fish to the spinach during the last 3 minutes of cooking to finish the dish. If you use scallops, add them to the spinach when you would have added the squid.*

1 tablespoon olive oil

6 cloves garlic, peeled and thinly sliced

1 2-ounce can anchovies packed in oil, drained and roughly chopped

⅛ to ¼ teaspoon red pepper flakes

½ cup white wine

2 pounds spinach, finely chopped, washed, and drained

1 pound cleaned squid bodies, cut into ¼-inch rings
   Pepper to taste

4 cups cooked hot couscous

4 teaspoons extra-virgin olive oil

1. Heat the olive oil in large Dutch oven over medium heat. Add the garlic, and sauté the garlic until it is fragrant, stirring it constantly.

2. Add the anchovies and red pepper flakes. Sauté the ingredients for 1 minute, stirring them constantly.

3. Raise the heat to high, and add the wine. Reduce the wine for 1 minute.

4. Add the spinach, and stir it until it is wilted. Reduce the heat, and continue cooking the spinach, stirring it often, until all of the liquid has evaporated, approximately 15 minutes.

5. Toss in the squid, and cook it only until it is done through, approximately 2 minutes. Season the ingredients with the pepper.

6. Spread the couscous on a large platter. Spoon the squid over the couscous, and drizzle the dish with the extra-virgin olive oil.

SQUID

Squid are a distant relative to mollusks, but they have no outer shell. They look like small octopuses, with long tentacles, white flesh, and spotted skin. Long popular in Asia and Italy (they are called "calamari" in Italian), only recently have Americans stopped shunning them. We are now just beginning to realize how flavorful, versatile, and nutritious squid can be. Squid are generally available fresh or frozen, whole or cleaned. If they are whole, a sweet smell, clear eyes, and smooth skin are indications of a fresh product. Their cleaned bodies can be stuffed and baked, or they can be sliced into rings and sautéed or added to soups and stews.

Swiss Chard Stuffed with Gnocchi

Although these neat rolls require forty-five minutes of preparation, they are well worth it. They are light and fresh-tasting and loaded with carbohydrates, vitamin C, iron, and calcium. The Swiss chard wrapping is rich in iron, and folic acid—a perfect pregnancy dish! **Tips:** *Select Swiss chard with large leaves and short stems. The stems need to be removed but they can be reserved and used in a pasta dish or soup. All of the preparation can be done up to 2 days in advance. Pour the sauce over the rolls just prior to placing them in the oven.*

PREPARATION: 45 minutes
BAKING: 20 minutes
YIELD: 4 to 6 main-course servings

1½ pounds green Swiss chard, stems removed and reserved
   Water to boil the chard plus 1 cup boiling water
½ cup sun-dried tomatoes
2 teaspoons olive oil
4 cloves garlic, peeled and finely chopped
1 cup sun-dried-tomato soaking water
1 28-ounce can whole tomatoes, drained and roughly chopped
   Salt to taste
   Pepper to taste
3 medium russet potatoes, baked until tender (about 30 to 35 minutes at 450°F) and peeled
1 egg, beaten
1 cup flour
4 ounces part-skim mozzarella, grated

1. Pour 2 inches of water into a Dutch oven, and bring the water to a boil. Carefully rinse the chard, and loosely tie the leaves together into 2 bunches. Add one bunch to the boiling water, and cook the chard for 5 minutes. Remove the chard, and submerge the chard in an ice bath to stop the cooking process. Drain the chard, and gently squeeze the leaves to remove the excess water. Repeat the procedure with the remaining bunch of chard. Set the chard aside.
2. While the chard is cooking, pour the 1 cup of boiling water over

the sun-dried tomatoes. Soak the tomatoes for 10 minutes, drain them, and reserve the soaking water. Finely chop the tomatoes, and set them aside.

3. Heat the olive oil in the Dutch oven over medium heat. Add the garlic, and sauté it until it is soft and fragrant, stirring it constantly. Add the reserved sun-dried-tomato soaking water, and simmer the garlic for 2 minutes. Add the canned tomatoes, and bring the liquid to a boil. Reduce the heat, and simmer the sauce for 15 minutes, stirring it often. Season the sauce to taste with the salt and pepper. Set the sauce aside.

4. Bring to a boil a stock pot half-filled with water and fitted with a strainer.

5. While the sauce is cooking, pass the potatoes through a ricer, or mash them well. Add the reserved sun-dried tomatoes, and season the potatoes with salt and pepper. Add the egg, and mix the ingredients well. Add the flour to form a dough. Turn the dough onto a lightly floured surface, knead the dough for 3 minutes, and form it into a ball.

6. Cut a 3-inch piece of dough from the ball. Place the piece of dough on a floured surface, and roll it into a long cylinder approximately ½ inch in diameter. Cut the cylinder into 2-inch lengths, and set the gnocchi aside. Repeat the procedure with the remaining dough.

7. Drop half the gnocchi into the boiling water, and cook them until they float, approximately 3 minutes. Drain the gnocchi, and submerge them in cold water. Quickly drain the gnocchi again, and set them aside. Repeat the procedure with the remaining gnocchi.

8. Heat the oven to 375°F.

9. Untie the steamed chard, and carefully separate the leaves. Open one leaf fully, and place 2 or 3 gnocchi at one end. Roll up the leaf, and tuck in the sides. Place the roll in a large casserole. Repeat the procedure with the remaining chard and gnocchi.

10. Pour the sauce over the rolls, and sprinkle the dish with the mozzarella.

11. Bake the rolls until the cheese is melted and the rolls are heated through, approximately 20 minutes.

MESTER

Cranberry-Corn Muffins · Classic French Bread · Cantaloupe-Banana Shake · Root-Vegetable Puree · Chicken Stock · White Bean and Roasted Butternut Squash Soup · Chicken Soup with Kale and Orzo · Ribollita (Bean, Bread, and Tomato Soup) · Herbed Basmati Rice with Tomatoes · "Oven-Fried" Potatoes · Rotelle, Tuna, and Summer Vegetables in a Balsamic Vinaigrette · Basic Polenta · Chicken and Lentil Stew with Rosemary · Farfalle with Chicken, Shiitake, Spinach, and Sage · Mexican Black Bean "Lasagna" · Pot Roast Pomodoro · Lime-Ginger Swordfish with Tomato-Avocado Salsa · Citrus Salmon with Mesclun and Raspberry Vinegar · Spaghetti with Turkey Sausage, Red Bell Peppers, Onions, and Tomatoes · Hamburgers with Spinach and Basil–Goat Cheese Pesto · Potatoes Stuffed with Spinach and Broccoli · Quinoa-Basil Tabbouleh · Grilled Tuna with Navy Bean Ragù · Potato, Onion, Spinach, and Goat Cheese Calzones · Penne with Chicken, Asparagus, Lemon, and Tarragon · Spinach Fettuccine with "Wild" Mushroom Sauce · Tricolor Farfalle with Tomato Sauce · Chicken with Peppers and Mushrooms · Steve and Julie's Cape Cod Scallops and Pasta

SUPPLEMENT A: RECIPES FOR GAINING WEIGHT
Whole-Wheat Bread with Cashews and Dates · Good-for-You French Toast · Three-Potato Home Fries with Corn, Scallions, and Cheese · Orecchiette with Squash, Broccoli Rabe, and Goat Cheese · Stuffed Roasted Bell Peppers · Mustard-Tarragon Chicken

SUPPLEMENT B: LOW-CALORIE RECIPES
White Bean, Escarole, and Tomato Soup · Chilled Sesame Noodles with Vegetables · Orvieto Chicken · Rigatoni with Wild Mushroom Ragù · Farmers' Market Pasta · Salt Cod, Chickpea, and Potato Soup

Cranberry-Corn Muffins

*These muffins pack a nutritional punch in a small package. They contain protein from yogurt and eggs, fiber from wheat flour and walnuts, and iron and folic acid from the molasses. They are an excellent choice for a quick breakfast and are ideal anytime if you are suffering from nausea and can tolerate little else. They can be frozen for future breakfasts or snacks. **Tip:** When you combine the wet and dry ingredients in quick breads, stir the ingredients only enough to moisten them. Overmixing the batter will toughen the final product.*

PREPARATION: 10 minutes
BAKING: 20 minutes
YIELD: 9 to 12 muffins

1 cup yellow corn meal
1½ cups unbleached, all-purpose flour
½ cup whole-wheat flour
1 tablespoon baking powder
¼ teaspoon salt
½ teaspoon cinnamon
2 eggs
1 cup nonfat plain yogurt
2 tablespoons unsalted butter, melted
4 tablespoons blackstrap molasses
2 tablespoons honey
1 cup dried cranberries
⅓ cup walnuts, chopped

1. Heat the oven to 400°F.
2. In a large mixing bowl, combine the corn meal, all-purpose flour, whole-wheat flour, baking powder, salt, and cinnamon, and mix the ingredients well.
3. In another large bowl, beat the eggs. Add the yogurt, melted butter, molasses, and honey. Mix the ingredients well.
4. Stir the dry ingredients into the wet ingredients just enough to moisten the dry ingredients. Gently fold the dried cranberries and walnuts into the batter.

5. Lightly butter the muffin tins. Fill each tin two-thirds full with batter.

6. Bake the muffins until they are lightly golden, approximately 20 minutes.

Classic French Bread

Bread is one of the best-tolerated foods for severely nauseated pregnant women, and the carbohydrates are just what your body needs for fuel for the baby. Homemade French bread is far superior to the soft, gummy, and tasteless supermarket product. And the smell of this delicious bread being baked may stimulate your appetite for the first time. **Tip:** *This bread dough can also serve as pizza, focaccia, or calzone dough. When preparing pizzas or calzone, the second rising can be eliminated.*

PREPARATION: 20 minutes
RISING: overnight plus 2 to 3 hours
BAKING: 35 minutes
YIELD: 2 loaves

2½ cups warm (95°F) water
2 tablespoons active dry yeast
3 cups plus 3 to 5 cups unbleached, all-purpose flour, divided
1 teaspoon salt
2 teaspoons olive oil
4 tablespoons corn meal
Flour for dusting

1. Place the water in a mixing bowl. Add the yeast, and gently stir it until it is dissolved. Allow the yeast to proof for 10 minutes.

2. Add 3 cups of the flour, stirring the dough with a wooden spoon until the dough is smooth. The dough will have the consistency of soft pudding.

3. Tightly cover the bowl with plastic wrap, and place the bowl in a warm, draft-free place for at least 8 hours or, preferably, overnight.

4. Add 1½ cups of flour and the salt to the bowl, and stir the dough

for 5 minutes. Stir in enough additional flour to make a soft dough.

5. Turn the dough out onto a lightly floured surface. Knead the dough until it is smooth and elastic, approximately 10 minutes, adding only enough flour to prevent the dough from sticking.

6. Place the oil on the bottom of a large bowl, and add the dough. Turn the dough around in the bowl to thoroughly coat it with the oil. Tightly cover the bowl with plastic wrap, and place the bowl in a warm, draft-free place until the dough has doubled in size, approximately 1 to 2 hours.

7. Remove the dough from the bowl, and allow the dough to rest for 5 minutes.

8. Meanwhile, sprinkle a large, heavy-duty baking sheet with the corn meal.

9. Divide the dough in half, and place it on a lightly floured work surface. Press the dough into a 10 × 5-inch rectangle. Starting at the long end, roll up the dough into a 10-inch loaf, pressing the seams to seal them. Lightly roll the loaf over the work surface, and place it on the tray seam side down. Repeat the procedure with the other piece of dough. Cover the loaves with a dry towel, and place them in a warm, draft-free place to rise for 1 hour.

10. Heat the oven to 450°F.

11. Slash three diagonal lines on the surface of each loaf, and dust the loaves with flour. Spray the bottom of the oven with water, and close the door. Wait 1 minute. Spray the oven again, and place the tray in the oven. Spray the oven every 7 minutes for 21 minutes, keeping the oven door open only as long as is necessary. Bake the breads until their crust is golden and crisp, approximately 35 minutes altogether.

Cantaloupe-Banana Shake

A fruit-and-skim-milk-based shake is an excellent choice for a quick, nutritious breakfast or an afternoon snack. Many women who are nauseated during pregnancy find that they can tolerate a liquid diet much better than a solid one. These drinks provide excellent nutrition, with plenty of protein, calcium, and vitamin C. **Tip:** *To make a three-berry shake, replace the banana and cantaloupe chunks with ½ cup each of frozen blueberries, raspberries, and strawberries, and add 1 tablespoon of honey. The remaining ingredients stay the same, as do the instructions.*

PREPARATION: 5 minutes
BLENDING: 1 minute
YIELD: 1 serving

1 large ripe banana, peeled, cut into chunks, wrapped tightly, and frozen for 24 hours
1 cup cantaloupe chunks, wrapped tightly and frozen for 24 hours
1¼ cups skim milk
½ cup nonfat dry milk powder
1 teaspoon vanilla

Place all of the ingredients in a blender, and process the mixture until it is smooth. Serve the shake immediately.

Root-Vegetable Puree

This smooth puree can be tolerated by even the most severely nauseated woman. Serve it at breakfast drizzled with maple syrup, at lunch as a main course, or at dinner as a soup thinned with vegetable stock or milk. **Tip:** *If yellow potatoes are unavailable, russets can be substituted.*

PREPARATION: 10 minutes
COOKING: 25 minutes
YIELD: 2 to 4 servings

1 tablespoon plus 1 tablespoon unsalted butter
1 2-inch piece gingerroot, peeled and finely chopped
1 turnip, peeled and cut into ½-inch chunks

2 medium carrots, peeled and cut into ½-inch chunks

2 medium yellow potatoes (Yellow Finns or Yukon Golds are good choices), scrubbed and cut into ½-inch chunks

1 large sweet potato or yam, scrubbed and cut into ½-inch chunks

2½ cups water

Salt to taste

Pepper to taste

1. Melt 1 tablespoon of the butter in a large Dutch oven over low heat. Add the gingerroot, and sauté it, stirring it constantly, until it is soft and fragrant. Add the turnip, carrots, potatoes, and sweet potato or yam, and sauté the vegetables for 3 minutes, stirring them constantly.

2. Raise the heat to high, and add the water. Cover the pot, and bring the liquid to a boil. Reduce the heat, and simmer the vegetables until they are tender, approximately 20 minutes.

3. Transfer the mixture to the work bowl of a food processor or blender. Be careful that the hot liquid does not splatter. Puree the mixture until it is smooth. Add the remaining 1 tablespoon of butter, and season the puree with the salt and pepper.

Chicken Stock

PREPARATION: 15 minutes
COOKING: 2 hours
YIELD: approximately 2 quarts

Plain chicken broth is a soothing way to fill your nauseated stomach. It will keep you hydrated while providing a small amount of calories and nutrients. If you feel up to it, try some cooked pasta or rice for extra carbohydrates. Tips: This recipe yields an excellent broth for a risotto, soup base, or sauce for those times when your stomach can handle more exciting dishes. As with all stocks, once it begins to boil it is critical to reduce the heat so that bubbles barely reach the surface. It is also important to skim the surface pe-

*riodically to remove any scum. By following these two steps, you will pro-
duce a stock that is fairly clear and grit-free. I prefer to make the stock a day
ahead and refrigerate it overnight. This improves the flavor and makes it simple to remove the fat, which has hardened on the surface.*

1 3- to 4-pound chicken, including the neck, left whole and rinsed
    well (save the liver, gizzard, and heart for another use)
2 medium carrots, scrubbed and coarsely chopped
2 ribs celery, coarsely chopped
1 medium onion, peeled and
    coarsely chopped
1 parsnip, scrubbed and
    coarsely chopped
4 cloves garlic, skin intact
5 sprigs parsley
5 to 6 fresh sage leaves
6 black peppercorns
3 quarts cold water

1. Combine all the ingredients in a large Dutch oven or stock pot.
   Cover the pot, and bring the water to a boil. Reduce the heat until
   the bubbles just reach the surface. Simmer the ingredients for 2
   hours, occasionally skimming the surface of the liquid.
2. Remove the chicken from the pot, and strain the remaining ingredients through a fine sieve into another pot. Press the vegetables in
   the sieve with the back of a large kitchen spoon against the side of
   the sieve to extract their liquid, and discard the vegetables. Remove
   the poultry meat from the carcass, save the meat for another use, and
   discard the carcass. Allow the stock to cool.
3. Strain the stock through a fine sieve again. Refrigerate the stock
   overnight to allow the fat to harden on its surface. Before using the
   stock, remove the fat.

White Bean and Roasted Butternut Squash Soup

This soup is warm and soothing yet full of nutrition and fiber. Pureed white beans give a creamy consistency to the soup without the added fat of dairy cream. **Tips:** *This soup can be prepared a day in advance and gently reheated in a double boiler or over low heat. It may be necessary to add water to thin it. If canned beans are used, don't cook them in step 1.*

PREPARATION: 10 minutes
COOKING: 50 minutes
YIELD: 4 to 6 servings

1 cup dried navy *or* cannellini beans, picked over, rinsed, and
    soaked overnight, *or* 2 cups canned beans, drained and rinsed

1 large butternut squash, peeled, seeded, and sliced into ½-inch
    pieces

1 medium sweet potato, peeled and sliced into ½-inch pieces

Salt to taste

Pepper to taste

1 tablespoon plus 1 teaspoon olive oil

2 teaspoons maple syrup

1 2-inch piece gingerroot, peeled and finely chopped

1 Spanish onion, peeled and diced

2 cups plus 3¾ cups water

½ cup cilantro, chopped

1. Place the dried beans in a pot, and cover them with water. Bring the water to a boil, reduce the heat, and simmer the beans until they are tender. Drain the beans, and transfer them to a blender or food processor. Process the beans until they are smooth, adding water if necessary. Set the beans aside.
2. While the beans are cooking, heat the oven to 400°F.
3. Combine the squash and potato in a bowl, sprinkle the vegetables with the salt and pepper, and drizzle over them the 1 tablespoon of olive oil and the maple syrup. Transfer them to a large roasting tray. Roast the vegetables until they are tender and slightly caramelized, approximately 45 minutes. Set the vegetables aside.

4. While the vegetables are roasting, heat the remaining 1 teaspoon of olive oil in a large Dutch oven over medium heat. Add the ginger, and sauté it until it is fragrant. Add the onion and a dash of salt. Sauté the onion, stirring it often, until it is soft. Add the 2 cups of water, and bring the liquid to a boil. Stir in the roasted vegetables, and simmer the ingredients, stirring them often, for 3 minutes.

5. Transfer the mixture to a food processor or blender, and puree until smooth. Return the mixture to the pot along with the reserved beans, and add the remaining 3¾ cups of water. Heat the soup. Just before serving the soup, add the cilantro, and adjust the seasonings, if necessary.

Chicken Soup with Kale and Orzo

This soup is simple to prepare, making it ideal for those with a busy lifestyle. The soup provides carbohydrates, calcium, folic acid, and iron in a very well-tolerated meal. And the combination of pasta and potatoes in a light chicken broth makes it particularly soothing. **Tips:** *Any type of potato, cooking green, and small pasta can be substituted for the ingredients in the recipe. Remember to adjust the cooking times to fit the ingredients you choose. Peasant bread and a green salad are the perfect accompaniments to this soup.*

PREPARATION: 15 minutes
COOKING: 30 minutes
YIELD: 4 servings

  1 tablespoon plus 1 teaspoon olive oil
  1 Spanish onion, peeled and diced
  5 cloves garlic, peeled finely chopped
  2 medium carrots, scrubbed and diced
  2 ribs celery, diced
    Salt
  2 yellow potatoes *or* purple potatoes *or* red potatoes, washed and thinly sliced into ⅛-inch thick rounds (Yukon Gold or Yellow Finn add lots of flavor)
 12 ounces kale, trimmed, roughly chopped, washed, and drained

8 cups chicken stock
½ cup orzo (rice-shaped pasta)
Meat from 1 cooked chicken, roughly chopped
½ cup mixed fresh herbs, such as cilantro, basil, thyme, oregano, parsley
Pepper to taste

1. Heat the olive oil in a Dutch oven over low heat. Add the onion, and sauté it until it is soft. Add the garlic, and sauté it until it is fragrant.
2. Add the carrots, celery, and a pinch of salt. Cover the pot, and cook the ingredients, stirring them often, for 6 minutes.
3. Add the potatoes and kale, and sauté them for 3 minutes. Pour in the stock, cover the pot, and bring the soup to a boil.
4. Reduce the heat, and simmer the soup until the potatoes are tender, approximately 3 minutes. Raise the heat, and return the soup to a boil.
5. Add the orzo, and cook the pasta for 5 minutes. Add the chicken, and simmer it for 3 minutes.
6. Before serving the soup, add the fresh herbs and pepper, and adjust the salt, if necessary.

Ribollita (Bean, Bread, and Tomato Soup)

Carbohydrates tend to be the best-tolerated nutrient in early pregnancy. This satisfying traditional Tuscan soup, which uses bread as its main ingredient, sits well if you are suffering from nausea. Since it gets better with time, you can reheat it in a microwave for a delicious high-fiber hot lunch. As is frequently the case with other dishes, there are as many versions of ribollita as there are cooks, but the basic ingredients remain the same. This version is one of our favorites. **Tip:** *If canned beans are used, skip step 1.*

PREPARATION: 15 minutes
COOKING: 1½ hours
YIELD: 4 to 6 main-course servings

1 cup dried cranberry, white, pinto, or red kidney beans, picked
   over, rinsed, and soaked for 8 hours, *or* 2 cups canned beans,
   drained and rinsed
4 cups water
2 tablespoons olive oil
1 Spanish onion, peeled and diced
5 cloves garlic, peeled and finely chopped
2 medium carrots, scrubbed and diced
2 ribs celery, diced
1 medium red bell pepper, cored, seeded, and diced
4 cups (¼ head) green cabbage, julienned
   Salt
1 pound dandelion greens *or* spinach, roughly chopped, washed,
   and drained
1 cup fresh basil, snipped
   Pepper to taste
1½ pounds stale crusty bread, cut into ½-inch cubes
1 28-ounce can whole tomatoes, drained and roughly chopped
10 cups hot chicken stock
   Extra-virgin olive oil for drizzling

1. Place the dried beans in a pot, and add the water. Bring the water to
   a boil, reduce the heat, and simmer the beans until they are tender,
   approximately 1 hour. Drain the beans, and set them aside.
2. Meanwhile, heat the oven to 350°F.
3. Heat the 2 tablespoons of olive oil in a Dutch oven over low heat.
   Add the onion, and sauté it until it is soft. Add the garlic, and sauté
   it until it is fragrant. Add the carrots, celery, red bell pepper, cabbage, and a pinch of salt. Cover the pot, and steam-sauté the vegetables, stirring them often, for 6 minutes.
4. Remove the pot from the heat, and stir in the dandelion greens or
   spinach, basil, and the reserved beans. Season the mixture with the
   salt and pepper.
5. In another large Dutch oven or oven-proof casserole, spread one-half
   of the vegetable-bean mixture evenly on the bottom. Then place one-

half of the bread evenly over the vegetables. Repeat the procedure with the remaining vegetables and bread.

6. Combine well the tomatoes and chicken stock. Season the mixture with the salt and pepper. Slowly pour the liquid over the bread-vegetable-bean layers.

7. Cover the pot or casserole, and bake the soup for 20 minutes. Remove the cover, and continue baking the soup 15 minutes longer.

8. Spoon the soup into individual bowls, and drizzle a tablespoon of the extra-virgin olive oil over each serving.

Herbed Basmati Rice with Tomatoes

A wonderful carbohydrate-rich dish to accompany any entree or to enjoy on its own if you are having trouble tolerating much else during early pregnancy.

PREPARATION: 10 minutes
COOKING: 30 minutes
YIELD: 4 side-dish servings

BASMATI RICE

Wonderfully aromatic, basmati rice, white and brown, is a staple in Indian cooking. More fragrant and flavorful than regular white rice, it is fabulous in cold rice salads, paellas, and side-dish recipes. Basmati rice is available in ethnic markets and many supermarkets.

1 tablespoon olive oil
1 medium Spanish onion, peeled and diced
3 cloves garlic, peeled and finely chopped
3 cups water
Salt to taste
1½ cups brown basmati rice *or* white basmati rice
½ cup flat-leaf (Italian) parsley, finely chopped
½ cup fresh basil, finely chopped
Pepper to taste
4 plum tomatoes, diced

1. Heat the olive oil in Dutch oven over medium-low heat. Add the onion, and sauté it until it is soft. Add the garlic, and sauté it until it is fragrant.

2. Pour in the water, and bring the ingredients to a boil.

3. Add a pinch of salt, and stir in the rice. Reduce the heat, cover the pot, and simmer the rice until the water has been absorbed and the rice is tender, approximately 30 minutes.
4. Stir in the parsley, basil, pepper, and tomatoes. Allow the rice to rest with the cover on for 5 minutes.

"Oven-Fried" Potatoes

Although French fries can never be part of a healthy diet, here is an alternative that may fool you. They have character, they are crisp and have a real potato flavor, and most importantly, they are loaded with complex carbohydrates and potassium but are low in fat. Try them the next time you have a hankering for fries. **Tip:** *The secret to making "fries" in the oven is in the technique. Both the oil and the oven need to be hot before the potatoes are added.*

PREPARATION: 10 minutes
BAKING: 30 minutes
YIELD: 4 to 6 servings

6 medium russet potatoes, scrubbed, dried, each cut lengthwise into 14 wedges
2 tablespoons olive oil
1 teaspoon salt
Pepper to taste

1. Heat the oven to 400°F.
2. Heat the olive oil in a large Dutch oven over high heat. Add the potatoes, salt, and pepper. Stir the potatoes well to coat them with the oil. Sauté the potatoes, stirring them constantly, for 3 minutes.
3. Transfer the potatoes to 2 large, heavy baking trays, spreading them out in a single layer. Bake them until they are golden and slightly crisp, approximately 30 minutes. Serve them immediately.

Rotelle, Tuna, and Summer Vegetables in a Balsamic Vinaigrette

PREPARATION: 15 minutes
CHILLING: 2 hours
YIELD: 4 main-course servings

This cold salad is carbohydrate-rich and packed with nutrients. Many pregnant woman find the tangy vinaigrette dressing appealing to their newly altered taste buds. Try it on days when your nausea has abated. It makes a nice addition to a picnic basket or a good main course on a warm evening. Rotelle is one of the best pastas for this dish since it absorbs the dressing well. **Tip:** *If possible, prepare this dish a day in advance to give the flavors a chance to develop.*

1 pound rotelle
1 tablespoon Dijon mustard
2 to 3 tablespoons balsamic vinegar
1 clove garlic, peeled and crushed
¼ cup extra-virgin olive oil
   Salt to taste
   Pepper to taste
2 cucumbers, peeled, seeded, and cubed
2 medium tomatoes, diced
1 small red onion, peeled and julienned
1 small red bell pepper, cored, seeded, and julienned
1 small yellow bell pepper, cored, seeded, and julienned
½ cup fresh basil, snipped
2 6½-ounce cans solid white tuna packed in water, drained and flaked

1. Bring a large pot of lightly salted water to a boil. Add the pasta, and cook it to just before the al dente stage, approximately 7 minutes (the vinegar in the dressing will continue to cook the pasta). Drain the pasta, and run it under cold water to stop the cooking process. Set the pasta aside.

2. Prepare the vinaigrette by whisking together the mustard, vinegar, and garlic. Slowly drizzle in the olive oil while continuing to whisk

the ingredients. Season the dressing with the salt and pepper, and set it aside.

3. In a large bowl, combine the cooked pasta with the remaining ingredients, and toss them well. Mix in the dressing, and adjust the seasonings. Cover the bowl tightly, and chill the salad for at least 2 hours.

Basic Polenta

Polenta is made from corn meal, which is carbohydrate-rich, very easily digested, and well tolerated during early pregnancy. Try it on its own if you are feeling nauseated or as a side dish if you are feeling well. **Tip:** *Using this basic recipe, you may also make a scallion polenta, which goes very well with the Chickpea and White Bean Ragù with Collard Greens on page 278. During the last 5 minutes of cooking, sauté 5 thinly sliced scallions in 1 teaspoon of olive oil, and add the scallions to the polenta.*

PREPARATION: 5 minutes
COOKING: 45 minutes
YIELD: 4 servings

6½ cups boiling water
2 cups yellow corn meal
2 tablespoons unsalted butter
½ cup grated Parmesan
    Salt to taste
    Pepper to taste

1. Pour the boiling water into a heavy pot. Slowly add the corn meal, whisking the mixture to prevent lumps from forming. After all the corn meal has been added, reduce the heat to low.

2. Stir the polenta almost constantly for 45 minutes to ensure even cooking. The polenta is done when it pulls away cleanly from the sides and bottom of the pot.

3. Remove the polenta from the heat, and add the butter and Parmesan. Season the polenta with the salt and pepper.

POLENTA

Polenta, the traditional corn-meal dish of northern Italy, is becoming increasingly popular in America. Polenta's desirability, like pasta's, is its versatility. Since its flavor is mild and neutral, polenta is able to absorb and enhance the flavors of whatever is being served with it.

There are other ways to serve polenta than simply as "mashed potatoes." It can be cooled on a board, sliced with a string (a traditional Italian technique), and baked with additional cheese. Or it can be sliced into decorative shapes and either grilled or fried. It can also serve as a pizza crust.

Chicken and Lentil Stew with Rosemary

Try this dish when your appetite is better. This hearty, lentil-based stew is flavored with the delicate taste of rosemary, making it very appealing in your newly pregnant state. The potatoes add extra carbohydrates, and the chicken is an excellent source of iron. Bring this to work in a plastic container, and heat it up in the microwave—the aroma will drive your coworkers crazy.
Tips: *If you prefer to use chicken legs or breasts or any combination of parts, do so. If chicken breasts are used and are large, cut them in half. If delicatta squash is not available, 2 cups of cubed butternut squash can be used. The dish can also be prepared several hours in advance and gently reheated. Accompany this stew with brown rice or tubular pasta.*

PREPARATION: 15 minutes
COOKING: 1½ hours
YIELD: 6 main-course serving

2 tablespoons olive oil
8 medium chicken thighs, skin removed and discarded
1 Spanish onion, peeled and diced
3 cloves garlic, peeled and finely chopped
1 tablespoon plus 1 teaspoon dried rosemary, crushed
1½ teaspoons dried basil
1 teaspoon dried thyme
2 medium carrots, scrubbed and diced
2 ribs celery, diced
1 large red bell pepper, cored, seeded, and diced
2 medium red potatoes, unpeeled and quartered
1 delicatta squash, peeled, seeded, and diced
　Salt to taste
1¼ cup lentils, thoroughly rinsed
1 cup dry red wine
5 to 6 cups chicken stock *or* water
½ pound fresh spinach, roughly chopped, washed, and drained
　Pepper to taste

1. Heat the olive oil in a large Dutch oven over high heat. Pat the chicken dry. Place four of the thighs, bone side up, in the oil. Sear the chicken pieces, turning them once, until a golden crust forms

on them. Remove the chicken pieces from the pan, and set them aside. Repeat this procedure with the other four thighs.

2. Reduce the heat slightly, and add the onion. Sauté the onion, stirring it often, until it is soft. Add the garlic, and sauté it until it is fragrant.

3. Add the rosemary, basil, and thyme, and sauté the ingredients for 30 seconds. Add the carrots, celery, red bell pepper, potatoes, squash, and salt. Reduce the heat, cover the pot, and cook the ingredients, stirring them often, for 5 minutes.

4. Add the lentils, and return the chicken to the pot. Stir the ingredients well, and cook them for 2 minutes. Raise the heat, add the wine, and simmer the ingredients until the wine has evaporated, approximately 5 minutes.

5. Pour in the stock or water, and bring the stew to a boil. Reduce the heat, cover the pot, and simmer the stew, stirring it occasionally, for 30 to 45 minutes or until the lentils are just tender.

6. Add the spinach, and cook the stew for 1 minute. Remove the chicken, and place it on a large serving platter. Season the sauce with the salt and pepper, and ladle it over the chicken.

Farfalle with Chicken, Shiitake, Spinach, and Sage

The abundance of intensely flavored fresh ingredients makes this recipe rich tasting without much fat to upset your stomach. The chicken and spinach are excellent sources of iron, and the unique flavor of the mushrooms will be particularly satisfying.

PREPARATION: 10 minutes
COOKING: 15 minutes
YIELD: 4 main-course servings

1 pound farfalle (bow-tie-shaped pasta)
1 tablespoon olive oil
1 pound boneless, skinless chicken breasts, trimmed of all visible fat and sliced into ¼-inch-thick strips

4 cloves garlic, peeled and finely chopped

12 ounces shiitake, stems removed and discarded, caps sliced

Salt to taste

½ cup white wine

1 pound spinach, stemmed, chopped, washed, and dried

4 tablespoons fresh sage, snipped

⅓ cup pasta cooking water

1 tablespoon unsalted butter

Pepper to taste

4 tablespoons grated Parmesan

1. Bring a large pot of lightly salted water to a boil. Add the pasta, and cook it while you prepare the sauce.
2. Heat the olive oil in a Dutch oven over medium heat. Add the chicken pieces, and sauté them for 5 minutes, turning them often. Add the garlic, and sauté it, stirring it often, until it is fragrant.
3. Raise the heat. Add the mushrooms and salt, and sauté them, stirring them constantly, until they are soft and their liquid has evaporated.
4. Add the wine, and simmer the ingredients until the wine has evaporated.
5. Add the spinach, sage, and pasta cooking water, and cook the ingredients, stirring them constantly, until the spinach is wilted. Stir in the butter. Season the sauce with the salt and pepper.
6. Drain the pasta, and add it to the sauce. Toss the ingredients well, and heat them for 1 minute. Divide the farfalle among 4 plates, topping each portion with 1 tablespoon of the Parmesan.

Mexican Black Bean "Lasagna"

This dish gets its name from the layering of tortillas and filling in a deep casserole. Try it when you are feeling good. It is packed with the nutrients required for pregnancy: pumpkinseeds for folic acid and calcium; kale for folic acid, calcium, and iron; black beans for fiber. This casserole is great for entertaining. Prepare it in a lovely ceramic dish for appealing presentation. ***Tips:*** To execute this recipe efficiently, you must be well organized. It is best to prepare the latter part of the bean recipe as well as the sauce while the beans are cooking. If you prepare the dish in this manner, the entire process should take just over an hour. If dried basil is used in the sauce, add it after the onions have been softened, and cook it for 2 minutes before the garlic is added. The casserole can be assembled a day in advance and baked for 30 minutes before serving it.

PREPARATION: 30 minutes
COOKING: 1¼ hours
YIELD: 6 main-course servings

BEANS

  1 pound black beans, picked over, rinsed, and soaked for 8 hours

  5 cups water

  1 tablespoon olive oil

  1 large Spanish onion, peeled and diced

  4 cloves garlic, peeled and finely chopped

  1 Scotch bonnet *or* serrano *or* jalapeño, finely chopped

  1 teaspoon chili powder

  1 teaspoon cumin powder

  1 teaspoon ground coriander

  1 pound kale chopped, washed, and drained

  3 ears fresh corn, kernels removed, *or* 2 cups frozen corn kernels, thawed

  ¾ cup cilantro, chopped

  Salt to taste

  Pepper to taste

SAUCE

  1 medium bulb garlic, loose skin removed

  1 tablespoon plus 1 tablespoon olive oil

  2 tablespoons water

  1 large Spanish onion, peeled and diced

  3 cloves garlic, peeled and finely chopped

  1 28-ounce can whole tomatoes, roughly chopped

  ½ cup roasted pumpkinseeds (available in many supermarkets and ethnic markets)

⅓ cup fresh basil, snipped, *or* 2 teaspoons dried basil
  Salt to taste
  Pepper to taste

Remaining Ingredients
  8 corn tortillas
  6 ounces Monterey jack, grated

1. To make the beans, place them in a large pot. Add the water, and bring it to a boil. Reduce the heat, and simmer the beans until they are tender, approximately 1 hour.
2. While the beans are cooking, make the sauce. Cut approximately ¼ inch off the top (nonstem side) of the garlic bulb, discard it, and place the bulb in a small bowl. Drizzle the garlic bulb with 1 tablespoon of the olive oil and the water. Cover the bowl tightly with plastic wrap, and microwave the garlic on high until it is soft, approximately 15 minutes. When the garlic bulb is cool, extract the pulp from the skin by gently squeezing each clove. Set the garlic aside.
3. Heat the remaining 1 tablespoon of olive oil in large Dutch oven over medium heat. Add the onion, and sauté it until it is soft. Add the chopped garlic, and sauté it until it is fragrant.
4. Heat the oven to 375°F.
5. Add the tomatoes, and bring the sauce to a boil. Reduce the heat, and simmer the sauce, stirring it often, for 15 minutes. Add the reserved garlic and the pumpkinseeds. Simmer the sauce 5 minutes longer.
6. Transfer the mixture to a blender or the work bowl of a food processor, and puree the sauce until it is smooth. Add the fresh basil, and season the sauce with the salt and pepper.
7. To complete the beans, while they are cooking, heat the olive oil in a large Dutch oven over low heat. Add the onion, and sauté it, stirring it often, until it is soft. Add the garlic, and sauté it until it is fragrant.
8. Add Scotch bonnet, serrano, or jalapeño, chili powder, cumin, and coriander, and sauté the mixture, stirring it often, for 2 minutes.

Add the kale, and steam it until it is tender, approximately 10 minutes. Add the corn and cilantro, and sauté them for 1 minute.

9. When the beans are done, drain them and stir them into the remaining bean ingredients. Season the beans with the salt and pepper.

10. To assemble the casserole, place 2 tortillas on the bottom of a 10 × 14-inch round casserole. Cover them with one-quarter of the bean mixture, followed by one-quarter of the sauce and one-quarter of the Monterey jack. Repeat the layering three more times, ending with the cheese.

11. Cover the casserole, and bake it until it is heated through, approximately 20 minutes.

Pot Roast Pomodoro

In this dish, tomatoes, white beans, and escarole add an Italian flavor to pot roast. Try this pot roast for an early-pregnancy iron boost. Beef is one of the best sources of iron, easily absorbed by the body in this form. In addition, the tomatoes are high in vitamin C, which will enhance your body's absorption of iron from the meat. **Tip:** *The keys to a moist and tender pot roast are a well-marbled cut of meat and long, very gentle cooking. If the meat is cooked over too high a heat, it will become tough.*

PREPARATION: 20 minutes
COOKING: 3 hours
YIELD: 6 main-course servings

4 pounds rump roast
12 cloves garlic, 8 peeled and left whole, 4 peeled and finely chopped
½ cup dried white beans, picked over, rinsed, and soaked for 8 hours
3 cups plus 2½ cups water
2 tablespoons olive oil
1 medium Spanish onion, peeled and diced

1 teaspoon dried oregano
1 teaspoon dried basil
½ cup brandy
2½ cups canned crushed tomatoes
2 medium carrots, scrubbed and sliced into 2-inch pieces
2 medium parsnips, scrubbed and sliced into 2-inch pieces
6 small white potatoes *or* yellow potatoes, sliced in half
1 medium head fennel, diced
3 cups escarole, roughly chopped, washed, and drained
Salt to taste
Pepper to taste

1. Stud the roast with the whole cloves of garlic.
2. Place the beans in a saucepan. Add the 3 cups of water, and bring the water to a boil. Reduce the heat, and simmer the beans until they are tender, approximately 1 hour. Drain the beans, and set them aside.
3. While the beans are simmering, heat the olive oil in a large Dutch oven over high heat. Add the rump roast, and sear it on all sides. Remove the roast, and set it aside.
4. Reduce the heat slightly, add the onion, and sauté it, stirring it constantly, until it is soft. Add the chopped garlic, and sauté it, stirring it constantly, until it is fragrant.
5. Add the oregano and basil, and sauté the ingredients, stirring them constantly, for 1 minute.
6. Raise the heat, and return the roast to the pot. Carefully pour in the brandy. Simmer the liquid until the brandy has evaporated, approximately 2 minutes.
7. Add the remaining 2½ cups of water and the tomatoes, and bring the liquid to a boil.
8. Quickly reduce the heat, tightly cover the pot, and simmer the ingredients over very low heat for 2¼ hours, turning the roast every 30 minutes.
9. Add the carrots, parsnips, potatoes, and fennel, and partially cover the pot. Simmer the roast 45 minutes longer.
10. Remove the roast from the pot, cover the roast loosely, and set it aside, keeping it warm.

11. Raise the heat under the pot, and add the escarole. Simmer the escarole, stirring it often, for 5 minutes.
12. Remove the pot from the heat, add the cooked beans, and season the sauce to taste with the salt and pepper.
13. Slice the roast, and ladle the sauce and vegetables over the slices.

Lime-Ginger Swordfish with Tomato-Avocado Salsa

*Try this nutritious fish dish in the first trimester when you are feeling good. Avocados are rich in folic acid, as is swordfish, which is also high in iron, both nutrients being important for you at this point in your pregnancy. The vitamin C in the lime and tomato will enhance your body's absorption of the iron. **Tips:** When preparing swordfish, it is best to use mild, fresh ingredients, which enhance its flavor. (Heavy sauces and powerful spices tend to mask its richness.) The salsa, minus the avocado, can be prepared 2 days in advance and refrigerated. Add the avocado just before serving the dish or the avocado will discolor. Other fish, including salmon, haddock, and tuna, may be substituted for the swordfish. Rather than broiling or grilling a less fatty fish such as haddock, I suggest roasting it.*

PREPARATION: 15 minutes
CHILLING: 2 hours
COOKING: 8 minutes
YIELD: 4 main-course servings

SALSA

    4 large tomatoes, diced
    1 teaspoon olive oil
    1 jalapeño, seeded and finely chopped
    2 scallions, trimmed and finely chopped
    1 small red onion, peeled and diced
    3 tablespoons cilantro, finely chopped
    1 tablespoon fresh mint, finely chopped
    1 tablespoon fresh lime juice
    1 tablespoon red-wine vinegar

½ teaspoon lime zest
1 large ripe avocado, peeled, pitted, and cut into ¼-inch chunks
Salt to taste
Pepper to taste

FISH

Juice 3 limes
1 tablespoon olive oil
1 2-inch piece gingerroot, peeled and finely chopped
3 tablespoons cilantro, finely chopped
Black pepper to taste
4 swordfish steaks, approximately ¾-inch thick

1. To prepare the salsa, in a medium bowl combine well the tomatoes, olive oil, jalapeño, scallions, red onion, cilantro, mint, lime juice, vinegar, and zest. Cover the bowl, and refrigerate the salsa for 2 hours.
2. While the salsa chills, prepare the fish marinade. Combine the lime juice, olive oil, gingerroot, cilantro, and black pepper in a bowl, and whisk the ingredients well. Place the fish steaks in a nonmetal bowl. Pour the marinade over steaks, and turn them so that they are evenly coated with the marinade. Cover the bowl, and refrigerate the fish steaks for 1 hour, turning them 2 or 3 times.
3. Light a charcoal grill, or heat the broiler.
4. Stir the avocado into the salsa, and season the salsa with the salt and pepper.
5. Drain the marinade from the fish steaks. Grill them, or broil them 4 inches from the heat, until they are just cooked through, turning them twice—approximately 8 minutes. Top each steak with some salsa.

Citrus Salmon with Mesclun and Raspberry Vinegar

Salmon, a very nutritious fish, is rich in omega-3 fatty acids and high in both iron and folic acid. Here, the absorption of the iron is enhanced by the citrus juices. This dish provides contrasting flavors and temperatures (tart, sweet, hot, and cold). The best method of preparing high-quality ingredients is often the simplest, and in this recipe the rich flavor of salmon is enhanced by fresh lemon and orange juices, the fillets then served on a bed of flavorful mesclun that has been tossed only in fruity olive oil and slightly sweet raspberry vinegar. Enjoy this dish now and throughout your pregnancy. **Tip:** *Mackerel or bluefish (not a source of iron) can be substituted for the salmon. The orange and lemon juices complement their oily flesh.*

PREPARATION: 10 minutes
COOKING: 7 minutes
YIELD: 4 main-course servings

---

    4 salmon fillets, approximately ¾-inch thick
      Salt to taste
      Pepper to taste
      Juice 1 orange
      Juice 1 lemon
   12 ounces mesclun, washed and dried
    2 tablespoons olive oil
    1 tablespoon raspberry vinegar

1. Heat the broiler.
2. Place the salmon on a heavy broiling tray. Sprinkle the fish with the salt and pepper. Drizzle the orange juice and lemon juice evenly over the fish.
3. Broil the fish 4 inches from the heat until the fillets are just cooked through, approximately 7 minutes.
4. Sprinkle the mesclun lightly with the salt and pepper. Drizzle the olive oil and raspberry vinegar over the mesclun, and toss the greens lightly.
5. Divide the mesclun evenly among 4 large plates. Place a fillet on each portion of greens.

MESCLUN

Mesclun is a mixture of seven to ten sweet and sharp-tasting baby greens. The greens can include arugula, tatsoi, baby bok choy, cress, and baby lettuces such as Lollo Rosso, Tango, Little Gem, red and green leaf, and mizuna. They are often available precut and prewashed, either in bulk or small packages.

Spaghetti with Turkey Sausage, Red Bell Peppers, Onions, and Tomatoes

If your cravings have started early and you have a hankering for Italian pork sausage but don't want the fat, calories, cholesterol, sodium, and nitrates it contains, try this dish. (When turkey sausage is properly spiced, it is difficult to tell that the sausage is not made with pork.) Excellent-quality turkey sausage is made with only ground white meat and spices. It is not only low in calories and fat, but is a fantastic source of protein, iron, and folic acid. And it may satisfy your craving for salty foods during pregnancy. **Tips:** *If dried herbs are used, add them when you add the bell peppers. The dish should be accompanied by crusty bread. In addition to serving it over pasta, the sauce may be served in crusty rolls for a hearty sandwich.*

PREPARATION: 10 minutes
COOKING: 50 minutes
YIELD: 4 to 6 main-course servings

1 tablespoon plus 1 tablespoon olive oil
1 pound lean sweet turkey sausage, cut in 2-inch pieces
1 medium Spanish onion, peeled and thinly sliced
1 medium red onion, peeled and thinly sliced
5 cloves garlic, peeled and finely chopped
2 large red bell peppers, cored, seeded, and thinly sliced
Dash red pepper flakes
1 35-ounce can whole tomatoes, roughly chopped
Salt to taste
Pepper to taste
⅓ cup fresh basil, snipped, *or* 2 teaspoons dried basil
2 tablespoons fresh oregano *or* 1 teaspoon dried oregano
1 pound spaghetti

1. Heat 1 tablespoon of the olive oil in a Dutch oven over medium-high heat. Add the sausage, and sear it until it is golden, turning it two or three times. Remove the sausage from the pot, and set it aside.

2. Reduce the heat to medium. Add the remaining 1 tablespoon of olive oil to the pot. Add the Spanish onion and red onion, and sauté

them, stirring them often, until they begin to soften. Add the garlic, and sauté it until it is fragrant.

3. Add the red bell peppers and the red pepper flakes, and sauté them, stirring them often, until the peppers begin to soften and sweat—approximately 5 minutes.

4. Raise the heat to high, and add the tomatoes. Bring the ingredients to a boil, reduce the heat, return the sausage to the pot, and gently stir the sauce.

5. Partially cover the pot, and simmer the sauce, stirring it occasionally, for 45 minutes.

6. Cook the pasta in boiling salted water until it is tender, drain it, and put it in a serving bowl or on individual plates. Ladle the sauce over the pasta.

Hamburgers with Spinach and Basil–Goat Cheese Pesto

*Here is a flavorful change of pace from the mundane that will satisfy your craving for red meat. The dish provides a double dose of iron from the beef and the spinach, and vitamin C–rich tomato to enhance the iron's absorption. Be certain your hamburger is well done. **Tips:** Although the iron content of the burgers will be reduced, ground turkey or chicken is a fine substitute for the beef. The pesto, which yields approximately 1 cup, also makes a wonderful, quick pasta and pizza sauce. Accompany this dish with the Orzo Salad with Spinach, Feta, and Roasted Pumpkinseeds (page 236).*

PREPARATION: 20 minutes
COOKING: 10 minutes
YIELD: 4 main-course serving

PESTO
2½ cups fresh basil leaves
2 cloves garlic, peeled and chopped
⅓ cup pine nuts
¼ cup olive oil

½ cup grated Parmesan

Black pepper to taste

REMAINING INGREDIENTS

3 tablespoons pesto (see above and step 1, below)

2 ounces goat cheese

1 tablespoon plus 2 teaspoons olive oil

3 cloves garlic, peeled and finely chopped

1 pound spinach, finely chopped, washed, and dried

1¼ pounds extra-lean ground beef

Salt to taste

Pepper to taste

4 large crusty rolls

1 large ripe tomato, cut into 4 slices

1. To make the pesto, combine the basil, garlic, and pine nuts in the work bowl of a food processor or in a blender. Process the ingredients until they are coarse. With the motor running, drizzle in the olive oil. Process the ingredients until they are smooth. Stir in the Parmesan, and add the pepper. Reserve 3 tablespoons of the pesto for use here, tightly covering and refrigerating the rest.

2. To make the hamburgers, combine the 3 tablespoons of pesto and the goat cheese, stirring the ingredients until they are smooth. Set the mixture aside.

3. Heat the 1 tablespoon of olive oil in a large skillet over medium-low heat. Add the garlic, and sauté it, stirring it constantly, until it is soft and fragrant. Add the spinach, and sauté it, stirring it constantly, until it is wilted. Transfer the spinach to a large mixing bowl.

4. Add the ground beef to the spinach, and sprinkle the ingredients with the salt and pepper. Combine the ingredients well. Form the mixture into 4 round patties.

5. Heat the remaining 2 teaspoons of olive oil in the skillet over high heat. Add the patties, and sear them on each side. Reduce the heat, and cook the burgers until they are well done.

6. Place each burger on a roll, add a slice of tomato, and spread one-quarter of the pesto–goat cheese mixture on the roll.

Potatoes Stuffed with Spinach and Broccoli

Potatoes are an excellent choice if you are nauseous. Just rub them with a little olive oil, and bake them. Then, when you feel a bit better, try this delicious preparation. Stuffed potatoes are a carbohydrate- and fiber-rich dish that, depending on your choice of additional ingredients, can be high in many nutrients. This version provides excellent amounts of calcium from the broccoli, and cheese. **Tip:** *These potatoes can be prepared a day in advance. Just wrap them tightly, refrigerate them, and bake them the following day.*

PREPARATION: 15 minutes
BAKING: 55 minutes
YIELD: 4 main-course servings

4 large baking potatoes (preferably russets)
1 tablespoon plus 1 tablespoon olive oil
1 large bunch broccoli, florets only
     (reserve the stems for another use)
2 cloves garlic, peeled and finely chopped
12 ounces cultivated white mushrooms, cleaned and sliced
     Salt to taste
1½ pounds spinach, roughly chopped, washed, and dried
1 large tomato, diced
1⅓ cups plus 1 cup grated Cheddar, firmly packed
     Pepper to taste

1. Heat the oven to 400°F.
2. Scrub and dry the potatoes thoroughly. Pierce them three or four times with a fork. Rub them with 1 tablespoon of the olive oil. Bake them until they are tender, approximately 45 minutes.
3. Remove the potatoes from the oven. Carefully slice them in half vertically, and allow them to cool.
4. While the potatoes are cooling, prepare the filling. Bring a pot of lightly salted water to a boil. Add the broccoli florets, and blanch them until they are tender-crisp. Drain and cool the florets under running water, and set them aside.
5. Heat the remaining 1 tablespoon of olive oil in a skillet over medium

heat. Add the garlic, and sauté it, stirring it constantly, until it is soft and fragrant. Add the mushrooms and salt. Sauté the mushrooms, stirring them constantly, until they are soft and all of their liquid has evaporated. Add the spinach, and sauté the ingredients, stirring them constantly, until the spinach has wilted. Transfer the mixture to a large bowl, add the reserved broccoli and tomato, and toss the ingredients well.

6. When the potatoes have cooled, scoop out their flesh, taking care not to tear the skins. Add the flesh to the vegetables, and blend the ingredients well. Be certain the potato is thoroughly mashed and evenly incorporated. Stir in the 1⅓ cups of Cheddar, and season the mixture with the salt and pepper.

7. Divide the stuffing among the 8 potato skins, filling them evenly. Sprinkle the remaining 1 cup of Cheddar on the top of each potato half.

8. Bake the potatoes until they are heated through, about 10 minutes.

Quinoa-Basil Tabbouleh

Preparation: 25 minutes
Chilling: 3 hours
Yield: 4 main-course servings

*Quinoa ("keen'-wah") is a grainlike product that once grew exclusively in Peru but is now being grown in the Colorado Rockies to meet the demands of the rapidly growing American market. Quinoa's flavor and texture are unique, its nutritional value almost unparalleled. It is carbohydrate-rich, contains complete, high-quality protein (the amino acid lysine is present, which is usually not present in plant sources), and boasts a large amount of iron. **Tip:** There are many varieties of quinoa available. When purchasing, choose the largest, whitest grains—their flavor will be lighter and sweeter than the darker grains.*

2 cups water
1 cup quinoa, rinsed
Juice 1½ lemons

2 tablespoons olive oil

2 cloves garlic, peeled and finely chopped

½ teaspoon allspice

1 medium red onion, peeled and finely chopped

1 cup fresh basil, snipped

½ cup flat-leaf (Italian) parsley, finely chopped

⅓ cup fresh mint, finely chopped

4 scallions, trimmed and finely chopped

1 medium cucumber, peeled, seeded, and chopped

1 large tomato, diced

1 medium red bell pepper, cored, seeded, and diced

   Salt to taste

   Pepper to taste

1. Bring the water to a boil in a medium-sized saucepan, and add the quinoa. Reduce the heat, and simmer the quinoa until the water is absorbed, approximately 15 minutes. Gently fluff the quinoa with a fork.

2. Add the lemon juice, olive oil, garlic, and allspice, and mix the ingredients well. Cover the pan tightly, and refrigerate the quinoa for 1 hour.

3. Add the remaining ingredients, and toss them well. Refrigerate the tabbouleh 2 hours longer.

Grilled Tuna with Navy Bean Ragù

Try this delicious dish for an early-pregnancy nutrition boost. Folic acid is present in both the tuna and the beans. The dish also supplies protein, carbohydrates, vitamin C, and iron. **Tips:** *If you can't locate kalamata and Sicilian olives in your local market, canned black olives can be substituted. The sauce can be prepared a day in advance and gently reheated before serving; it may be necessary to add a small amount of water to thin it. Although tuna*

PREPARATION: 15 minutes
COOKING: 1 hour
YIELD: 4 main-course servings

is a fish that many prefer medium-rare, make sure that your portion is well done. Polenta (see page 125), unmatched for soaking up juices from ragùs and stews, is the perfect compliment to the aggressive flavors of the sauce and fish.

1¼ cups dried navy beans, picked over, rinsed, and soaked for 8
    hours
5 cups water
1 tablespoon plus 1 tablespoon olive oil
  Juice 1 lemon
2 tablespoons fresh rosemary, finely chopped
  Pepper to taste
4 tuna steaks, ¾-inch thick
4 cloves garlic, peeled and finely chopped
  Pinch red pepper flakes
6 medium tomatoes, peeled, seeded, and chopped, *or* 2 cups
    canned whole tomatoes, chopped
16 kalamata olives, pitted and finely chopped
6 Sicilian olives, pitted and finely chopped
⅓ cup fresh basil, snipped
  Salt to taste

1. Place the beans in a pot, add the water, and bring the water to a boil. Reduce the heat, and simmer the beans until they are tender, approximately 45 minutes. Drain the beans, reserving ¾ cup of the cooking water. Set both the beans and the reserved water aside.
2. While the beans are cooking, combine 1 tablespoon of the olive oil, the lemon juice, and rosemary in a nonmetal bowl. Grind pepper on both sides of the tuna steaks. Place the steaks in the marinade, turning them to coat them well. Cover the fish, and refrigerate it for 45 minutes.
3. While the fish is marinating, prepare the ragù by heating the remaining 1 tablespoon of olive oil in a Dutch oven over medium heat. Add the garlic, and sauté it, stirring it constantly, until it is soft and fragrant. Add the red pepper flakes and tomatoes, and bring the sauce to a boil. Reduce the heat to a low, add the kalamata and Sicilian

olives, cover the pot, and simmer the ragù for 15 minutes, stirring it often.

4. Add all but 1 cup of the cooked beans to the ragù. Puree the reserved cup of beans in a blender or food processor (if necessary, add a bit of water) until they are smooth. Add the puree to the ragù.

5. Add the reserved bean cooking water and basil to the ragù, and simmer the ragù 5 minutes longer. Season the ragù with the salt and pepper.

6. Heat the grill or broiler.

7. Grill or broil the fish steaks until they are cooked through. Ladle a portion of the ragù on the bottom of each of 4 dinner plates, and place a tuna steak on top of each portion.

Potato, Onion, Spinach, and Goat Cheese Calzones

*Calzones are wonderfully versatile: they can be filled with any combination of vegetables, cheeses, herbs, meats, poultry, and seafood. In this recipe, slightly crisp roasted potatoes are mixed with sweet onions, spinach, and creamy goat cheese. Although the ingredients sound rich, the recipe serves 6 and the overall fat and calorie contents are surprisingly low. The potatoes and crust provide a double dose of carbohydrates, the spinach is rich in iron, and the goat cheese a relatively low-fat source of calcium. **Tips:** Many pizza shops sell their pizza dough, which can then be used here. This is an excellent (and quicker) alternative to making your own. The onions and spinach can be prepared a day in advance.*

Preparation and rising: 1 hour
Baking: 20 minutes
Yield: 6 main-course servings

Dough
　　2 cups warm tap water (about 95°F)
　　1 tablespoon sugar
　　1 tablespoon active dry yeast

1 tablespoon olive oil plus extra for greasing the bowl

5 to 5½ cups unbleached, all-purpose flour

1 teaspoon salt

FILLING

1 tablespoon plus 1 tablespoon olive oil

3 medium russet potatoes, scrubbed, dried, and sliced into
⅛-inch rounds

Salt to taste

Pepper to taste

2 medium Spanish onions, peeled and thinly sliced

2 tablespoons sugar

1 pound spinach, finely chopped, washed, and drained

8 ounces goat cheese, cut into 6 pieces

4 tablespoons corn meal

1. To make the dough, pour the water into a large mixing bowl. Add the sugar, and sprinkle in the yeast, stirring the ingredients with a fork to dissolve the yeast. Let the yeast proof for 5 minutes. (At this point, the yeast should be foaming.)

2. Add the olive oil, 2 cups of the flour, and the salt to the yeast mixture. Stir the ingredients with a wooden spoon for 3 minutes. Allow the mixture to rest for 15 minutes.

3. Add 2 more cups of the flour, and stir the dough for an additional 3 minutes. When the dough begins to pull away from the sides of the bowl, it is ready to be kneaded.

4. Sprinkle some of the remaining flour over your work surface. Remove the dough from the bowl, and coat the dough with the flour. Begin kneading the dough, using the heels of your hands, by pushing it out in front of you and then folding in the sides. Add only enough flour to your hands and the work surface to prevent the dough from sticking. When the dough is no longer sticky, stop adding flour, but continue to knead the dough until it is soft, smooth, and elastic. Step 4 should take approximately 10 minutes.

5. Lightly grease a large bowl with the olive oil. Roll the dough in the

oil to coat it, and tightly cover the bowl with plastic wrap. Place the dough in a warm, draft-free place to rise.

6. Heat the oven to 450°F.

7. While the dough is rising, prepare the filling. Heat 1 tablespoon of the olive oil in Dutch oven over high heat. Add the potatoes, and sprinkle them with the salt and pepper. Sauté the potatoes, stirring them often, for 2 minutes. Transfer the potatoes to a baking tray, and place the tray in the oven. Roast the potatoes until they are slightly crisp. Remove them from the oven, and set them aside. Keep the oven on.

8. While the potatoes are roasting, prepare the onions and spinach. Heat the remaining 1 tablespoon of olive oil over medium heat. Add the onions and a pinch of salt. Sauté the onions, stirring them often, until they are very soft. Add the sugar, and sauté the onions until they have caramelized, approximately 3 minutes. Add the spinach, and stir the ingredients until the spinach has wilted. Set the onion-spinach mixture aside.

9. When the dough has doubled in bulk, deflate it by bringing its edges toward the center of the bowl. Allow the dough to rest for 5 minutes.

10. Sprinkle 2 heavy baking sheets with the corn meal. Divide the dough into 6 equal pieces, and shape each into a ball. Flatten the balls lightly, and place 5 of them under a towel while you roll 1 out.

11. Lightly flour a work surface. Roll 1 ball of dough into a 12 × 7-inch oval. Transfer it to a baking sheet. Place a layer of potatoes on one-half of the dough leaving a ½-inch border around the edge. Then place a layer of some onions and spinach (be certain most of the liquid is pressed out of the mixture or the calzone will be soggy), and top with some goat cheese. Fold the other half of the dough over the filling, making the edges meet. Seal the edges, crimp with a fork, and prick the top in two or three places. Repeat the procedure with the 5 remaining pieces of dough and the rest of the filling. You should have 3 calzones on each tray.

12. Bake the calzones until they are golden, approximately 20 minutes.

Penne with Chicken, Asparagus, Lemon, and Tarragon

PREPARATION: 10 minutes
COOKING: 15 minutes
YIELD: 4 main-course servings

This pasta dish is quick and easy to prepare, and contains all the necessary nutrients for a first-trimester entrée. Asparagus is a delicious source of folic acid, and chicken is a well-absorbed source of iron. And the lemon-tarragon sauce is sure to appeal to your palate. **Tip:** *Shrimp, squid, scallops, or any combination of the three can be substituted for the chicken. It is best to add them after the butter has been incorporated into the sauce. If seafood is used, eliminate the Parmesan.*

1½ pounds asparagus, trimmed
1 pound penne
1 tablespoon olive oil
1 pound skinless and boneless chicken breasts, trimmed of all
    visible fat and cut in ¼-inch-thick strips
4 cloves garlic, peeled and finely chopped
⅓ cup white wine
2 tablespoons fresh tarragon
½ cup asparagus blanching water
   Juice 1 to 2 lemons
1 tablespoon unsalted butter
   Salt to taste
   Pepper to taste
4 tablespoons grated Parmesan

1. Bring a medium-sized pot of lightly salted water to a boil. Add the asparagus, and blanch them until they are tender-crisp. Drain them, reserving ½ cup of the blanching water, and immediately submerge the asparagus in an ice bath to stop the cooking. Drain the asparagus again, and set them aside.
2. Bring a large pot of lightly salted water to a boil. Add the penne.
3. While the pasta is cooking, heat the olive oil in a Dutch oven over medium heat. Add the chicken, and sauté it, turning it often, for 5

minutes. Add the garlic, and sauté it, stirring it often, until it is fragrant.

4. Raise the heat, and add the wine. Simmer the liquid until it has evaporated.

5. Add the tarragon, blanching water, and the reserved asparagus. Cook the asparagus until they are heated through. Add the lemon juice, and swirl in the butter. Season the sauce with the salt and pepper.

6. Drain the pasta, and add it to the sauce. Toss the ingredients well, and heat them through for 1 minute. Divide the pasta among 4 serving plates, garnishing each serving with 1 tablespoon of the Parmesan.

Spinach Fettuccine with "Wild" Mushroom Sauce

This quick, easy pasta is satisfying because of its high-carbohydrate content. The spinach noodles provide more iron than plain pasta, while the "wild" mushrooms add a lovely buttery flavor. This meal will sit well with those who are nauseated. **Tip:** *Many mushrooms—shiitake, portabella, crimini, and oyster—that were once considered wild are now cultivated.*

PREPARATION: 10 minutes
COOKING: 15 minutes
YIELD: 4 main-course servings

  1 pound spinach fettuccine
  2 teaspoons extra-virgin olive oil
  4 cloves garlic, peeled and finely chopped
1¼ pounds mixed "wild" mushrooms (shiitake, portabella, and crimini are excellent choices and widely available)
    Salt to taste
  ¾ cup homemade chicken stock *or* low-sodium canned chicken broth
  ⅓ cup pasta cooking water
  ½ cup flat-leaf (Italian) parsley, finely chopped

2 teaspoons unsalted butter
Pepper to taste

1. Bring a large pot of lightly salted water to a boil, and add the fettuccine.
2. While the pasta is cooking, heat the olive oil in a Dutch oven over low heat. Add the garlic, and sauté it, stirring it often, until it is soft and fragrant. Raise the heat to medium, and add the mushrooms and a pinch of salt. Sauté the mushrooms, stirring them constantly, until they are very soft and all their liquid has evaporated, approximately 5 minutes.
3. Raise the heat to high, and add the chicken stock or broth and pasta cooking water. Stir in the parsley. Simmer the sauce for 2 minutes.
4. Stir in the butter, and season the sauce with the salt and pepper.
5. Drain the pasta, add it to the sauce, and toss the ingredients well. Heat the pasta and sauce over low heat, stirring them often, for 2 more minutes.

Tricolor Farfalle with Tomato Sauce

Enjoy this meal in the first trimester and throughout your pregnancy. **Tips:** *This basic tomato sauce may be prepared ahead of time and kept in the freezer for part of an easy homemade meal. I use vegetable farfalle in this version to add color and fun to the dish; but if it is not available, your favorite pasta will do just fine.*

PREPARATION: 5 minutes
COOKING: 30 minutes
YIELD: 4 main-course servings

2 teaspoon olive oil
4 cloves garlic, peeled and finely chopped
1 small Spanish onion, peeled and diced
Salt to taste
1 teaspoon dried basil

1 teaspoon dried oregano

½ teaspoon dried thyme

⅔ cup water

1 35-ounce can plum tomatoes, roughly chopped

    Pepper to taste

1 pound plain farfalle *or* vegetable farfalle

4 tablespoons grated Parmesan

1. Heat the olive oil in a Dutch oven over medium heat. Add the garlic, and sauté it, stirring it constantly, until it is soft and fragrant. Add the onion and a pinch of salt. Sauté the onion, stirring it often, until it is soft. Stir in the basil, oregano, and thyme, and sauté the ingredients 2 minutes longer.

2. Raise the heat, add the water, and simmer the ingredients for 2 minutes. Add the tomatoes, and bring the sauce to a boil. Reduce the heat, and simmer the sauce, stirring it often, for 20 minutes. Season the sauce with salt and pepper.

3. Cook the pasta in lightly salted, boiling water until the pasta is tender, approximately 8 minutes. Drain the pasta, and divide it among 4 individual plates. Ladle a portion of sauce over each serving of pasta. Sprinkle each serving with 1 tablespoon of the Parmesan.

Chicken with Peppers and Mushrooms

This easily-put-together chicken dish is true comfort food, ideal for a cold evening. With only a hint of garlic, the wonderfully sweet flavor of the bell peppers and the earthy mushrooms are the stars. **Tips:** *Serve this dish with a simple baked potato to supply the carbohydrates, and you have a nutritionally perfect first-trimester entrée. This dish can also be accompanied by polenta (see page 125) or pasta.*

PREPARATION: 15 minutes

COOKING: 1 hour

YIELD: 4 to 6 main-course servings

2 teaspoons olive oil

8 chicken thighs, skin removed and discarded

Salt to taste

Pepper to taste

4 cloves garlic, peeled

1 red bell pepper, cored, seeded, and diced

1 green bell pepper, cored, seeded, and diced

1 yellow bell pepper, cored, seeded, and diced

2 teaspoons dried rosemary

1 pound cultivated white mushrooms, sliced

1 cup white wine

3 tablespoons red-wine vinegar

1 28-ounce can whole tomatoes, chopped

1. Heat the olive oil in a large Dutch oven over high heat. Pat the chicken dry, and season it with the salt and pepper. Carefully place the chicken in the hot oil bone side up. Sear the chicken on both sides, turning it once. Remove the chicken from the pot, and set it aside. Pour off all but 2 teaspoons of the pan drippings.

2. Reduce the heat to medium, and add the garlic to the pot. Sauté the garlic, turning it often, until it is golden. Remove the garlic, and reserve it as "a cook's treat" for later.

3. Add the red, green, and yellow bell peppers and a dash of salt. Sauté the peppers, stirring them often, until they begin to soften. Add the rosemary, mushrooms, and another dash of salt. Sauté the ingredients, stirring them often, until the mushrooms are soft and all of their liquid has evaporated, approximately 5 minutes.

4. Raise the heat to high, and return the chicken to the pot along with any accumulated juices. Add the wine and vinegar, and reduce the liquid for 2 minutes. Stir in the tomatoes, and bring the liquid to a boil. Reduce the heat, and simmer the ingredients, stirring them occasionally, for 45 minutes. Season the dish with salt and pepper.

Steve and Julie's Cape Cod Scallops and Pasta

*Steve Ferzoco and Julie Miner are friends with whom we try to spend a few days every summer on Cape Cod. Julie's parents, Lydia and Jerry Miner, have been vacationing in Wellfleet for more than twenty years. While there, all of us gather oysters and clams, and feast on some of the local fresh fish for dinner. We never go to a restaurant, but chip in with the cooking and make great dinners every night. This is one of our favorite dishes. Scallops are a rich source of protein, and pasta provides the needed carbohydrates for energy. **Tip:** If sea scallops are not available, it is fine to use the delicate bays. However, do not sear them. Add them to the sauce after the butter has been incorporated.*

PREPARATION: 10 minutes
COOKING: 15 minutes
YIELD: 4 main-course servings

1 pound fettuccine
1 tablespoon extra-virgin olive oil
1 pound sea scallops, rinsed and dried, attached muscle removed and discarded
4 cloves garlic, peeled and finely chopped
1 medium red bell pepper, cored, seeded, and diced
½ cup white wine
½ cup pasta cooking water
6 plum tomatoes, diced
1 tablespoon unsalted butter
¾ cup fresh basil, snipped
Salt to taste
Pepper to taste

1. Bring a large pot of lightly salted water to a boil, and add the pasta.
2. While the pasta is cooking, heat the olive oil in a Dutch oven over high heat. Add the scallops, and sear them on each side until they are golden. Remove the scallops, and set them aside.
3. Reduce the heat, and add the garlic to the pan. Sauté the garlic, stirring it constantly, until it is fragrant. Add the red bell pepper, and

sauté the ingredients, stirring them constantly, for 3 minutes.

4. Raise the heat, and add the wine. Reduce the wine for 1 minute. Add the pasta water, tomatoes, and butter.

5. Return the scallops to the pan along with any accumulated juices. Cook the scallops until they are just done, approximately 2 minutes.

6. Reduce the heat, and add the basil. Cook the sauce 1 minute longer. Season the sauce with the salt and pepper.

7. Drain the pasta, and add it to the sauce. Toss the ingredients well, heating them through for 1 minute.

SUPPLEMENT A
RECIPES FOR GAINING WEIGHT

꩜

Whole-Wheat Bread with Cashews and Dates

This bread is packed with nutrients: iron from wheat germ and dates, calcium from buttermilk, protein from cashews, and plenty of fiber. Toast a slice or two of this carbohydrate-rich bread and spread the slice(s) with a fruit preserve for a quick breakfast, or use the slices in one of the French toast recipes in this book. **Tips:** *The cracked wheat can be prepared a day in advance, covered tightly, and refrigerated. The dough can also be prepared through the first flour additions, covered, and left at room temperature. This will give the bread a slightly sour but pleasing flavor.*

PREPARATION: 30 minutes
PROOFING/BAKING: 3¾ hours
YIELD: 1 large loaf

1½ cups water
⅓ cup cracked wheat
1 cup water, warmed (approximately 95°F)
⅓ cup honey
2 tablespoons active dry yeast (about 2 packages)
1 cup buttermilk, warmed
2 cups whole-wheat bread flour
5 cups (approximately) unbleached, all-purpose flour, divided
⅓ cup wheat germ, toasted
1 teaspoon salt

1¼ cups date pieces, roughly chopped
1 cup raw cashew pieces
2 teaspoons peanut oil
4 tablespoons corn meal
Flour for dusting

TO KNEAD YEAST DOUGHS

Kneading a yeast dough is a push, fold, and turn technique. After the dough has been mixed in a bowl, lightly flour a work surface and your hands. Turn the dough onto the surface, and begin kneading by firmly pressing down on the dough with the heel of your hands and pushing it away from you. Fold the dough, and turn it slightly. Repeat this push, fold, and turn technique until the dough is soft and elastic. Add only enough flour to prevent the dough from sticking to the work surface. If too much flour is used, the dough will be tough and will not rise well.

It is impossible to tell how long yeast-based doughs should be kneaded. Yeast doughs contain

1. Place the 1½ cups of water in a small saucepan, and bring the water to a boil. Stir in the cracked wheat, reduce the heat, and simmer the cracked wheat until it is soft. Transfer the cracked wheat to a large plate, spreading it over the plate. Allow the wheat to cool to room temperature.

2. Place the 1 cup of warm water in a large bowl. Add the honey, stirring it well. Add the yeast, and stir the ingredients gently until the yeast has dissolved. Allow the yeast to proof at room temperature for 10 minutes.

3. Add the warm buttermilk, and stir the mixture well. Add the whole-wheat bread flour and 3 cups of the all-purpose flour. Stir the dough with a wooden spoon for 5 minutes. The dough will be sticky and wet.

4. Add the cooled cracked wheat, toasted wheat germ, 1 more cup of the all-purpose flour, and the salt. Stir for 2 minutes. Add the dates and cashews, and stir the ingredients until they are well incorporated. Add enough of the remaining all-purpose flour to form a soft dough.

5. Turn the dough out onto a lightly floured work surface. Knead the dough for approximately 10 minutes, adding only enough flour to the work surface to prevent the dough from sticking. The dough will be smooth and elastic. Form the dough into a ball.

6. Place the oil on the bottom of a large, clean nonmetal bowl. Place the dough in the oil, and turn the dough to coat it all over with the oil. Cover the bowl tightly with plastic wrap, and allow the dough to rise in a warm, draft-free place until it has doubled in bulk, approximately 2 hours.

7. The dough will now be soft and elastic. Pull the sides of the dough toward the center, and deflate the dough by pressing it in the middle to allow the air to escape. Turn the dough onto a very lightly

floured work surface, and allow the dough to rest for 5 minutes. Shape the dough into a 10-inch round loaf that is 1 inch high. Sprinkle the corn meal on a heavy baking sheet. Place the dough on the sheet, and cover the dough with a dry towel. Return the dough to a warm, draft-free spot to rise until it has doubled in size, approximately 1 hour.

8. Heat the oven to 400°F.

9. With a sharp knife, slash 3 evenly spaced lines approximately ½ inch deep on the top of the loaf. Dust the loaf with the flour.

10. Spray the bottom of the oven with water. Close the oven door, and wait 1 minute. Spray the oven floor again, and place the bread on the middle rack. Spray the oven at 10-minute intervals for 30 minutes. Bake the bread approximately 10 minutes longer without spraying or until the crust is crisp and the bread sounds hollow when tapped.

11. Carefully remove the hot loaf from the oven, and place it on a rack to cool.

different flours with different characteristics, each of which requires different kneading times. For example, a classic French bread made only with water, yeast, flour, and salt will require only 10 minutes of kneading. On the other hand, a bread made with buckwheat and whole-wheat flours is heavier and denser, and will require several minutes more of work. Properly kneaded dough is smooth and elastic.

Good-for-You French Toast

*Although traditional French toast is loaded with carbohydrates, it also contains a considerable amount of fat from egg yolks and whole milk in the batter, not to mention the butter in which it is fried. I have been preparing a lower-fat version for years. This recipe uses eggs and egg whites, and skim milk in place of whole, to keep the fat and cholesterol down. This version is still a significant source of calories if you are trying to gain weight. The toasted pecans add great flavor and a nutty texture, and are a healthful, calorie-dense addition. **Tips:** To quicken the cooking process, use two skillets. To adapt the recipe to a reduced-fat and -calorie version, substitute 3 egg whites for the whole eggs.*

PREPARATION: 10 minutes
COOKING: 10 minutes
YIELD: 2 to 3 servings

⅓ cup pecans

4 tablespoons skim milk

2 eggs

4 egg whites

1 teaspoon vanilla

2 tablespoons maple syrup *or* honey

1 teaspoon cinnamon

6 slices whole-wheat bread from a bakery-style loaf, sliced 1-inch thick

1 teaspoon unsalted butter

Maple syrup, warmed

1. Place the pecans in a small skillet over low heat. Toast the pecans, tossing them often, until they are fragrant. Transfer them to the work bowl of a food processor or blender, and puree them until they have turned into a paste. Add the milk, and puree the ingredients until they are smooth. Set the mixture aside.

2. Place the eggs and egg whites in a large bowl, and whisk them very well. Add the vanilla, maple syrup or honey, and cinnamon, and whisk the ingredients well. Add the nut-milk mixture, and combine the ingredients well. Transfer the batter to a large, shallow bowl.

3. Place 2 slices of the bread in the batter. Pierce the bread lightly with a fork 3 or 4 times, and allow the slices to sit in the batter for 1 minute. Turn the bread over, and let the slices sit in the batter 1 minute longer.

4. Heat a skillet or griddle over medium heat. Add the butter to the pan, swirling the butter to coat the pan. Add the 2 slices of bread. Cook the bread until one side is golden, flip the bread over, and cook the bread on the other side until the slices are golden.

5. While the first 2 slices of bread are cooking, dip 2 more slices in the batter. Repeat steps 3 and 4 until all of the bread is cooked. Accompany the French toast with the warm maple syrup.

Three-Potato Home Fries with Corn, Scallions, and Cheese

This hearty dish may be eaten for breakfast or lunch and is a rich source of carbohydrates, calcium, folic acid, and fiber. The versatile, nutritious potato often plays a supporting role in a meal. In this recipe, however, it is worthy of star status. Three varieties of potato, sharp and mild cheeses, red bell pepper, garlic, scallions and tomatoes make this dish as pleasing to the eye as it is to the palate. **Tips:** To prepare this dish properly, it is important to use a heavy, nonstick skillet and to keep the heat high. This will allow you to use a minimum amount of oil to brown the potatoes and prevent them from sticking.

PREPARATION: 15 minutes
COOKING: 35 minutes
YIELD: 4 main-course servings

1 large sweet potato, scrubbed
4 medium red potatoes, scrubbed
4 medium Yellow Finn *or* Yukon Gold potatoes, scrubbed
3 tablespoons olive oil
1 medium red onion, peeled and thinly sliced
4 scallions, trimmed, thinly sliced, with white and green parts separated
4 cloves garlic, peeled and finely chopped
1 medium red bell pepper, cored, seeded, and thinly sliced
2 ears fresh corn, kernels removed, *or* 1½ cups frozen corn kernels, thawed
Salt to taste
Pepper to taste
1 large tomato, diced
⅓ cup grated, packed Cheddar
⅓ cup grated, packed Monterey jack

1. Heat the oven to 375°F.
2. Place the sweet potato, red potatoes, and Yellow Finn or Yukon Gold potatoes in a pot, cover them with cold water, and bring the water to a boil. Cook the potatoes until they are just tender, ap-

proximately 15 minutes. They should be a bit resistant when poked with a fork. Drain them, and rinse them under cold water until they are cool. Cut the potatoes into ⅓-inch cubes, and set them aside.

3. Heat the olive oil in a large, nonstick skillet over high heat. When the oil is hot, add the potatoes. Sauté them, tossing them often, until they begin to take on color. Add the onion and the white part of the scallions, and sauté the ingredients, tossing them often, 2 minutes longer. Add the garlic, and sauté it, stirring it constantly, for 1 minute.

4. Add the red bell pepper and corn, and sauté the ingredients, tossing them often, until the potatoes are well browned. Add the green part of the scallions, and season the home fries with the salt and pepper.

5. Transfer the mixture to a casserole or cast-iron pan (the latter will add extra iron to the meal). Sprinkle the home fries with the tomato, Cheddar, and Monterey jack. Bake the home fries until the cheese melts, approximately 10 minutes.

Orecchiette with Squash, Broccoli Rabe, and Goat Cheese

PREPARATION: 45 minutes
COOKING: 10 minutes
YIELD: 4 main-course serving

This dish provides excellent amounts of folic acid and calcium. It is one of our favorites. Broccoli and broccoli rabe are vastly different vegetables—both in appearance and taste. Broccoli rabe figures prominently in Italian cooking. It has an intense, slightly pungent flavor, thin, spinach-sized stems, and dark-green leaves with greenish-yellow buds. It is best to only rinse rabe since soaking it tends to make it bitter. **Tips:** *The majority of the preparation time is devoted to the roasting of the squash. To save time, roast the squash a day in advance. The following day, heat it in the oven while the pasta is cooking.*

1 large butternut squash, peeled, seeded, and cut into ¾-inch
   cubes
2 tablespoons plus 1 tablespoon olive oil
2 tablespoons brown sugar
   Salt to taste
   Pepper to taste
4 cloves garlic, peeled and lightly crushed but still whole
1 pound orecchiette ("little ears" pasta)
1 to 1½ pounds broccoli rabe, trimmed, coarsely chopped, and
   rinsed under cold running water
½ cup pasta cooking water
6 ounces goat cheese

1. Heat the oven to 400°F.
2. Place the squash in a large bowl. Drizzle it with the 2 tablespoon of olive oil, and sprinkle it with the brown sugar, salt, and pepper. Place the squash on a large baking tray. Roast the squash until it is soft and golden, approximately 45 minutes. Set it aside.
3. Bring a large pot of lightly salted water to a boil.
4. Once the water reaches a boil, heat the remaining 1 tablespoon of olive oil in a Dutch oven over medium heat. Add the garlic, and sauté it, turning it often, until it is golden. Remove the garlic, and set it aside for a "cook's treat."
5. Add the pasta to the water.
6. Raise the heat under the garlic oil to high. Add the broccoli rabe. The water clinging to the broccoli rabe should be sufficient to steam it while it cooks in the oil. If necessary, add more water to prevent the vegetable from burning. Sprinkle the broccoli rabe with salt, and cover the pot. Steam the vegetable, stirring it often, until it is tender, approximately 5 minutes. Add the pasta cooking water.
7. Drain the pasta, and add it to the broccoli rabe. Reduce the heat to low. Gently cook the mixture, stirring it often, for 2 to 3 minutes. Season the mixture to taste with salt and pepper.
8. Spoon the pasta into 4 bowls. Distribute the roasted squash evenly among the bowls. Garnish each serving with the goat cheese.

Stuffed Roasted Bell Peppers

This dish contains vitamin C, complex carbohydrates, protein, potassium, fiber, pyridoxine (vitamin B_6), and folic acid. And the avocados are high in fat. **Tips:** Except for adding the avocado and cheese, the recipe can be prepared 1 day in advance. Twenty minutes before serving the dish, stir in the avocado, and dot the peppers with the cheese. To adapt the recipe to a lower-fat, lower-calorie version, eliminate the avocado, and decrease the cheese to 3 ounces. If you are using canned beans, skip step 1.

PREPARATION: 90 minutes
(including bean cooking)
BAKING: 10 minutes
YIELD: 4 main-course servings

½ cup dried Great Northern beans, picked over, rinsed, and soaked overnight, *or* 1½ cups canned white beans, drained and rinsed

⅓ cup pine nuts

6 medium red bell peppers, halved and roasted (see page 161)

2½ cups water

Salt to taste

1¼ cups couscous

2 tablespoons olive oil

2 cloves garlic, peeled and finely chopped

2 medium tomatoes, diced

3 ears fresh corn, kernels removed, *or* 2 cups frozen corn kernels, thawed

½ cup cilantro, finely chopped

Juice 1 lemon

Juice 2 limes

Pepper to taste

1 large avocado, peeled, pitted, and cubed

6 ounces goat cheese

1. Place the dried beans in a pot, cover them with water, and bring the water to a boil. Reduce the heat, and simmer the beans until they are tender, approximately 45 minutes. Drain the beans, cool them, and set them aside.

ROASTED BELL PEPPERS

6 bell peppers
3 to 4 tablespoons extra-virgin olive oil
  Black pepper

1. Heat the broiler.
2. Cut the peppers in half lengthwise, and remove the stems, seeds, and ribs.
3. Place the peppers on a rack or broiling pan skin side up approximately 3 inches from the heat. Broil the peppers until the skin is completely charred, approximately 6 minutes.
4. Remove the peppers from the broiler, and place them in a plastic bag. Seal the bag with a tie or twist it tightly closed, and steam the peppers for approximately 10 minutes. Remove the peppers from the bag, and peel the skin off, making sure that all the black is removed. (It is sometimes easier to remove the skin under cool running water.)
5. Place the peppers in a jar, cover them with the olive oil, and grind some black pepper over them. Cover the jar tightly, and refrigerate the peppers—they will keep for approximately 1 week.

Notes: (1) If you desire, add chopped garlic and fresh rosemary to the peppers before you seal the jar. After marinating for several days in the seasonings, the peppers will be bursting with flavor. (2) An alternative method of roasting bell peppers is to roast them whole over a gas burner on top of the stove. If you use this method, it is necessary to turn them often.

2. While the beans are cooking, place the pine nuts in a small skillet over very low heat. Toast them, tossing them often, until they are golden. Remove them from the pan, and set them aside.
3. Bring the water to a boil in a small saucepan, add a dash of salt and the couscous, and stir the couscous well. Return the water to a boil, remove the pot from the heat, and cover the pot tightly.
4. Heat the oven to 375°F.
5. While the couscous is steaming, heat the olive oil in a large skillet over medium heat. Add the garlic, and sauté it until it is fragrant. Add the tomatoes, and sauté them, stirring them often, for 1 minute.

Add the corn, and sauté the ingredients, stirring them often, for 2 minutes. Add the cilantro. Transfer the mixture to a large bowl.

6. Add the lemon juice and lime juice. Stir in the reserved pine nuts and the cooked beans.

7. Fluff the couscous with a fork. Add it to the vegetable mixture. Season the mixture with the salt and pepper, and stir in the avocado.

8. Generously stuff each pepper half. Dot the top of each half with goat cheese. Bake the peppers until the filling is hot and the cheese is melted, approximately 10 minutes.

Mustard-Tarragon Chicken

PREPARATION: 5 minutes
COOKING: 10 minutes
YIELD: 4 main-course servings

This delicious chicken dish is a rich source of iron. It is more calorie-dense than most chicken dishes because of the cream. Serve it with pasta or potatoes to complement the meal. **Tip:** *When preparing this dish, it is critical to add the mustard during the last minute of cooking. If you simmer the sauce for much longer than a minute with the mustard added, there is a chance that the sauce will curdle. I use 1 heaping tablespoon of mustard, but you can adjust the amount to taste.*

1 tablespoon plus 1 tablespoon olive oil
2 large whole boneless, skinless chicken breasts, trimmed of all visible fat, cut in half, flattened to ¼-inch thickness, and thoroughly dried
Salt to taste
Pepper to taste
3 medium shallots, peeled and finely chopped
¾ teaspoon dried tarragon
½ cup white wine
1 ½ cups whipping cream
1 tablespoon Dijon mustard

1. Heat 1 tablespoon of the olive oil in a large sauté pan over medium-high heat.
2. Sprinkle the chicken with the salt and pepper. Carefully place the chicken in the hot oil, and sear the chicken for 2 to 3 minutes on each side, turning the chicken once, until it is golden. Remove the chicken, and keep it warm.
3. Reduce the heat slightly, and add the remaining 1 tablespoon of olive oil. Add the shallots and tarragon, and sauté the ingredients, stirring them constantly, until the shallots are soft, approximately 45 seconds.
4. Raise the heat to high, and add the wine. Reduce the liquid for 2 minutes.
5. Add the cream, and reduce it, stirring the mixture often, until the sauce thickens, approximately 5 minutes.
6. Reduce the heat, and return the chicken to the pan. Simmer the chicken until it is cooked through, approximately 2 minutes. Remove the chicken, and place it on a serving platter.
7. Spoon the mustard into the sauce, and stir it until it is well incorporated. Adjust the seasonings, and spoon the sauce over the chicken.

SUPPLEMENT B
LOW-CALORIE RECIPES

White Bean, Escarole, and Tomato Soup

PREPARATION: 15 minutes

COOKING: 1½ hours

YIELD: 4 to 6 first or main-course servings

*The leafy greens in this soup provide an excellent source of folic acid, and the beans are rich in fiber. You may accompany the soup with a slice of crusty bread or a salad to complete the meal. If you add the pasta, you have a well rounded dish by itself, one that is very low in calories and fat yet is quite satisfying. **Tips:** The dried beans can be cooked a day in advance. If you use canned beans, eliminate 3 cups of the water and the bean cooking water. When available, ½ cup of fresh herbs such as basil or parsley can be added during the last 2 minutes of cooking to provide a burst of flavor. Swiss chard is a good substitute for the escarole. If you use Swiss chard, separate the stems from the leaves. Add the stems during the sauté stage of cooking and the leaves during the last 7 minutes.*

**TO PREPARE
DRIED BEANS**

There are four important steps that need to be followed in the preparation of a successful bean dish.

1. Since beans come directly from the field and are not

1 cup dried white beans, picked over, rinsed, and soaked
     overnight, *or* 2 cups canned white beans, drained and rinsed

4 cups plus 5 cups water

1 tablespoon olive oil

1 medium Spanish onion, peeled and diced

3 cloves garlic, peeled and finely chopped

2 medium carrots, scrubbed and diced

2 ribs celery, diced

1 teaspoon fennel seed, lightly crushed

...e to include some of the leaves)

...es

...ly chopped, washed, and drained (optional)

...oven, cover them with the 4 cups ...boil. Reduce the heat, and simmer ...approximately 45 minutes. Drain ...ooking water.

...the olive oil in a Dutch oven over low heat. Add the onion, and sauté it until it is soft. Add the garlic, and sauté it until it is fragrant. Add the carrots, celery, fennel seed, diced fennel, and a pinch of salt. Cover the pot, and steam-sauté the ingredients over medium-low heat, stirring them often, for 6 minutes.

3. Add the tomatoes, the reserved bean water, the reserved beans, and the remaining 5 cups of water. Bring the soup to a boil, reduce the heat, and simmer the soup until the vegetables are tender, approximately 15 minutes.

4. Add the escarole, and simmer the soup 5 minutes longer. Add the fresh herbs, if desired. Season with the salt and pepper.

processed, it is critical to sort through them and remove any dirt or pebbles.

2. You should thoroughly rinse your beans in a colander or swirl them in two or three changes of water to remove any dust.

3. I recommend soaking beans for approximately 8 hours before cooking them. It will reduce their cooking time by 20 to 30 minutes. It is not necessary to soak split peas or lentils.

4. Beans should be simmered in 3 to 4 times their bulk in water (3 to 4 cups of water per 1 cup of beans).

In addition, a pinch of salt added to the beans after they have been cooked will bring out their full flavor.

Chilled Sesame Noodles with Vegetables

Light and flavorful cold sesame noodles can be a side dish or a low-fat lunch or dinner. Broccoli, red bell pepper, and sugar snap peas provide an abundance of flavor, texture, and nutrition. Broccoli is an excellent low-fat source of calcium. **Tip:** *The flavor of this dish is improved after a day of chilling.*

PREPARATION: 15 minutes
COOKING: 10 minutes
YIELD: 4 main-course servings

6 scallions, trimmed and thinly sliced

1 pound thin spaghetti *or* linguine

1 large bunch broccoli, separated into florets and stems, stems peeled and sliced into disks

½ pound sugar snap peas, strings removed

1 tablespoon peanut oil

2 cloves garlic, peeled and finely chopped

2-inch piece gingerroot, peeled and finely chopped

1 red bell pepper, cored, seeded, and diced

3 tablespoons tamari *or* low-sodium soy sauce

2 tablespoons rice vinegar

1 tablespoon sugar

1 tablespoon sesame oil

Pepper to taste

1. Place the scallions in a large bowl.
2. Bring a large pot of lightly salted water to a boil, and add the pasta. Three minutes before it is done, add the broccoli to the same water. Two minutes later add the sugar snap peas.
3. When the pasta is tender, drain it and the vegetables well, and thoroughly cool the ingredients under cold running water. (Be certain the vegetables are cool, or they will continue to cook.) Add the pasta and vegetables to the scallions, and toss the ingredients well.
4. Heat the peanut oil in a medium-sized skillet over medium-low heat. Add the garlic and ginger. Sauté the ingredients, stirring them often, until they are soft and fragrant. Add the red bell pepper, and sauté it until it begins to soften.
5. Add the tamari or soy sauce, rice vinegar, and sugar. Cook the sauce for 2 minutes. Remove the pan from the heat, and allow the sauce to cool.
6. When the sauce is cool, pour it over the noodles. Add the sesame oil, and season the dish with the pepper.

Orvieto Chicken

Orvieto, a small hilltop town in the lush Italian countryside, is known for its wonderful white wines. While Hope was pregnant with Joey, we visited Orvieto and enjoyed this unbelievably simple chicken dish there. The chicken is skinless, yet the searing gives it a marvelous crisp crust. If you accompany it with "Oven-Fried" Potatoes (page 123), you will not believe that you could eat this well for so little in terms of calories and fat. **Tip:** *Searing the chicken properly is the key to this dish. If the chicken is thoroughly dried and the oil hot enough, the flesh will crisp nicely and still maintain its moistness.*

PREPARATION: 5 minutes
COOKING: 25 minutes
YIELD: 4 to 6 main-course
   servings

1 tablespoon olive oil
8 chicken thighs, skin removed and discarded, washed, and
    thoroughly dried
Salt to taste
Pepper to taste

1. Heat the oven to 400°F.
2. Heat the olive oil in a heavy Dutch oven or large cast-iron skillet over high heat. Sprinkle the chicken liberally with the salt and pepper.
3. When the oil begins to smoke, carefully place the chicken in the pan bone side up (watch for splattering oil). Sear the chicken for 3 to 5 minutes on each side or until a crust forms.
4. Transfer the chicken to a tray, and bake it until it is done through, approximately 15 minutes.

Rigatoni with Wild Mushroom Ragù

Ragù in Italian cooking refers to a long-simmered tomato-based sauce. The sauce may contain a variety of meats such as lamb, veal, pork, and beef. Our variation contains no meat, simply wild mushrooms (a good source of folic acid). This substitution keeps the calories and fat low but the end product amazingly

PREPARATION: 15 minutes
COOKING: 1³/₄ hours
YIELD: 4 main-course servings

hearty, flavorful, and thick. **Tips:** *It is important to use dried mushrooms in this dish because of the intense flavor they impart to the sauce. If dried porcini are not available, use dried shiitake. The sauce can be prepared 2 to 3 days in advance and refrigerated. This is not only convenient, but improves its flavor. Accompany this dish with a green salad and crusty bread.*

1 tablespoon olive oil
1 medium Spanish onion, peeled and finely chopped
4 cloves garlic, peeled and finely chopped
1 large carrot, scrubbed and finely chopped
1 rib celery, finely chopped
  Salt to taste
¾ pound portabellas, stems peeled and diced, caps wiped clean
    and sliced
1 ounce dried porcini, soaked in ⅔ cup boiling-hot water for 30
    minutes and drained, soaking liquid reserved
¾ cup Marsala
  Mushroom soaking liquid
1 28-ounce can crushed tomatoes
½ cup fresh basil, snipped
  Pepper to taste
1 pound rigatoni *or* other tubular pasta
  Grated Parmesan

TO SOAK DRIED MUSHROOMS

Dried mushrooms have a tendency to be gritty. Their soaking water contains both dirt and tremendous flavor. Care needs to be taken to prevent the grit from being passed on to the food by means of the soaking water. To do this, first strain the soaking water through a double layer of paper towels. Second, when adding the soaking water to the sauce, pour it slowly so that any grit not caught by the paper towels will remain at the bottom of the bowl.

1. Heat the olive oil in a Dutch oven over medium heat. Add the onion, and sauté it until it is soft.
2. Add the garlic, and sauté it until it is fragrant. Add the carrot, celery, and a pinch of salt. Cover the pot, and steam-sauté the vegetables, stirring them often, until they begin to soften.
3. Add the portabellas, and sauté the mushrooms, stirring them often, until they are soft. Stir in the porcini, and cook them for 1 minute.
4. Add the wine and the reserved mushroom soaking liquid. Simmer the mixture for 3 minutes.
5. Add the tomatoes, and bring the sauce to a boil. Reduce the heat, cover the pot, and simmer the sauce, stirring it often, for 1½ hours. Remove the cover during the last 15 minutes of cooking. Stir in the

basil, and season the sauce with salt and pepper.

6. Bring a large pot of lightly salted water to a boil, and add the pasta. When the pasta is done, drain it, and divide it among 4 bowls. Ladle the sauce over the pasta, and sprinkle each serving with Parmesan.

Farmers' Market Pasta

On a warm afternoon, stop by your local farmers' market and choose the best and freshest ingredients for your evening meal. This recipe, written to take advantage of the wonderful produce available at farmers' markets, is an example of a quick pasta dish using a few seasonal vegetables. It is rich in carbohydrates and extremely low in fat. And folic acid, potassium, and vitamin A are all well represented here. Follow it exactly, or use it as an inspiration for your own creation. **Tips:** *The key ingredients in this dish are the extra-virgin olive oil, balsamic vinegar, and eggplant. The other ingredients can be altered according to availability and taste. Use any ingredients that catch your eye at the market. White eggplant contains fewer seeds and is milder and less bitter than the purple variety, but it can be difficult to locate. Small purple eggplants (also called Italian or Japanese eggplants) may be substituted.*

PREPARATION: 10 minutes
COOKING: 15 minutes
YIELD: 4 main-course servings

  1 pound farfalle
  2 tablespoons extra-virgin olive oil
  4 cloves garlic, peeled and finely chopped
  1 large red bell pepper, cored, seeded, and diced
1¼ pounds white eggplant, cut into ½-inch cubes
  2 tablespoons balsamic vinegar
  ½ cup pasta cooking water
  2 ears fresh corn, kernels removed
  ½ cup fresh basil *or* cilantro, snipped
     Salt to taste
     Pepper to taste
     Grated Romano

1. Bring a large pot of lightly salted water to a boil, and add the pasta.
2. While the pasta is cooking, heat the olive oil in a Dutch oven over medium heat. Add the garlic, and sauté it, stirring it constantly, until it is fragrant. Add the red bell pepper, and sauté it, stirring it often, until it begins to soften.
3. Add the eggplant, and sauté it, stirring it often, until it begins to soften. Add the balsamic vinegar, and simmer the ingredients for 30 seconds. Add the pasta water, fresh corn, and basil or cilantro. Season the vegetables with the salt and pepper.
4. Drain the pasta, and return it to the pot. Add the vegetables, and stir the ingredients over low heat for 2 minutes. Divide the pasta among 4 serving dishes. Sprinkle some Romano over each serving.

Salt Cod, Chickpea, and Potato Soup

This is a great pantry dish. You may already have most of the ingredients on hand. Salt cod can be kept in your refrigerator for 2 weeks and will not deteriorate in quality. The potatoes, chickpeas, and fish make this a filling and rich-tasting soup that is low in calories and fat, and high in fiber. **Tip:** *Many seafood soups have a rich fish broth as a base. This recipe relies on the richness of salt cod. Salt cod is so flavorful and firm that it can be simmered for 15 minutes, maintain its texture, and infuse intense flavor into the soup base.*

PREPARATION: 10 minutes
COOKING: 40 minutes
YIELD: 4 first-course or main-course servings

    1 tablespoon olive oil
    3 cloves garlic, peeled and finely chopped
    1 large Spanish onion, peeled
       and diced
    1 large potato, peeled and
       cut into ⅓-inch cubes
    ½ cup brown rice

10 cups water

1 teaspoon saffron threads

1 cup canned chickpeas, drained and rinsed

1 pound salt cod, thoroughly rinsed and soaked for 16 hours in 4 changes of cold water

1½ cups frozen peas

Salt to taste

Pepper to taste

1. Heat the olive oil in large Dutch oven over medium heat. Add the garlic, and sauté it, stirring it constantly, until it is fragrant. Add the onion, and sauté it, stirring it often, until it is soft. Add the potato, and sauté it for 1 minute.
2. Stir in the rice, raise the heat to high, and add the water. Bring the liquid to a boil, add the saffron, reduce the heat, and simmer the ingredients for 20 minutes.
3. Add the chickpeas and salt cod. Simmer the soup 10 minutes longer. Add the peas, and season the soup with the salt and pepper.

SAFFRON

Saffron, the world's most expensive spice, is the dried stigmas of the saffron crocus. It is hand-picked, and approximately 210,000 stigmas make 1 pound! Besides being the one ingredient you must have in paella, it is also found in fish stews and other seafood dishes as well as risotto.

13 SECOND TRIMESTER

Orange-Apple-Apricot Scones · Irish Soda Bread · Blueberry-Corn Pancakes · Potato and Egg Medley · Cannellini Bean Hummus · Grilled Eggplant Rolls · Hope's Potato Salad · Tomato-Bread Salad · Roasted New Potatoes with Red Bell Peppers, Thyme, and Fennel · Pan-Seared Monkfish with Corn-Avocado Relish · Broiled Swordfish with Mango-Kiwi Salsa · Spaghetti with Turkey Meatballs · Strip Steak with Mushrooms, Garlic, and Gorgonzola · Penne with Swiss Chard and Pine Nuts · Linguine with Monkfish, Pecans, Thyme, and Raspberry Vinegar · Paella with Salt Cod · Salt Cod and Squid Stew · Cashew and Black Bean Chili · Curried Basmati Rice and Chicken · Turkey Sausage with White Beans, Tomatoes, and Sage · Red Lentil and Bulgur Salad with Cashews and Corn · Chickpeas with Kale, Sun-Dried Tomatoes, and Pine Nuts · Potato Gnocchi with Butter and Parmesan · Classic Risotto · Pappardelle with Spinach-Mushroom Sauce · Pork Piccata · Tuscan Pork Chops · Spicy Eggplant-Shrimp Bruschetta · Herb-Crusted Salmon · Farfalle with Spicy Sausage, Squid, Tomatoes, and Onions · Penne with Broccoli Rabe and Spicy Turkey Sausage · Farfalle with Eggplant, Zucchini, Mushrooms, and Tomatoes

Orange-Apple-Apricot Scones

*These whole-grain scones make a wonderful breakfast or snack anytime during pregnancy. The dried fruit is nutrient-dense and particularly rich in fiber, making it an ideal way to prevent constipation, which commonly begins in the second trimester. And the wheat germ is packed with iron, which your body now needs in large amounts. **Tips:** Equal amounts of raisins, dates, or prunes can be substituted for the apples and apricots. Serve the scones plain or with your favorite fruit jam.*

PREPARATION: 15 minutes
COOKING: 12 minutes
YIELD: 6 scones

1 cup unbleached, all-purpose flour
½ cup whole-wheat flour
½ cup toasted wheat germ
1 tablespoon baking powder
½ teaspoon salt
¾ teaspoon cinnamon
3 tablespoons cold unsalted butter, cut into 6 pieces
2 tablespoons honey
2 eggs
1 tablespoon finely chopped orange rind
½ cup skim milk
⅔ cup dried apricots, roughly chopped
⅓ cup dried apple, roughly chopped

1. Heat the oven to 425°F.
2. Lightly grease or spray a heavy-duty baking sheet.
3. In a large bowl, combine well the all-purpose flour, whole-wheat flour, wheat germ, baking powder, salt, and cinnamon.
4. With a pastry cutter or your fingers, cut the butter into the dry ingredients.
5. In a medium-sized bowl, whisk together the honey, eggs, orange rind, and milk.
6. Stir the liquid ingredients into the dry ingredients, mixing them only until the dry ingredients are just moistened. The dough will be

sticky. Fold in the apricots and apples.

7. Turn the dough onto a lightly floured work surface. Flatten the dough with your hands into approximately a ¾-inch-thick rectangle. Cut the rectangle into 6 triangular wedges.

8. Place the scones ½-inch apart on the prepared baking sheet. Bake the scones until they are golden-brown, approximately 12 minutes.

Irish Soda Bread

If you are suffering from heartburn or are one of the few who still have morning sickness, this bread will make a soothing breakfast or snack. Simply toast it, and spread lightly with your favorite jam. This recipe provides fiber from the wheat flour and iron from the wheat germ.

PREPARATION: 15 minutes
BAKING: 30 minutes
YIELD: 1 loaf

  3 tablespoons corn meal
1¼ cups unbleached, all-purpose flour plus additional flour for
     sprinkling
  1 cup whole-wheat flour
  ½ cup rolled oats
  ¼ cup toasted wheat germ plus additional wheat germ for
     sprinkling
  2 tablespoons sugar
  1 teaspoon salt
  1 teaspoon baking soda
  1 teaspoon baking powder
  3 tablespoons unsalted butter, at room temperature
  1 cup raisins
  ¼ cup walnuts, coarsely chopped
1⅓ cups nonfat plain yogurt
  ¼ cup honey
  2 teaspoons grated orange rind

1. Heat the oven to 425°F.
2. Sprinkle a heavy-duty baking tray with corn meal, and set it aside.
3. In a large bowl, combine the all-purpose flour, whole-wheat flour, oats, wheat germ, sugar, salt, baking soda, and baking powder.
4. With a pastry cutter or your fingers, cut the butter into the flour mixture. Stir in the raisins and walnuts.
5. In a medium bowl, combine the yogurt, honey, and orange rind, and mix the ingredients well.
6. Stir the wet ingredients into the flour mixture until the dry ingredients are just moistened.
7. Lightly flour a work surface. Turn the sticky dough onto the work surface, and knead the dough for 1 to 2 minutes.
8. Shape the dough into a ball, and place it on the prepared baking tray. With a sharp knife, cut a cross into the top of the dough approximately ½ inch deep. Sprinkle the top of the loaf with the additional flour and wheat germ.
9. Bake the bread for 30 minutes. Allow it to cool completely before cutting it.

Blueberry-Corn Pancakes

These pancakes have a slightly coarse texture from the corn meal, making them interesting and filling. They are a great cure for heartburn by virtue of their ability to absorb stomach acid. We often prepare them for a Sunday evening dinner. **Tip:** *To reduce the cooking time, use two skillets.*

PREPARATION: 10 minutes
COOKING: 12 minutes
YIELD: 8 large pancakes

1⅓ cups unbleached, all-purpose flour
½ cup yellow corn meal
¼ teaspoon salt
2 teaspoons baking powder
1 teaspoon baking soda
2 eggs

1 tablespoon unsalted butter, melted, plus 1 teaspoon unsalted
butter for greasing skillet
2 tablespoons honey
1 teaspoon vanilla
1 cup skim milk
2 cups fresh blueberries *or* frozen blueberries, thawed
Maple syrup, warmed

1. In a large bowl, combine well the all-purpose flour, corn meal, salt, baking powder, and baking soda.
2. In another bowl, beat the eggs very well. Add the melted butter, honey, vanilla, and skim milk, and mix the ingredients well.
3. Add the dry ingredients to the wet ones, stirring them until the dry ingredients are just moistened.
4. Preheat a griddle or skillet over medium heat. When it is hot, add ½ teaspoon of butter, and quickly spread it over the surface of the pan.
5. Add ½ cup of the batter to the pan. Sprinkle the pancake with some of the blueberries, and cook the pancake until bubbles appear. Flip the pancake over, and cook it on the other side.
6. Repeat this procedure until all of the batter and blueberries are used up. Add more butter to the pan as needed.
7. Top each serving with additional blueberries, and accompany the pancakes with the warm syrup.

Potato and Egg Medley

Cooking potatoes and eggs together in a flat (not rolled) omelet is a Spanish technique. The famous Valencian dish Spanish Tortilla (see page 225) consists of cubed potatoes, onions, garlic, olive oil, and eggs. In this adaptation, the eggs are scrambled with scallions, tomatoes, and goat cheese. It is a soothing carbohydrate- and protein-rich dish that can be prepared quickly for breakfast or any time, making it a good choice for busy pregnant women. Accompany these eggs with toasted bagels that have been drizzled with olive oil.

PREPARATION: 10 minutes
COOKING: 20 minutes
YIELD: 2 breakfast or main-
course servings

1 tablespoon plus 1 teaspoon extra-virgin olive oil

2 medium Yellow Finn *or* Yukon Gold potatoes, cut into ⅛-inch cubes

2 eggs

4 egg whites

1 tablespoon skim milk

4 scallions, trimmed, white and green parts separated, and thinly sliced

1 medium tomato, diced

3 ounces goat cheese

Salt to taste

Pepper to taste

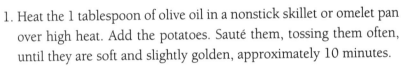

1. Heat the 1 tablespoon of olive oil in a nonstick skillet or omelet pan over high heat. Add the potatoes. Sauté them, tossing them often, until they are soft and slightly golden, approximately 10 minutes.

2. While the potatoes are cooking, beat the eggs and egg whites very well, and stir in the milk. Set the mixture aside.

3. When the potatoes are cooked, add the white part of the scallions to them, and toss the ingredients. Sauté the potatoes for 2 minutes. Add the green part of the scallions and the tomato, and toss the ingredients. Sauté the ingredients for 1 minute. Remove the mixture from the pan, and set the mixture aside.

4. Heat the remaining teaspoon of olive oil in the skillet over medium heat. When it is hot, add the egg mixture. Allow the eggs to set for 45 seconds. Add the potato mixture, and stir the ingredients. Allow the eggs to cook 30 seconds longer. Stir the eggs again, and allow them to set for 15 seconds.

5. Remove the eggs from the heat, and stir in the goat cheese. Season the eggs with the salt and pepper.

Cannellini Bean Hummus

This is an offbeat version of a traditional hummus, the lemon-garlic-tahini-chickpea spread. Using cannellini beans, scallions, and tomatoes, the flavor is similar to the more common version but creamier and less nutty. It will appeal to your renewed second-trimester palate. It makes a wonderful sandwich spread and can be tossed with pasta. We like to accompany it with crusty bread and the Roasted and Chilled Sweet-Potato Salad (page 230) for a cool, high-fiber dinner. Cannellini beans are surprisingly high in calcium. **Tips:** For a different flavor, eye-catching pink color, and larger doses of folic acid and fiber, substitute red kidney beans for the cannellini beans. If canned beans are used, skip step 1.

PREPARATION: 10 minutes
COOKING: 45 minutes
YIELD: about 3 cups

1½ cups dried cannellini beans, picked over, rinsed, and soaked
    overnight, *or* 3 cups canned beans, drained and rinsed
3 cloves garlic, peeled and minced
Juice 2 lemons
3 tablespoons tahini
1 teaspoon extra-virgin olive oil
½ to ¾ cup water
Salt to taste
Pepper to taste
5 scallions, trimmed and thinly sliced
2 medium tomatoes, diced

1. Place the dried beans in a pot, cover them with water, and bring the water to a boil. Reduce the heat, and simmer the beans until they are tender, approximately 45 minutes. Drain and cool the beans.
2. Place the cooled beans in the bowl of a food processor or blender. Add the garlic, lemon juice, tahini, olive oil, and ½ cup of water. Blend the ingredients until they are smooth. Add additional water, if necessary, to attain the desired consistency. Season the spread with the salt and pepper.
3. Stir in the scallions and tomatoes.
4. Refrigerate the hummus for 3 hours.

Grilled Eggplant Rolls

These unique treats provide a calcium boost from the relatively low-fat, delicious goat cheese. One of our favorites! **Tips:** *The eggplant slices can be prepared a day in advance and refrigerated. The flavor and texture of these rolls are best at room temperature. Remove them approximately 1 hour before they are to be served.*

PREPARATION: 35 minutes
COOKING: 10 minutes
YIELD: 4 appetizer servings

⅓ cup sun-dried tomatoes
2 medium purple eggplants, ends trimmed and each cut lengthwise into 5¼-inch-thick pieces
2 tablespoons plus 1 teaspoon extra-virgin olive oil
4 ounces goat cheese
1 cup fresh basil, finely chopped
1 clove garlic, peeled and minced
    Salt to taste
    Pepper to taste

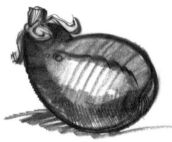

1. Light a charcoal fire, or heat the broiler or a skillet-grill.
2. Place the sun-dried tomatoes in a bowl, cover them with boiling water, and allow them to macerate for 20 minutes.
3. Brush the eggplant slices on each side with the 2 tablespoons of the olive oil. Grill the eggplant slices on each side, turning them once, until they are soft, approximately 5 to 10 minutes. Set the eggplant aside while you prepare the filling.
4. Combine the goat cheese, basil, sun-dried tomatoes, garlic, and remaining teaspoon of olive oil in a bowl, mixing the ingredients well. Season the filling with the salt and pepper.
5. Divide the filling into 10 equal portions. Place a portion of filling on top of each eggplant slice, and roll the eggplant around the filling.

Hope's Potato Salad

Hope craved potato salad during the second trimester. But a traditional potato salad is often laden with mayonnaise, which is loaded with fat. Although nonfat mayonnaise is now available, it tastes artificial. Hope suggested this fine-tasting, nutritious alternative. In this recipe, pureed white beans replace the mayonnaise. There is more texture in this potato salad, as compared to one prepared with mayonnaise, the flavor is unique, and the salad low in fat. **Tip:** *If canned beans are used, skip step 1.*

PREPARATION: 15 minutes
COOKING: 55 minutes
CHILLING: 3 hours
YIELD: 4 to 6 side-dish
   servings

¾ cup dried white beans, picked over, rinsed, and soaked for 8
      hours, *or* 1½ cups canned white beans, drained and rinsed
2½ pounds medium red potatoes, scrubbed and cut into ½-inch
      cubes
1 large tomato, diced
1 medium cucumber, peeled, seeded, and diced
1 small red onion, peeled and finely chopped
2 ribs celery, diced
2 hard-boiled eggs, roughly chopped (remove the yolks, if
      desired)
2 tablespoons nonfat plain yogurt
1 tablespoon sugar
1 tablespoon extra-virgin olive oil
1 tablespoon red-wine vinegar
⅓ to ½ cup water
   Salt to taste
   Pepper to taste

1. Place the dried beans in a pot, cover them with water, bring the water to a boil, and reduce the heat. Simmer the beans until they are tender, approximately 45 minutes. Drain the beans, and cool them.
2. While the beans are simmering, place the potatoes in a pot, cover them with cold water, bring the water to a boil, and cook the potatoes until they are tender, approximately 20 minutes. Do not over-

cook the potatoes, or they will fall apart in the salad. Drain them, cool them under running water, and transfer them to a large bowl.

3. Add the tomato, cucumber, onion, celery, and eggs.

4. Transfer the cooked beans to the work bowl of a food processor. Add the yogurt, sugar, olive oil, and vinegar. Turn on the processor, and, with the motor running, add ⅓ cup of water. Puree the mixture until it is smooth, adding additional water, if necessary, to attain the desired consistency.

5. Pour the bean mixture over the potato mixture, and mix the ingredients well. Season the salad with the salt and pepper. Cover the bowl tightly, and chill the salad for 3 hours.

Tomato-Bread Salad

PREPARATION: 10 minutes
CHILLING: 2 hours
YIELD: 4 side-dish servings

This is one of our favorite dishes. We started eating it during the second trimester because because Hope had iron-deficiency anemia. It is rich in vitamin C, and Hope would take her iron supplement with it or we would serve it with a high-iron main course to boost the absorption of the iron. We became addicted to it and ate it whenever good tomatoes were available. By no means is tomato-bread salad a new idea—it is an old Tuscan specialty. In keeping with the Tuscan tradition, the ingredients list is small and the quality of the dish high because only the best ingredients are used. Vine-ripened tomatoes, Parmesan (one of the most calcium-rich of cheeses), extra-virgin olive oil, and chewy bread will make a memorable salad that is quick and easy to prepare.

3 to 4 large tomatoes, diced (approximately 4 cups)
4 cups crusty day-old bread, cubed
2 tablespoons extra-virgin olive oil
½ cup grated Parmesan
½ cup fresh basil, snipped

Salt to taste

Pepper to taste

Combine the tomatoes, bread cubes, olive oil, Parmesan, and basil in a large, nonmetal bowl, and toss the ingredients well. Season the salad with the salt and pepper. Cover the bowl tightly, and chill the salad for 2 hours.

Roasted New Potatoes with Red Bell Peppers, Thyme, and Fennel

This dish provides a delicious alternative to traditional roasted potatoes. The thyme and fennel add a unique flavor that many pregnant women find particularly appealing in the second trimester. Use the potatoes as a side dish, or make them in advance and reheat them for lunch. They are rich in complex carbohydrates and are an ideal food to support a growing baby. **Tips:** *The bell peppers can be roasted 3 days in advance and refrigerated. Some supermarkets and Italian grocery stores stock roasted peppers; these are an excellent choice if you don't roast your own.*

PREPARATION: 20 minutes
COOKING: 35 minutes
YIELD: 4 side-dish servings

2 tablespoons olive oil

1 medium fennel bulb, diced

4 cloves garlic, peeled and finely chopped

8 medium red potatoes, scrubbed and dried

4 large tomatoes, peeled, seeded, and chopped

2 medium red bell peppers, roasted (see page 000) and thinly sliced

3 tablespoons fresh thyme

Salt to taste

Pepper to taste

1. Heat the oven to 400°F.
2. Heat the olive oil in a large sauté pan over medium heat. Toss in the fennel, and sauté it, stirring it often, until it begins to soften. Add the garlic, and sauté it, stirring it constantly, until it is fragrant.
3. Add the potatoes, tomatoes, and roasted peppers, stirring the ingredients. Sauté the vegetables for 1 minute, and add the thyme. Season the vegetables with the salt and pepper.
4. Transfer the mixture to a large roasting pan. Bake the potatoes until they are tender, approximately 25 minutes.

Pan-Seared Monkfish with Corn-Avocado Relish

PREPARATION: 15 minutes
CHILLING: 2 hours
COOKING: 15 minutes
YIELD: 4 main-course servings

The distinct, delicious flavor of avocado will satisfy many cravings during pregnancy. Although a high-fat fruit, it has many important nutrients, including folic acid. Enjoy the distinct blend of this dish's tastes and textures now and throughout your pregnancy. **Tips:** *The corn-avocado relish can be prepared without the avocado 1 day in advance and refrigerated. Stir in the avocado just before serving time. Be certain that the membrane surrounding the monkfish fillet is removed before the fish is cooked.*

3 ears fresh corn, kernels removed
1 large tomato, diced
1 clove garlic, peeled and minced
1 small red onion, peeled and finely chopped
1 small red bell pepper, cored, seeded, and diced
2 scallions, trimmed and thinly sliced
½ cup cilantro, finely chopped
1 tablespoon plus 2 tablespons olive oil
  Juice 1 lemon
  Salt to taste

Pepper to taste

1 large avocado, diced

1½ to 2 pounds monkfish fillets, membrane removed, cut into 3-inch pieces

1. To prepare the relish, in a large bowl combine the corn, tomato, garlic, onion, bell pepper, scallions, cilantro, 1 tablespoon of the olive oil, and lemon juice. Mix the relish well. Season it with the salt and pepper. Cover the bowl and refrigerate the relish for 2 hours. Stir in the avocado.
2. Heat the oven to 450°F.
3. Heat the remaining 2 tablespoons of olive oil in a large skillet over medium-high heat. Pat the monkfish dry, and sprinkle it with salt and pepper. Place 3 or 4 pieces in the hot oil, and sear the fish on each side, turning the pieces once, until a golden crust forms. Remove the fish, and place the pieces in a shallow roasting pan. Repeat the procedure with the remaining fish. If necessary, add a bit more oil to the skillet to prevent the fish from sticking.
4. Place the fish in the hot oven, and roast the fish until it is just done.
5. To serve, place a portion of the relish on a plate, and put 2 or 3 pieces of the fish on top.

MONKFISH

Monkfish—also known as goosefish, bellyfish, lotte, anglerfish, and "poor man's lobster"—has been a favorite of Mediterranean cooks for generations but has long been considered a trash fish in America. This is now changing—we are falling in love with its sweet flavor. The monkfish is a markedly homely creature with a huge head, bulging eyes, and loose black skin. Only its tail is edible, the tail's flesh being firm, white, and mild, its meaty texture making it a good choice for fish soups, paella, and sautéed dishes.

Broiled Swordfish with Mango-Kiwi Salsa

This fresh-tasting salsa is addictive and will satisfy the common craving for fruit that many women have in the second trimester. We have used it on fish in this recipe, but it is versatile and can also accompany poultry or vegetables. Mangoes and kiwis are both high in calcium. **Tips:** *Salmon, monkfish, halibut, or any mild white-fleshed fish can be substituted for the swordfish. If a soft-fleshed fish (for example, haddock) is used, it is best to bake or broil it. An Anjou or Bosc pear can be used in place of the Asian pear.*

PREPARATION: 10 minutes
CHILLING: 2 hours
COOKING: 10 minutes
YIELD: 4 main-course servings

SALSA

    1 ripe mango, peeled and cut into ⅓-inch cubes

    1 Asian pear, cut into ¼-inch cubes

    1 small red pepper, cored, seeded, and cut into ¼-inch cubes

    1 small red onion, peeled and thinly sliced

    2 kiwis, peeled and thinly sliced

    Juice 2 lemons

    ½ cup cilantro, chopped

    2 to 3 tablespoons plum sauce (available at Asian markets and at some supermarkets)

FISH

    4 ¾-inch-thick swordfish steaks (approximately 1½ pounds)

    Olive oil for rubbing on the swordfish

1. Combine all of the salsa ingredients in a nonmetal bowl, mixing them well. Transfer half of the salsa to the work bowl of a food processor or blender, and process the salsa until it is smooth. Add the puree to the remaining salsa, and mix the salsa well. Cover the bowl, and refrigerate the salsa for 2 hours.
2. Heat the broiler.
3. Rub the fish steaks with the olive oil. Place the steaks on a broiling tray, and broil them 4 inches from the heat until they are just cooked through, turning them only once, approximately 8 minutes.
4. Transfer the steaks to a large platter. Remove their skin, and discard it. Top each steak with the salsa.

Spaghetti with Turkey Meatballs

Ground turkey breast, now widely available, is a delicious low-fat, iron-rich substitute for ground beef—so delicious that you may never make meatballs with red meat again! You will find this a filling, satisfying dish, one that the whole family will love. **Tip:** *Both the meatballs and the sauce can be prepared 1 day in advance, then gently reheated 30 minutes before serving it.*

PREPARATION: 30 minutes
COOKING: 1 hour
YIELD: 8 main-course servings

MEATBALLS

⅔ cup bread crumbs
½ cup skim milk
2¼ pounds ground turkey breast
2 egg yolks
1 cup grated Parmesan
½ teaspoon salt
½ teaspoon pepper
4 teaspoons olive oil, divided
3 cloves garlic, peeled and finely chopped
1 medium Spanish onion, peeled and very finely chopped
1½ teaspoons dried basil
1 teaspoon dried oregano
1 cup water

SAUCE

2 teaspoons olive oil
6 cloves garlic, peeled and finely chopped
2 medium Spanish onions, peeled and diced
Salt to taste
2 teaspoons dried basil
1 teaspoon dried oregano
1 teaspoon dried thyme
1 cup pan juices
2 28-ounce cans whole tomatoes, roughly chopped
Pepper to taste
1¾ pounds spaghetti

1. To make the meatballs, combine the bread crumbs and milk, and allow the ingredients to sit for 5 minutes. Meanwhile, in another bowl combine the ground turkey, egg yolks, Parmesan, salt, and pepper. Add the soaked bread crumbs to the turkey mixture, and mix the ingredients well.

2. Heat 1 teaspoon of the olive oil in a skillet over medium heat. Add the garlic, and sauté it, stirring it constantly, until it is soft and fragrant. Add the onion and a pinch of salt, and sauté the onion, stirring it often, until it is soft. Stir in the basil and oregano, and sauté the ingredients for 2 minutes. Add this mixture to the ground-turkey mixture, thoroughly combining the ingredients.

3. Roll the mixture into 36 1½-inch meatballs.

4. Heat another teaspoon of the olive oil in a large skillet over high heat. Add 12 of the meatballs to the hot oil, and sear them on all sides. Remove the meatballs, and clean the pan. Repeat the procedure two more times.

5. After the third batch of 12 meatballs has been browned, remove them and deglaze the pan with the water. Set the meatballs and the pan juices aside, while you prepare the sauce.

6. To prepare the sauce, heat the olive oil in a Dutch oven over medium heat. Add the garlic, and sauté it, stirring it constantly, until it is soft and fragrant. Add the onions and a dash of salt, and sauté them, stirring them often, until they are soft. Add the basil, oregano, and thyme, and sauté them 2 minutes longer.

7. Raise the heat, and add the reserved pan juices. Simmer the mixture for 1 minute. Stir in the tomatoes, and bring the mixture to a boil.

8. Add the meatballs, reduce the heat, and simmer the meatballs, carefully stirring them occasionally, for 30 minutes.

9. Remove the meatballs from the sauce, and simmer the sauce for 20 minutes. Season the sauce with salt and pepper. Return the meatballs to the sauce.

10. Add the pasta to a large pot of lightly salted boiling water, and cook the pasta until it is tender. Divide the pasta among 8 individual plates, and accompany each portion with sauce and meatballs.

Strip Steak with Mushrooms, Garlic, and Gorgonzola

Many women crave red meat during the second trimester, probably reflecting an increased need for iron, which prevents anemia in the mother and is necessary for the creation of red blood cells in the baby. Heme iron, the type of iron contained in meats, is particularly well absorbed. This recipe combines high-quality steak and a unique sauce flavored with the sweet taste of roasted garlic.

PREPARATION: 15 minutes

COOKING: 15 minutes

YIELD: 4 main-course servings

2 teaspoons plus 1 teaspoon olive oil

6 ounces shiitake, stems removed and discarded, caps sliced

6 ounces crimini, sliced

Salt to taste

4 6-ounce top-loin (New York, Kansas City, or Delmonico) strip steaks, pounded to ¼-inch thickness

Black pepper to taste

⅓ cup brandy

1 cup beef stock

1 medium bulb roasted garlic, pureed

2 ounces Gorgonzola

1. Heat the 2 teaspoons of olive oil in a large sauté pan over medium heat. Add the shiitake, crimini, and a pinch of salt, and sauté the mushrooms, stirring them constantly, until they are soft and all of their liquid has evaporated. Remove them from the pan, and set them aside.

2. Wipe the pan, and raise the heat to high. Add the remaining 1 teaspoon of olive oil.

3. Pat the steaks dry, and sprinkle them with the salt and pepper. Place the steaks in the pan, and sear them on each side until a crust forms, turning them once. If necessary, do this in two batches. Remove the steaks, and set them aside.

ROASTED GARLIC

Cook the garlic in a slow oven to allow the sugar to caramelize and the flavors to intensify. And remember to save the liquid that the garlic is cooked in—it will add great flavor to mashed potatoes, soups, sauces, and stews.

3 bulbs garlic
   Extra-virgin olive oil
   Salt to taste
   Pepper to taste
$1/4$ cup white wine
$1/2$ cup chicken stock *or* water

1. Preheat the oven to 275°F.
2. Prepare the garlic bulbs by removing any loose skin and cutting $1/4$ inch off the top (non-stem side) of each bulb to expose the raw cloves. Place the garlic in a baking dish, drizzle the bulbs with the olive oil, and sprinkle them with the salt and pepper. Pour the wine and the stock or water on the bottom of the dish.
3. Bake the garlic for $1^{1}/4$ hours or until the inner cloves are very soft.
4. Remove the garlic from the oven, and allow the bulbs to cool. Press the soft garlic out of the loose skin.

Note: Although the flavor will not be as sweet and intense, the garlic can also be "roasted" in a microwave oven. Follow the procedure given for a conventional oven, but use a microwave-safe bowl, covered tightly with plastic wrap. It will take approximately 10 to 20 minutes to cook the garlic (cooking times will vary, depending on the power of the microwave oven).

---

4. Carefully pour the brandy in the pan, and flame it. When the flame dies down, add the stock and roasted-garlic puree. Reduce the sauce until it begins to thicken, and season it with salt and pepper.

5. Return the steaks to the pan along with any accumulated juices. Add the mushrooms, and simmer the sauce for 1 minute, turning the steaks once.

6. Place the steaks on a platter. Spoon the sauce over the steaks, and sprinkle them with the Gorgonzola.

Penne with Swiss Chard and Pine Nuts

This quickly prepared meal is loaded with key nutrients important during pregnancy: the chard provides significant amounts of fiber, iron, and folic acid; the pine nuts provide both protein and folic acid; and the pasta is rich in carbohydrates. This may be a perfect pregnancy meal. Swiss chard is a popular cooking green in Italy. The leaves can be either red or green and have an earthy flavor; the stems are sweet. **Tips:** *As you toast the pine nuts, monitor them closely and toss often since they burn easily. The stems of Swiss chard take approximately 3 minutes longer to cook than the leaves.*

PREPARATION: 15 minutes
COOKING: 15 minutes
YIELD: 4 main-course servings

⅓ cup pine nuts
1½ pounds green Swiss chard *or* red Swiss chard, stems and leaves
    separated, leaves roughly chopped and stems trimmed and
    julienned
1 tablespoon extra-virgin olive oil
5 cloves garlic, peeled and finely chopped
1 pound penne
    Salt to taste
½ cup pasta cooking water
1 tablespoon unsalted butter
    Pepper to taste
    Grated Parmesan

1. Bring a large pot of lightly salted water to a boil.
2. Meanwhile, place the pine nuts in a small skillet over low heat, and sprinkle them lightly with salt. Toast them, tossing them often, until they are golden. Set them aside.
3. Fill a sink with cold water, and put the chard leaves in the sink. Place a colander in the water, and put the chard stems in the colander.
4. Heat the olive oil in a large Dutch oven over medium heat. Add the garlic, and sauté it until it is soft and fragrant.
5. Remove the colander from the water, drain the stems, and add the

stems to the pot. Sauté the stems, stirring them constantly, for 2 minutes.

6. Add the pasta to the boiling water.

7. Raise the heat under the Dutch oven to high. Drain the chard leaves, and add them to the pot along with a pinch of salt. Cook the chard, stirring it often, until it is tender. (The water that is clinging to the leaves should be sufficient to steam the chard.)

8. Add the pasta cooking water and the butter. Season the chard with salt and pepper.

9. Drain the pasta, and add it to the chard. Add the toasted pine nuts. Stir the ingredients well, and gently cook them, stirring them often, for 2 minutes.

10. Divide the pasta among 4 individual plates. Sprinkle the Parmesan on each serving.

Linguine with Monkfish, Pecans, Thyme, and Raspberry Vinegar

Preparation: 10 minutes
Cooking: 15 minutes
Yield: 4 main-course servings

Your second-trimester palate will be delighted by this fish dish. The raspberry vinegar provides the sweetness and the fresh thyme the flavor you are craving after the difficult first-trimester months. **Tips:** *The firm texture of monkfish makes it a good choice for a quickly sautéed pasta dish. However, halibut, scallops, shrimp, or cooked lobster meat can be substituted for the monkfish in this recipe with equally fine results. If you use cooked lobster meat, add it just before you add the tomatoes. It is best to use fresh thyme here since it provides the critical intense burst of flavor that makes this dish sublime.*

1 teaspoon plus 2 teaspoons unsalted butter
¼ cup whole pecans
1 pound linguine
1 tablespoon olive oil

1½ pounds monkfish fillets, cut into 3-ounce pieces
    (approximately 8) and thoroughly dried
2 medium leeks, trimmed, thoroughly washed, and thinly sliced
2 tablespoons shallots, peeled and finely chopped
⅓ cup raspberry vinegar
1 cup chicken stock
5 medium plum tomatoes, diced
2 tablespoons fresh thyme
  Salt to taste
  Pepper to taste

1. Melt the 1 teaspoon of butter in a skillet over very low heat. Add the pecans, tossing them well. Gently sauté the pecans, tossing them often, for 5 minutes. Remove the nuts, and set them aside.
2. Bring a large pot of lightly salted water to a boil. Add the pasta.
3. Heat the olive oil in a large sauté pan over high heat. Add the monkfish, and sear the pieces on each side until a golden crust forms. Remove the fish from the pan, and set it aside.
4. Reduce the heat to medium, and add the remaining 2 teaspoons of butter. Add the leeks, and sauté them, stirring them constantly, until they are soft but not browned. Add the shallots, stirring them constantly, and sauté them until they begin to soften.
5. Raise the heat to high, and add the vinegar. Reduce the vinegar for 1 minute. Add the chicken stock, and bring the liquid to a boil.
6. Return the monkfish to the pan along with any accumulated juices, and cook the fish until it is just done.
7. Add the tomatoes, the reserved pecans, and thyme, and cook the ingredients for 1 minute. Season the mixture with the salt and pepper.
8. Drain the pasta, and add it to the sauce. Toss the ingredients well, being careful not to break up the monkfish, and cook the pasta over low heat for 1 minute.

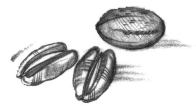

Paella with Salt Cod

The craving for salt is common during pregnancy. Since you do not have to limit salt intake during pregnancy, you can salt your food to taste. Salt cod, long a staple in Mediterranean cooking, is becoming increasingly popular with American cooks. And for the pregnant woman craving salty food, salt cod is perfect. This dish is rich in iron from three sources: salt cod, spinach, and chickpeas. The recipe comes from my Spanish grandmother. **Tips:** *You have to plan in advance when cooking with salt cod: the fish must be soaked in several changes of cold water over a 16-hour period. Accompany this dish with lemon wedges.*

PREPARATION: 20 minutes

COOKING: 45 minutes

YIELD: 4 to 6 main-course servings

PAELLA

Paella is the traditional saffron-flavored rice dish from Spain. It contains a variety of ingredients that may include shrimp, mussels, clams, chicken, sausage, salt cod, green beans, lima beans, chickpeas, cauliflower, and spinach. Although paella takes only 45 minutes to cook, to assemble its many ingredients is time-consuming. It is sometimes accompanied by a garlic sauce and lemon wedges.

Paella is traditionally made outdoors in huge *paelleras* (paella pans) over an open flame but is frequently

2 tablespoons olive oil

1 medium Spanish onion, peeled and diced

4 cloves garlic, peeled and finely chopped

2 medium tomatoes, diced

1½ teaspoons saffron threads

2 cups Arborio rice

3½ cups water *or* chicken stock

Pepper to taste

1 pound salt cod, thoroughly rinsed, soaked for 16 hours in 4 changes of cold water, and cut into 2-inch pieces

10 ounces frozen cauliflower, defrosted

10 ounces frozen chopped spinach, defrosted

1 16-ounce can chickpeas, drained and rinsed

1. Heat the olive oil in a 12-inch paella pan or cast-iron skillet over medium-low heat. Add the onion, and sauté it, stirring it often, until it is soft. Add the garlic, and sauté it until it is fragrant. Add the tomatoes and saffron, and sauté them, stirring them constantly, until the tomatoes are very soft.

2. Add the rice, and stir it to coat it with the onion-tomato mixture. Sauté the rice, stirring it constantly until the rice is lightly toasted, approximately 2 minutes.

3. Raise the heat to high. Add the water or stock, and bring the ingredients to a boil. Season the mixture with the pepper. Reduce the heat, and simmer the mixture for 5 minutes.

4. Add the codfish to the pan, distributing the pieces well and submerging them in the simmering liquid. Simmer the paella for 15 minutes.

5. Add the cauliflower, spinach, and chickpeas to the pan, evenly distributing them around the pan and submerging them slightly into the cooked rice. Simmer the paella until all the liquid is absorbed, and the rice is tender, approximately 10 minutes.

cooked indoors. Paella pans come in various sizes, from small ones (serving 2 people) to very large ones (serving 15 to 20). If you don't have a paella pan, the dish can be prepared in a heavy cast-iron skillet. Its bright, contrasting colors and its various flavors and textures make paella a great party dish. We have eaten this at practically every family gathering for as long as I can remember.

Salt Cod and Squid Stew

Here is another salt-cod dish for those who cannot seem to satisfy their craving for salt. In this recipe, salt cod is combined with tender squid, potatoes, and tomatoes to create a intensely flavored stew, one that is satisfying and hearty and that tastes great reheated the next day. **Tip:** *The stew can be accompanied by crusty bread, or try serving it with couscous in large, shallow bowls.*

PREPARATION: 15 minutes
COOKING: 25 minutes
YIELD: 6 main-course servings

2 medium Yellow Finn potatoes *or* 1 large russet potato, rinsed and cut into small cubes

2 teaspoons olive oil

4 cloves garlic, peeled and finely chopped

1 Spanish onion, peeled and diced

1 medium leek, trimmed, thoroughly washed, and thinly sliced

1 rib celery, diced

Salt to taste

1 cup potato cooking water

1 28-ounce can whole tomatoes, chopped

1 pound salt cod, thoroughly rinsed and soaked for 16 hours in 4

changes of cold water, and cut into ¾-inch pieces

2 teaspoons fresh sage

Pepper to taste

½ pound squid bodies, cut into ¼-inch-thick rounds

1. Place the potatoes in a pot, and cover them with cold water. Bring the water to a boil, and simmer the potatoes until they are tender but still a bit firm, approximately 15 minutes. Drain the potatoes, reserving 1 cup of their cooking water. Rinse the potatoes under cold water, and set them aside.

2. While the potatoes are cooking, heat the olive oil in a large Dutch oven over medium heat. Add the garlic, and sauté it, stirring it constantly, until it is soft and fragrant. Add the onion, and sauté it, stirring it often, until it is soft. Add the leek, celery, and a pinch of salt, and sauté the ingredients, stirring them often, until the celery begins to soften.

3. Add the potato cooking water and tomatoes, and bring the liquid to a boil. Reduce the heat, and carefully stir in the salt cod and cooked potatoes. Simmer the stew for 15 minutes, carefully stirring it often (vigorous stirring will cause the fish to shred).

4. Add the sage, and season the stew with the pepper. Raise the heat to high, and add the squid. Cook the stew only until the squid turns bright white, approximately 1 minute.

Cashew and Black Bean Chili

Preparation: 15 minutes

Cooking: 1½ hours

Yield: 6 main-course servings

Chili is something you probably would not have considered eating during the first trimester. But now you can indulge. This mildly spicy bean dish will satisfy your craving for spicy foods without giving you indigestion. Black beans are not only a good source of folic acid and calcium, but will keep you regular since they have a large amount of fiber. **Tips:** *If canned beans are used,* *decrease the water to 2½ cups. Accompany the chili with brown rice, and top each portion with a dollop of plain yogurt.*

1 pound dried black beans, picked over, rinsed, and soaked for 8
    hours, *or* 4 cups canned black beans, drained and rinsed
8 cups plus 1 cup water
1 tablespoon olive oil
1 large onion, peeled and diced
4 cloves garlic, peeled and finely chopped
2 medium red bell peppers, cored, seeded, and diced
2 jalapeños, finely chopped
2 medium carrots, scrubbed and diced
1 tablespoon chili powder
2 teaspoons cumin
2 teaspoons ground coriander
1 teaspoon cayenne
  Salt to taste

1 28-ounce can whole tomatoes, coarsely chopped
1 cup raw cashew pieces
1½ cups bean cooking water
1 cup fresh *or* frozen corn kernels
½ cup flat-leaf (Italian) parsley, chopped
  Juice 1 lemon
  Pepper to taste

1. Place the dried beans in a large pot. Add the 8 cups of water, and bring it to a boil. Reduce the heat, and simmer the beans until they are tender, approximately 1 hour. Drain the beans, reserving 1½ cups of their cooking water.
2. Meanwhile, heat the olive oil in a Dutch oven over low heat. Add the onion, and sauté it until it is soft. Add the garlic, and sauté it until it is fragrant.
3. Add the red bell peppers, jalapeños, carrots, chili powder, cumin, coriander, cayenne, and a pinch of salt. Cover the pot, and steam-sauté the ingredients, stirring them often, for 6 minutes.

4. Pour in the remaining 1 cup of water. Add the tomatoes and cashews, and simmer the ingredients until the carrots are tender, approximately 15 minutes.

5. Add half of the cooked black beans with the reserved cooking water to the work bowl of a blender or food processor, and puree the beans until they are smooth. Combine the bean puree with the whole beans, stirring the mixture well.

6. Stir the beans into the vegetable-nut-spice mixture. Add the corn, parsley, and lemon juice. Season the chili with salt and pepper.

Curried Basmati Rice and Chicken

This dish is a delicious source of fiber and iron. The brown rice provides the fiber your body needs to counteract the constipating effect of the hormone progesterone, which begins to reach high levels during the second trimester, and the chicken is an excellent low-fat source of heme iron, which is very well absorbed. Your second-trimester palate will delight in the delicate sweetness of the basmati rice and distinctly contrasting assertive curry flavor. **Tip:** *Medium- or long-grain brown rice can be substituted for the basmati rice.*

PREPARATION: 15 minutes
COOKING: 30 minutes
YIELD: 4 to 6 main-course servings

1 tablespoon plus 1 tablespoon olive oil
1 medium Spanish onion, peeled and diced
4 cloves garlic, peeled and finely chopped
1 tablespoon peeled and finely chopped gingerroot
2 medium carrots, scrubbed and diced
2 ribs celery, diced
  Salt to taste
1 tablespoon plus 1 teaspoon good-quality curry powder
1 teaspoon cumin
2 teaspoons coriander

¼ teaspoon nutmeg

1 teaspoon cinnamon

4 cups water *or* chicken stock

2 cups brown basmati rice

1 large red bell pepper, cored, seeded, and diced

1 large green bell pepper, cored, seeded, and diced

1½ pounds skinless, boneless chicken breast, trimmed of all visible fat and thinly sliced

5 scallions, trimmed and thinly sliced

Pepper to taste

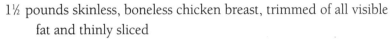

1. Heat 1 tablespoon of the olive oil in large Dutch oven over medium-low heat. Add the onion, and sauté it, stirring it often, until it is soft. Add the garlic and gingerroot, and sauté them, stirring them constantly, until the garlic is fragrant.

2. Add the carrots, celery, a pinch of salt, the 1 tablespoon of curry powder, cumin, coriander, nutmeg, and cinnamon. Stir the ingredients well, and cover the pot. Steam-sauté the ingredients, stirring them often, for 5 minutes.

3. Raise the heat, and add the water or stock. Bring the liquid to a boil. Stir in the rice, cover the pot, and reduce the heat. Simmer the ingredients until the water is absorbed and the rice is tender, approximately 20 minutes.

4. While the rice is cooking, heat the remaining 1 tablespoon of oil in a large sauté pan over medium-low heat. Add the red bell pepper and green bell pepper, sauté them until they begin to soften.

5. Add the remaining 1 teaspoon of curry powder, and stir the peppers well.

6. Add the chicken, and sauté it, stirring it often, until it is thoroughly cooked.

7. Remove the pan from the heat, and stir in the scallions.

8. Add the chicken and peppers to the rice, fluffing the rice with a fork. Season the dish with salt and pepper.

Turkey Sausage with White Beans, Tomatoes, and Sage

The poultry and beans provide the iron and fiber that you require in the second trimester. By substituting turkey sausage for traditional pork sausage, the fat content of this meal is minimized. **Tips:** *This traditional Italian combination of ingredients makes a fabulous sauce that can be accompanied with polenta. If there are any leftovers, they can be used as a sandwich or calzone filling or even as a hearty pizza sauce. If canned beans are used, skip step 1.*

PREPARATION: 10 minutes
COOKING: 1 hour
YIELD: 6 main-course servings

ALCOHOL IN COOKING

~~~~~~~~~~

Wine or other alcohol is safe to use in cooking during pregnancy as long as it is simmered for at least 5 minutes. The cooking process will evaporate the alcohol, leaving the flavor behind.

1 cup dried Great Northern beans, picked over, rinsed, and soaked for 8 hours, *or* 2 cups canned Great Northern beans, drained and rinsed
1 tablespoon plus 1 teaspoon olive oil
1 pound sweet turkey sausage *or* hot turkey sausage, cut into ½-inch pieces
1 medium Spanish onion, peeled and diced
5 cloves garlic, peeled and finely chopped
½ cup white wine
1 28-ounce can whole tomatoes, roughly chopped
¼ cup fresh sage, chopped
   Salt to taste
   Pepper to taste
1 pound rigatoni, cooked and drained

1. Place the dried beans in a medium-sized pot, cover them with water, and bring the water to a boil. Reduce the heat, and simmer the beans until they are tender, approximately 45 minutes. Drain the beans, and set them aside.

2. While the beans are cooking, heat the 1 tablespoon of olive oil in a Dutch oven over high heat. Add the sausage, and sear the pieces on all sides until they are golden. Remove the sausage pieces, and set them aside.

3. Reduce the heat to medium, and add the 1 teaspoon of olive oil. Add the onion, and sauté it, stirring it often, until it is soft. Add the garlic, and sauté it, stirring it constantly, until it is fragrant. Raise the heat, and add the wine, simmering it until it has evaporated.

4. Add the tomatoes and the reserved cooked sausage, and bring the mixture to a boil. Reduce the heat, and simmer the sauce, stirring it occasionally, for 20 minutes.

5. Add the sage and cooked beans, and simmer the sauce for 5 minutes. Season the sauce with salt and pepper.

6. Serve the sauce over the pasta.

Red Lentil and Bulgur Salad with Cashews and Corn

This bulgur dish combines red lentils, cilantro, basil, corn, and cashews to provide contrasting flavors, textures, and colors that will appeal to you. The salad contains both the fiber and iron you need in the second trimester and supplies all of the essential amino acids to form a complete protein. **Tip:** *Don't overcook the lentils. After the water returns to a boil, they will be tender in 3 to 5 minutes.*

PREPARATION: 25 minutes
CHILLING: 3 hours
YIELD: 4 main-course servings

1¾ cups boiling water
1 teaspoon salt
1 cup bulgur
1 cup red lentils, picked over and rinsed
1 small red bell pepper, cored, seeded, and finely chopped
4 scallions, trimmed and finely chopped
1 ear fresh corn, kernels removed
12 ounces fresh spinach, finely chopped, washed, and spun dry
1 clove garlic, peeled and minced

½ cup raw cashew pieces

3 tablespoons cilantro, finely chopped

3 tablespoons fresh basil, finely chopped

Juice 2 lemons

2 tablespoons olive oil

Salt to taste

Pepper to taste

1. Add the 1 teaspoon salt to the boiling water, and gradually stir in the bulgur. Remove the pot from the heat, and cover it tightly. Allow the bulgur to steam for 20 minutes or until it is tender.

2. Place the lentils in a pot, and cover them with water. Bring the water to a boil, reduce the heat, and simmer the lentils until they are tender, approximately 3 to 5 minutes. Drain the lentils, and rinse them under cool running water.

3. Combine the lentils and bulgur in a large nonmetal mixing bowl, and mix them well.

4. Stir in all of the remaining ingredients. Cover the bowl tightly, and chill the salad for at least 3 hours, preferably overnight.

Chickpeas with Kale, Sun-Dried Tomatoes, and Pine Nuts

PREPARATION: 15 minutes
COOKING: 2 hours
YIELD: 4 main-course servings

*One of the most nutritious of all beans, chickpeas (also called garbanzo beans and ceci) are rich in iron, calcium, and folic acid. Since the kale is packed with the same nutrients, you get a double dose of important vitamins and minerals. This dish is also fiber-rich. **Tips:** I like to serve these chickpeas with a fragrant rice (such as jasmine or basmati) laced with fresh herbs, toss it with penne, or simply accompany it with crusty bread and a sliced-tomato salad. If canned beans are used, skip step 1.*

1 pound dried chickpeas, picked over, rinsed, and soaked for 8
    hours, *or* 4 cups canned chickpeas, drained and rinsed
6 cups water plus additional water, if necessary
    Salt to taste
½ cup sun-dried tomatoes
2 tablespoons olive oil
1 large Spanish onion, peeled and diced
1 medium red bell pepper,
    cored, seeded, and diced
6 cloves garlic, peeled and
    finely chopped
1¼ pounds kale, trimmed, chopped,
    washed, and drained
    Pepper to taste
⅓ cup pine nuts, toasted (see page 191)
    Grated Parmesan

1. Place the dried chickpeas in a large pot. Add the 6 cups of water, bring the water to a boil, reduce the heat, and simmer the chickpeas until they are tender, approximately 2 hours. Sprinkle the chickpeas with the salt, drain them, and set them aside.

2. While the beans are cooking, place the sun-dried tomatoes in a bowl, cover them with boiling water, and allow them to macerate for 20 minutes. Drain the tomatoes, julienne them, and set them aside.

3. Heat the olive oil in a large Dutch oven over medium heat. Add the onion, and sauté it, stirring it often, until it is soft. Add the red bell pepper, and sauté it, stirring it often, for 2 minutes. Add the garlic, and sauté it until it is fragrant.

4. Add the kale, and cook it, stirring it often, until it is tender. The water that clings to the leaves should be sufficient to cook the kale. If necessary, add additional water to the pot to prevent the kale from burning.

5. Add the sun-dried tomatoes. Season the vegetables with salt and pepper.

6. Add the cooked chickpeas, and gently simmer the mixture, stirring it often, for 5 minutes.

7. Garnish the chickpeas with the toasted pine nuts and the Parmesan.

Potato Gnocchi with Butter and Parmesan

PREPARATION: 40 minutes
COOKING: 5 minutes
YIELD: 3 to 4 main-course
servings

Gnocchi, Italian dumplings that are boiled, are often made with potatoes, winter squash, or ricotta that has been combined with flour. They are topped with grated cheese or creative sauces that may be olive oil-, tomato-, or butter-based. In short, gnocchi is a versatile dish whose ingredients are limited only by the imagination. This version, with potatoes and cheese, is "comfort food." Potatoes are great for preventing heartburn and stomach upset, and are easily digested. **Tips:** *Gnocchi are a fantastic way to use up leftover baked potatoes. If you are preparing baked potatoes, make several extra for gnocchi. It will cut the preparation time for gnocchi in half.*

3 medium russet potatoes, scrubbed

¾ cup unbleached, all-purpose flour

1 teaspoon olive oil

1 egg yolk

½ cup grated Parmesan plus additional for sprinkling

½ teaspoon salt

½ teaspoon pepper

2 tablespoons unsalted butter

1. Place the potatoes in a large pot, and cover them with cold water. Bring the water to a boil, and cook the potatoes until they are very tender, approximately 30 minutes. Drain the potatoes, and let them cool.

2. When the potatoes are cool, slip off their skins. Mash their flesh until it is smooth, or pass it through a food mill. Transfer the mashed potatoes to a large mixing bowl.

3. Stir in the flour, olive oil, egg yolk, the ½ cup of Parmesan, salt, and pepper.

4. Turn the dough onto a lightly floured work surface. Knead the dough for 3 minutes, and form it into a ball.

5. Slice a 3-inch piece of dough from the ball. On a lightly floured surface, roll the piece into a long cylinder approximately the width of your thumb. Cut the cylinder crosswise into ¾-inch pieces. Set the pieces aside on a lightly floured plate. Repeat the procedure with the remaining dough.

6. Bring a large pot of water to a boil. Add the gnocchi. Cook the gnocchi until they float to the surface, approximately 3 minutes. Drain the gnocchi, toss them with the butter, and sprinkle them with the additional Parmesan.

Classic Risotto

This risotto, with no added fat from a large amount of butter or cream, is creamy because of the cooking method. Thus, it is an ideal dish for those suffering from heartburn since the calories are derived largely from carbohydrates and chicken stock, which will cause little reflux. Risotto, of course, can be an elaborate dish, but this is a basic version. There are more complex risottos for you to try (if your stomach can tolerate them) on pages 243 and 247.

PREPARATION: 10 minutes
COOKING: 30 minutes
YIELD: 4 main-course servings

6 to 8 cups chicken stock
1 tablespoon olive oil
1 medium Spanish onion, peeled and diced
2 cups Arborio rice
1 cup white wine
1 tablespoon unsalted butter

RISOTTO

Risotto, the wonderful northern Italian specialty, has been aptly called "the porridge of the Gods." The main ingredient in risotto is Arborio rice, a highly polished medium-grain rice that is slightly longer than it is wide. It grows in Italy's Po Valley and gives risotto its fabulous creamy consistency. During the cooking process, Arborio rice absorbs large amounts of liquid without loosing its shape or popping. This releases starch, which allows the grains to cling together while not becoming too sticky. The rice should be cooked until it is al dente, its texture remaining firm but tender.

Although there are rules for preparing risotto, there are no boundaries as to what can be added. The best guideline is to use whatever is fresh and of high quality.

⅔ cup grated Parmesan
  Salt to taste
  Pepper to taste

1. Pour the stock into a large saucepan, and bring the stock to a boil. Reduce the heat to a low simmer.
2. Heat the olive oil in a Dutch oven over low heat. Add the onion, and sauté it, stirring it often, until it is soft.
3. Add the rice, and mix it well with the onion. Sauté the rice, stirring it constantly, until it is lightly toasted, approximately 2 minutes.
4. Raise the heat, add the wine, and simmer the rice, stirring it often, until the wine has been absorbed by the rice.
5. Pour in 1 cup of the hot stock, and stir the ingredients well. Simmer the rice, stirring it often to prevent it from sticking, until the liquid is absorbed.
6. Add another 1 cup of stock, and repeat the procedure.
7. Continue adding the stock ½ cup at a time, stirring the rice well. *Remember:* only add additional stock when the previous amount has been almost completely absorbed. The rice is done when it is creamy and tender but al dente. This will take approximately 20 to 25 minutes.
8. Remove the rice from the heat, and stir in the butter and Parmesan. Season the risotto with the salt and pepper, and serve it immediately.

Pappardelle with Spinach-Mushroom Sauce

This pasta dish is quick and easy to toss together, and the garlicky olive-oil flavor is sure to delight your palate. Eat this throughout your pregnancy for a carbohydrate- and nutrient-rich meal. **Tip:** *Pappardelle, a versatile pasta, are ideal with all sauces, which tend to cling to these wide noodles.*

1 pound pappardelle
2 teaspoons olive oil
5 cloves garlic, peeled and finely chopped
12 ounces cultivated white mushrooms, sliced
   Salt to taste
1 pound fresh spinach, stems discarded, leaves roughly chopped,
   washed, and drained
¾ cup homemade chicken broth *or* low-sodium canned chicken
   broth
⅓ cup pasta cooking water
   Pepper to taste
4 tablespoons grated Parmesan

1. Bring a large pot of lightly salted water to a boil, and add the pasta.
2. Heat the olive oil in a Dutch oven over medium heat. Add the garlic, and sauté it, stirring it often, until it is soft and fragrant.
3. Raise the heat to high, and add the mushrooms and a pinch of salt. Sauté the mushrooms until they are soft and all of their liquid has evaporated, approximately 5 minutes.
4. Add the spinach, and cook it, stirring it constantly, until it is wilted.
5. Add the chicken broth and pasta cooking water. Season the sauce with the salt and pepper.
6. When the pasta is cooked, drain it, add it to the sauce, and toss the ingredients well. Heat the pasta and sauce, stirring the ingredients often, for 2 minutes over low heat. Divide the pasta among 4 individual plates, sprinkling 1 tablespoon of the Parmesan over each serving.

PREPARATION: 10 minutes
COOKING: 15 minutes
YIELD: 4 main-course servings

Pork Piccata

*Pork, an excellent source of niacin, has reemerged as a legitimate lean meat due to the way pigs are raised today. Here it is substituted for the more traditional and expensive veal. This quick, easy meal is full of appeal because of the sharp flavors of lemon and capers. **Tip:** Capers and canned chicken broth (even the low-sodium version) are salty, so the dish may not require much additional salt.*

PREPARATION: 10 minutes
COOKING: 15 minutes
YIELD: 4 to 6 main-course
servings

1½ pounds pork tenderloin, trimmed of all visible fat and cut into 8
pieces
1 tablespoon olive oil
Salt to taste
Pepper to taste
3 medium shallots, peeled and finely chopped
⅓ cup white wine
1½ cups homemade chicken broth *or* low-sodium canned chicken
broth
Juice 2 lemons
¼ cup capers in brine, drained
1 tablespoon unsalted butter

CAPERS

Capers are the unopened flower buds of the caper plant. They provide a sharp pickle flavor to a dish and are especially good with chicken, pork, and fish. They also add tang to a robust tomato-based puttanesca sauce. They are most often pickled in brine or vinegar but may be found packed in salt. If small capers are available, purchase them— they are more delectable than the larger ones.

1. Flatten the pork pieces, cut side up, under plastic wrap by pounding them with a mallet until they are approximately ⅛ inch thick.
2. Heat the olive oil in a large sauté pan over medium-high heat. Lightly salt and pepper the pork. Add the pork to the pan, and sear the meat on both sides. Remove the pork, and set it aside.
3. Add the shallots to the pan, and sauté them, stirring them constantly, until they are soft.
4. Raise the heat to high, and add the wine. Reduce the wine for 1 minute. Add the chicken broth, and bring the liquid to a boil. Reduce the liquid for 2 minutes.
5. Add the lemon juice and capers, and simmer the sauce 1 minute longer.

6. Add the butter, and simmer the sauce 2 minutes longer. Return the pork and its juices to the pan.
7. Season the sauce with the salt and pepper.
8. Place the pork on a serving platter, spooning the sauce over the meat.

Tuscan Pork Chops

Pork chops are lean, tender, and flavorful. The loin and rib are the two best cuts. You and your family will love this easy-to-prepare favorite. **Tip:** *You may accompany this dish with pasta or the Classic Risotto (page 205).*

PREPARATION: 15 minutes
COOKING: 50 minutes
YIELD: 4 main-course servings

1 tablespoon olive oil
4 cloves garlic, peeled and lightly crushed but still intact
4 pork loin chops *or* pork rib chops, ½-inch thick
  Salt to taste
  Pepper to taste
1 large Spanish onion, peeled and thinly sliced
1 medium red bell pepper, cored, seeded, and thinly sliced
1 bulb fennel, trimmed and thinly sliced
1 teaspoon fennel seed, lightly crushed
1 pound cultivated white mushrooms, sliced
⅓ cup red-wine vinegar
½ cup white wine
1 28-ounce can whole tomatoes, finely chopped
2 tablespoons capers in brine, drained
½ cup fresh basil, snipped

1. Heat the olive oil in a large Dutch oven over medium heat. Add the garlic, and sauté it, turning it often, until it is golden. Remove it, reserving it as a "cook's treat."
2. Sprinkle the pork with the salt and pepper. Raise the heat, and care-

PORK

The diet for pigs has undergone drastic changes in the past 20 years. The result has been a more muscular animal that yields leaner cuts. As a matter of fact, well-trimmed pork tenderloin is leaner than white-meat chicken.

Since the entire pig is edible, pork provides a variety of eating and lends itself to many preparations. When buying fresh pork, look for meat that is pinkish-white to pink and well-marbled. The leanest and most tender cuts come from the loin; they are best sautéed and grilled. The tenderloin can be roasted whole in a fashion similar to beef tenderloin, or it can be sliced, flattened, and quickly sautéed like veal scallops.

It is very important when preparing pork to cook it thoroughly. In the past, it was necessary to cook pork until it reached an internal temperature of 185°F to kill trichinae, which cause the disease trichinosis. But studies have shown that the trichinae are killed at 150°F, so it is perfectly safe to cook pork to 160°F or 170°F.

fully place the chops in the hot oil. Sear the chops on each side, turning them once, until a crust forms. Remove the chops, and set them aside.

3. Reduce the heat, and add the onion and a dash of salt. Sauté the onion, stirring it often, until it is soft.

4. Add the bell pepper, fennel bulb, and fennel seed. Reduce the heat, cover the pot, and steam-sauté the ingredients, stirring them often, for 5 minutes.

5. Uncover the pot, and raise the heat. Add the mushrooms, and sauté them until they are soft and all of their liquid has evaporated.

6. Add the vinegar and wine, and simmer the ingredients for 2 minutes. Add the tomatoes.

7. Return the pork to the pot along with its juices. Reduce the heat, cover the pot, and simmer the ingredients, stirring them occasionally, for 20 minutes. Uncover the pot, and simmer the ingredients, stirring them often, 10 minutes longer.

8. Add the capers and basil, and season the sauce with the salt and pepper.

Spicy Eggplant-Shrimp Bruschetta

You could never have eaten this dish in the first trimester. But try it now. Tender eggplant, smoky bread, a piquant sauce, and light, crisp shrimp enhanced by fresh tomatoes all contribute to its texture and flavor. **Tips:** *If possible, use small Italian or Japanese eggplants—they are more tender, less bitter, and contain fewer seeds than the large purple variety. A green salad is the perfect accompaniment.*

PREPARATION: 15 minutes
COOKING: 30 minutes
YIELD: 4 to 6 main-course servings

1 tablespoon olive oil
1 medium Spanish onion, peeled and diced
½ teaspoon red pepper flakes

5 cloves garlic, peeled and finely chopped, plus 2 cloves garlic, peeled and lightly crushed

1½ pounds Italian or Japanese eggplant, cut into ½-inch cubes
 Salt to taste

¾ cup water

2 pounds fresh tomatoes, peeled, seeded, and chopped, *or* 2 cups canned whole tomatoes, drained and chopped

14 kalamata olives, pitted and finely chopped

⅓ cup capers in brine, drained

½ cup fresh basil, snipped

8 ¾-inch-thick slices of peasant boule (round loaf)
 Extra-virgin olive oil for brushing on the bread

1½ pounds large shrimp, peeled and deveined
 Pepper to taste

1. Heat the olive oil in a Dutch oven over medium heat. Add the onion, and sauté it, stirring it often, until it is soft. Add the red pepper flakes and the chopped garlic, and sauté the garlic until it is fragrant. Add the eggplant and a dash of salt. Sauté the eggplant, stirring it constantly, until it begins to soften, approximately 3 minutes.
2. Heat the grill or broiler.
3. Add the water to the Dutch oven, and simmer the ingredients for 2 minutes. Add the tomatoes, and stir the sauce well. Bring the sauce to a boil, reduce the heat, and simmer the sauce, stirring it often, for 15 minutes. Add the olives and capers, and simmer the sauce 5 minutes longer. Add the basil, and set the sauce aside.
4. Rub each side of the sliced bread with the lightly crushed garlic. Brush each slice of bread lightly on both sides with the extra-virgin olive oil. Grill or broil the bread until the slices are golden.
5. Return the sauce to the stove, and bring the sauce to a simmer over high heat. Add the shrimp, and cook them, stirring them constantly, until they just turn pink, approximately 2 minutes. Season the shrimp with the salt and pepper. (Keep in mind that the capers and olives are salty.)
6. Place 1 or 2 slices of bread on a plate, and spoon some of the eggplant and shrimp over the bread.

Herb-Crusted Salmon

PREPARATION: 5 minutes
COOKING: 10 minutes
YIELD: 4 main-course servings

You should begin to eat fish now since it is a delicious low-fat source of protein. This salmon dish is simple to prepare and provides a healthy amount omega-3 fatty acids. Serve it with potatoes or pasta to keep your carbohydrate intake up. **Tip:** *The quality of this dish depends on the quality of the dried herbs that are used: if the herbs are old and flavorless, the taste will suffer. Fortunately, excellent Italian Seasoning and herbes de Provence are widely available. You can also make your own mixture by combining basil, thyme, oregano, sage, marjoram, and rosemary. Herbes de Provence may also include fennel seeds, lavender, summer savory, and bay.*

⅔ cup Italian Seasoning *or* herbes de Provence
Salt to taste
Pepper to taste
1½ pounds salmon fillet (cut from the thick end), skinned and cut into 4 pieces
2 egg whites, very well beaten
1 tablespoon olive oil
1 lemon, quartered

1. Heat the oven to 400°F.
2. Place the Italian Seasoning or herbes de Provence in a bowl. Sprinkle them with the salt and pepper, and mix the ingredients well.
3. Dip the salmon fillets in the egg whites, allowing the excess egg to drain off. Then dredge the fillets in the herbs, coating the fillets on each side and patting the herbs onto the surface of the fillets to help the herbs adhere to the fish.
4. Heat the olive oil in a large sauté pan over medium-high heat. Carefully place the fillets in the oil, and sear them on each side until a crust forms, turning them once.
5. Remove the fillets from the pan, transfer them to a baking tray, and place them in the oven. Bake the fillets until they are just cooked through, approximately 5 minutes. Accompany each portion with a lemon wedge.

Farfalle with Spicy Sausage, Squid, Tomatoes, and Onions

Although your inclination may initially be "Squid and sausage—a combination only a pregnant woman could love," your whole family will delight in this interesting contrast of flavors and textures. The hot sausage is complemented by the mild squid and smoky tomatoes, and the onions provide a hint of sweetness. A welcome and hearty dish after the difficult months of the first trimester, it provides a satisfying dose of carbohydrates to energize your and nourish your growing baby. **Tips:** *The tomatoes and the onion can be prepared a day in advance. Bring the onion to room temperature before garnishing each serving.*

PREPARATION: 15 minutes

COOKING: 30 minutes

YIELD: 6 main-course servings

  2 teaspoons plus 4 teaspoons olive oil, plus olive oil for rubbing
      on the tomatoes
10 plum tomatoes
  1 large red onion, peeled and thinly sliced
      Salt to taste
  1 tablespoon sugar
  ½ pound spicy turkey sausage, cut into ½-inch pieces
  1 pound farfalle
  4 cloves garlic, peeled and finely chopped
  2 teaspoons fresh sage, snipped
  ⅓ cup fresh basil, snipped
  1 pound squid, sliced into ¼-inch thick rounds
      Pepper to taste

1. Heat the broiler.
2. Lightly rub the tomatoes with the olive oil. Place them on a tray, and broil them, turning them once or twice, until they are charred. Remove them, and allow them to cool. When they are cool, slip off their skins, and puree the tomatoes in a blender or food processor until they are smooth.
3. While the tomatoes are roasting, heat the 2 teaspoons of olive oil in

a skillet over medium heat. Add the onion and a dash of salt, reduce the heat to low, and sauté the onion, stirring it often, until it is golden, approximately 20 minutes. Add the sugar, and sauté the onion 2 minutes longer. Set the onion aside.

4. Bring a large pot of lightly salted water to a boil.

5. While the onion is cooking, heat the remaining 4 teaspoons of olive oil in a Dutch oven over high heat. Add the sausage, and sear it on all sides. Reduce the heat, and cook the sausage until it is done, approximately 5 minutes.

6. Add the pasta to the water.

7. Add the garlic to the sausage, and sauté the garlic, stirring it constantly, until it is fragrant. Add the puréed tomatoes, and bring the sauce to a simmer. Add the sage, basil, and squid, and cook the sauce just until the squid turns bright white, approximately 2 minutes. Season the sauce with the salt and pepper.

8. Drain the pasta, and add it to the sauce. Heat the ingredients over low heat for 1 minute.

9. Divide the pasta and sauce among 6 individual plates. Garnish each serving with the reserved caramelized onion.

Penne with Broccoli Rabe and Spicy Turkey Sausage

Earthy broccoli rabe, spicy sausage, and sweet sun-dried tomatoes provide a wonderful array of flavors that will delight your second-trimester palate.

PREPARATION: 35 minutes
COOKING: 15 minutes
YIELD: 6 main-course servings

⅓ cup sun-dried tomatoes
1 tablespoon plus 1 tablespoon olive oil
1 pound spicy turkey sausage, sliced into 1-inch pieces
1 pound penne

1 chipotle *or* your favorite chili, finely chopped

6 cloves garlic, peeled and finely chopped

1½ pounds broccoli rabe, roughly chopped, washed, and drained

1 cup pasta cooking water

Salt to taste

Pepper to taste

1. Place the sun-dried tomatoes in a bowl, cover them with boiling water, and allow them to macerate for 20 minutes. Drain the tomatoes, julienne them, and set them aside.
2. Heat 1 tablespoon of the olive oil in a large Dutch oven over high heat. Add the sausage, and sear it on all sides. Reduce the heat, and cook the sausage through, turning it often, approximately 5 minutes. Remove the sausage, and set it aside.
3. Bring a large pot of lightly salted water to a boil. Add the pasta.
4. Heat the remaining 1 tablespoon of olive oil in the Dutch oven over medium heat. Add the chipotle, and sauté the pepper, stirring it often, for 1 minute. Add the garlic, and sauté it, stirring it constantly, until it is soft and fragrant. Raise the heat, and add the broccoli rabe. Sauté it, stirring it constantly, for 1 minute. Add the pasta cooking water, and steam the broccoli rabe until it is tender. Add the sun-dried tomatoes, and reduce the heat to low.
5. Drain the pasta, and add it to the vegetables. Toss the ingredients well, and season them with the salt and pepper. Add the cooked sausage.

Farfalle with Eggplant, Zucchini, Mushrooms, and Tomatoes

This dish is sure to please—especially after the difficult months of the first trimester, when bland foods were all you could tolerate. Your palate will delight in the varied flavors that the many vegetables provide here. The vegetables are loaded with the necessary nutrients for the second trimester, and the pasta is an excellent source of the carbohydrates that your baby needs during this rapid time of growth. **Tip:** *The sauce can be prepared 1 day in advance and gently reheated 20 minutes before serving. The overnight chilling will give the flavors time to develop and intensify.*

PREPARATION: 15 minutes
COOKING: 35 minutes
YIELD: 4 main-course servings

1 tablespoon olive oil
5 cloves garlic, peeled and finely chopped
1 large Spanish onion, peeled and diced
   Salt to taste
1 tablespoon dried basil
1 teaspoon dried oregano
1 teaspoon dried thyme
1 large red bell pepper, cored, seeded, and diced
1 large eggplant, cut into ⅓-inch cubes
1 medium zucchini, cut into ⅓-inch cubes
8 ounces cultivated white mushrooms, sliced
1 28-ounce can whole tomatoes, chopped
   Pepper to taste
1 pound farfalle
4 tablespoons grated Parmesan

1. Bring a large pot of lightly salted water to a boil.
2. Heat the olive oil in a large Dutch oven over medium heat. Add the garlic, and sauté it, stirring it constantly, until it is soft and fragrant. Add the onion and a pinch of salt, and sauté the onion, stirring it often, until it is soft. Stir in the basil, oregano, thyme, and red bell pepper, and cook the ingredients for 2 minutes.

3. Add the eggplant, and cook it for 3 minutes. Add the zucchini and mushrooms, and sauté the mushrooms until they are soft and all of their liquid has evaporated, approximately 6 minutes.

4. Add the tomatoes, and bring the sauce to a boil. Reduce the heat, and simmer the sauce, stirring it often, for 15 minutes. Season the sauce with the salt and pepper.

5. Add the pasta to the boiling water, and cook the pasta until it is tender. Add the pasta to the sauce, tossing the ingredients until they are well combined.

6. Divide the pasta and sauce among 4 individual plates. Sprinkle 1 tablespoon of the Parmesan over each serving.

14 THIRD TRIMESTER

Gravid Granola · Dried Cranberry and Walnut Scones · Brown Rice, Tofu, and Eggs · Oatmeal-Prune-Walnut Muffins · Blueberry-Corn Muffins · Spanish Tortilla · Chilled Couscous Salad · Twice-Cooked Potatoes with Corn, Shiitake, and Sun-Dried Tomatoes · Roasted and Chilled Sweet-Potato Salad · Sweet-Potato Wedges with Coriander · Jalapeño-Corn-Cheddar Muffins · Curried Acorn Squash, Red Lentil, and Apple Soup · Chilled Chickpea Salad with Raisins, Pine Nuts, Vegetables, and Yogurt · Orzo Salad with Spinach, Feta, and Roasted Pumpkinseeds · Herb-Garden Haddock · Gingered Scallops with Summer Vegetables · Grilled Sesame-Tamari Pork Tenderloin · Glazed Salmon on Garlicky Greens · Risotto with White Beans, Spinach, and Shiitake · Tomato and Swiss Chard Bruschetta · Broiled Kale, Tomato, and Mozzarella Sandwiches · Shrimp, Scallop, and Squid Risotto · Roasted Chicken with Potatoes and Garlic · Spinach-Potato Gnocchi with Uncooked Fresh Tomato Sauce · Linguine with Clams, Spinach, and Tomatoes · Southwestern White Bean, Bulgur, and Vegetable Stew

Gravid Granola

PREPARATION: 5 minutes
COOKING: 20 minutes
YIELD: 4 cups

This granola is superior in both flavor and nutrition to many of the mass-produced varieties: there are no heavy syrups; the only fat is that which occurs naturally in the ingredients; the ingredients are dry-roasted, which results in a deep toasted flavor; and the granola's nutritional profile—vitamin B_6, zinc, iron, fiber, and carbohydrates—is complete. When you do not have time for a full meal, mix it, with fresh fruit, into nonfat plain yogurt, or have it with skim milk for breakfast. **Tip:** *The granola will remain fresh for 1 week.*

1½ cups regular rolled oats (not quick-cooking)
⅓ cup raw cashew pieces, roughly chopped
⅓ cup pecans, roughly chopped
⅓ cup sesame seeds
⅓ cup sunflower seeds
¼ teaspoon salt
¾ cup toasted wheat germ
⅓ cup brown sugar
¼ teaspoon nutmeg
1 teaspoon cinnamon
1⅓ cup raisins

1. Heat a heavy skillet (cast iron works well) or Dutch oven over medium-low heat. Add the oats, cashews, and pecans, and cook the ingredients, stirring them often, until they begin to toast, approximately 5 to 7 minutes.
2. Add the sesame seeds and sunflower seeds, and cook them, stirring them often, for another 10 minutes. Add the salt, wheat germ, and brown sugar, and cook the ingredients, stirring them constantly, until the sugar has melted.
3. Reduce the heat, and add the nutmeg and cinnamon, and cook the ingredients for 1 minute.
4. Transfer the granola to a large baking tray. Add the raisins, and spread the granola over the tray so the granola can cool quickly. When the granola is cool, place it in an airtight container.

Dried Cranberry and Walnut Scones

Scones are a wonderful carbohydrate-rich bedtime snack or breakfast food. They are fast and easy to prepare, and they can be frozen. Serve them plain or with your favorite fruit jam. **Tips:** *This is a basic recipe that may be altered to suit your taste: raisins, prunes, dried cherries or strawberries, or any other dried fruit can be substituted for the dried cranberries; grated orange or lemon rind can be added; the corn meal can be eliminated, and an equal amount of flour or toasted wheat germ can be substituted; whole-wheat flour can be substituted for part of the white, if you need extra fiber. Enjoy the creative process, and develop your favorite variation.*

PREPARATION: 10 minutes
BAKING: 12 minutes
YIELD: 6 scones

2 cups unbleached, all-purpose flour
1 tablespoon baking powder
½ teaspoon salt
¼ cup sugar
4 tablespoons cold unsalted butter, cut into 8 pieces
2 eggs, room temperature
½ cup skim milk
½ cup dried cranberries
⅓ cup walnuts, finely chopped

1. Heat the oven to 425°F.
2. Lightly grease or spray a heavy-duty baking sheet.
3. In a large bowl, combine the flour, baking powder, salt, and sugar. Mix the ingredients well.
4. With a pastry cutter or your fingers, cut the butter into the dry ingredients.
5. In a medium-sized bowl, whisk together the eggs and milk.
6. Stir the liquid ingredients into the dry ingredients, and mix only until the dry ingredients are just moistened. The dough will be sticky. Fold in the dried cranberries and walnuts.
7. Turn the dough out onto a lightly floured surface. Flatten the dough into a rectangle that is ¾-inch thick. Cut the dough into 6 wedges,

and place the wedges ½ inch apart from one another on the baking sheet.

8. Bake the scones until they are golden brown, approximately 12 minutes.

Brown Rice, Tofu, and Eggs

This delicious breakfast dish is packed with fiber and will get even the most stubborn of bowels moving in the third trimester. At first glance, the ingredients may seem odd, but the combination works. The inspiration for the dish came from Aaron Park, who served it for brunch in his restaurant, the West Side Cafe, in Portland, Maine.

PREPARATION: 15 minutes
COOKING: 15 minutes
YIELD: 3 to 4 servings

1 tablespoon peanut oil
1 1-inch piece gingerroot, peeled and finely chopped
1 medium red bell pepper, cored, seeded, and diced
6 ounces snow peas, strings removed, sliced into thirds
4 scallions, trimmed and thinly sliced, white and green parts separated
2 tablespoons tamari *or* low-sodium soy sauce
2 teaspoons sesame oil
1 teaspoon sugar
3 cups cooked brown rice (approximately 1 cup raw)
10 ounces tofu (bean curd), roughly chopped
2 eggs, well beaten
Pepper to taste

1. Heat the peanut oil in a Dutch oven over medium heat. Add the gingerroot, and sauté it, stirring it often, until it is fragrant. Add the red bell pepper, and sauté it, stirring it often, until it begins to soften.

Add the snow peas and the white part of the scallions, and sauté them until the snow peas turn bright green. Add the tamari or soy sauce, sesame oil, and sugar.

2. Add the rice, and stir the ingredients well. Add the tofu, and continue to stir the ingredients until they are mixed.

3. Add the eggs, and stir them until they have set. Stir in the green part of the scallions. Season the dish with the pepper.

Oatmeal-Prune-Walnut Muffins

Cooked bulgur provides texture and moistness in these muffins, which are rich in fiber and complex carbohydrates and ideal for a quick third-trimester breakfast or snack. Make a double batch, and freeze the extras.

½ cup plus ½ cup regular rolled oats (not quick-cooking)
1 tablespoon dark-brown sugar
1⅓ cups unbleached, all-purpose flour
½ cup whole-wheat flour
1 tablespoon baking powder
½ teaspoon baking soda
½ teaspoon salt
½ cup cooked bulgur
2 eggs
1 cup skim milk
2 tablespoons unsalted butter, melted, plus additional for buttering the tins
½ cup honey
1⅓ cups pitted prunes, roughly chopped
½ cup walnuts, roughly chopped

PREPARATION: 15 minutes
BAKING: 20 minutes
YIELD: 9 to 12 muffins

1. Heat the oven to 400°F.
2. Place ½ cup of the oats in a small skillet over low heat. Toast the oats, tossing them often, until they are golden. Remove the skillet from the heat, and add the brown sugar, stirring the ingredients until the sugar has melted. Set the toasted oats aside.
3. Pulverize the remaining oats in a food processor or blender. Set the oat powder aside.
4. In a large mixing bowl, combine the all-purpose flour, whole-wheat flour, baking powder, baking soda, salt, toasted oats, and oat powder, mixing the ingredients well. Add the cooked bulgur.
5. In another large bowl, beat the eggs. Add the milk, the 2 tablespoons of butter, and honey, mixing the ingredients well.
6. Stir the dry ingredients into the wet ingredient until the dry ingredients are just moistened. Gently fold in the prunes and walnuts.
7. Lightly butter some muffin tins. Fill each tin two-thirds full.
8. Bake the muffins for 20 minutes or until they are lightly golden.

Blueberry-Corn Muffins

PREPARATION: 10 minutes
BAKING: 20 minutes
YIELD: 9 to 12 muffins

*Try these muffins just before your due date for a carbohydrate-loading breakfast. They are not the mundane variety you purchase in a market—their texture and flavor make them unique: the corn meal and toasted wheat germ contribute to their slightly grainy texture and the vanilla yogurt to their flavor. **Tip:** Raspberries, cranberries, or strawberries can be substituted for the blueberries.*

2 cups unbleached, all-purpose flour
¾ cup yellow corn meal
⅓ cup toasted wheat germ
1 tablespoon baking powder

2 tablespoons sugar

½ teaspoon salt

2 eggs

1 cup nonfat vanilla yogurt

2 tablespoons unsalted butter, melted, plus additional for
   buttering the tins

½ cup honey

1½ cups fresh blueberries *or* frozen blueberries, defrosted

1. Heat the oven to 400°F.
2. In a large mixing bowl, combine the flour, corn meal, wheat germ, baking powder, sugar, and salt.
3. In another large bowl, beat the eggs, and add the yogurt, butter, and honey, mixing the ingredients well.
4. Stir the dry ingredients into the wet ingredients until the dry ingredients are just moistened. Gently fold in the blueberries.
5. Lightly butter some muffin tins. Fill each tin two-thirds full.
6. Bake the muffins for 20 minutes or until they are lightly golden.

Spanish Tortilla

*This egg-and-potato dish is an excellent source of low-fat protein and carbohydrates, a perfect combination for an energizing third-trimester meal. A traditional Spanish tortilla is prepared like an omelette but is served flat, like the Italian frittata. Also, a classic tortilla is loaded with fat from whole eggs and a large amount of olive oil. This recipe uses a fraction of both ingredients to keep the fat content to the recommended levels. **Tip:** Another traditional Spanish tortilla is made with scallions. To prepare this version, substitute 1 large bunch of thinly sliced scallions for the potatoes, and eliminate the cubanelle and garlic.*

PREPARATION: 10 minutes

COOKING: 15 minutes

YIELD: 2 breakfast or main-course servings

1 tablespoon plus 1 tablespoon olive oil
2 medium red potatoes, scrubbed, dried, and cut into ¼-inch
  cubes
1 medium Spanish onion, peeled and diced
1 cubanelle, diced (a bell pepper can be substituted)
3 cloves garlic, peeled and
  finely chopped
2 eggs
4 egg whites
1 tablespoon water
  Salt to taste
  Pepper to taste

1. Heat 1 tablespoon of the olive oil in an omelette pan or a nonstick skillet over high heat. Add the potatoes, and sauté them, tossing them often, until they just begin to take on color, approximately 10 minutes.
2. Add the onion and pepper, and sauté the vegetables, tossing them often, until they are soft. Add the garlic, and sauté it until it is fragrant. Transfer the potato mixture to a plate, and wipe the pan clean.
3. Reduce the heat to medium, and add the remaining 1 tablespoon of olive oil to the pan.
4. Beat the eggs and the egg whites with the water. Sprinkle the egg mixture with the salt and pepper. Add the eggs to the hot oil, and cook them until they are almost set but still a bit runny. Occasionally lift the edges of the tortilla to allow the eggs to run onto the hot pan.
4. Gently scatter the potato mixture over the eggs.
5. Loosen the sides and the bottom of the tortilla with a spatula. Place a large plate over the tortilla, and invert the pan onto the plate. Remove the pan, slide the tortilla, which is now on the plate, back into the pan, and cook the other side for 1 to 2 minutes. Remove the tortilla, and serve it immediately.

Chilled Couscous Salad

Couscous, an excellent source of complex carbohydrates, is perfect for the carbohydrate-loading days preceding labor. As a North African specialty, couscous is often accompanied by a long-simmered meat (frequently chicken or mutton) and served in a light broth. It also makes a unique chilled salad, as is evident from this recipe. Its delicate texture and sweet flavor will make it a staple in your kitchen. **Tip:** This recipe is just a guideline. Experiment with a variety of vegetables, nuts, seeds, and herbs to create a salad you love.

PREPARATION: 35 minutes
COOKING: 20 minutes
CHILLING: 2 hours
YIELD: 4 to 6 side-dish or main-course servings

1 cup sun-dried tomatoes
4 cups water
  Salt to taste
1 pound fresh peas in the pod, shelled, *or* 1 cup frozen peas, defrosted
3 ears fresh corn, kernels removed, *or* 2 cups frozen corn kernels, defrosted
2 cups uncooked couscous
1 medium cucumber, peeled, seeded, and diced
1 large tomato, diced
3 scallions, trimmed and thinly sliced
1 clove garlic, peeled and minced
½ cup fresh basil, snipped
2 tablespoons extra-virgin olive oil
1 tablespoon red-wine vinegar
½ teaspoon sugar
  Pepper to taste
⅓ pound feta, crumbled

1. Place the sun-dried tomatoes in a bowl, cover them with boiling water, and allow them to macerate for 20 minutes. Drain the tomatoes, julienne them, and set them aside.
2. Combine ice cubes and cold water in the sink.
3. Pour the 4 cups of water into a large pot, and add a dash of salt. Bring the water to a boil. Add the peas, and blanch them for 1 minute. Add

the corn, and blanch it for 45 seconds. Drain the water into another pot, reserving the liquid. Submerge the peas and corn in the ice bath, quickly cooling the vegetables. Drain the vegetables, and set them aside.

4. Return the cooking water to a boil. Add the couscous, stirring it well, and cook it for 1 minute. Remove the pot from the heat, and cover it tightly. Steam the couscous until all of the water has been absorbed, approximately 15 minutes. Uncover the pot, and fluff the couscous with a fork. Transfer the couscous to a baking tray, and spread it evenly over the surface of the tray to cool.

5. In a large bowl, combine the reserved peas and corn, the cucumber, tomato, scallions, sun-dried tomatoes, garlic, and basil, and toss the ingredients well. Stir in the cooled couscous.

6. In another bowl, whisk together the olive oil, vinegar, and sugar. Pour the dressing over the couscous and vegetables, and mix the salad well. Season the salad with the salt and pepper, and garnish it with the crumbled feta. Cover the bowl tightly, and chill the salad for 2 hours.

Twice-Cooked Potatoes with Corn, Shiitake, and Sun-Dried Tomatoes

*This delicious side dish will boost the carbohydrate content of your meals in the days preceding labor or anytime you need an energy boost. It's a wonderful change of pace from roasted or mashed potatoes. **Tips:** Serve these potatoes with grilled or roasted meat or poultry. The leftovers are great cold for lunch the following day. During the summer, use the freshest and sweetest corn available.*

PREPARATION: 50 minutes
BAKING: 40 minutes
YIELD: 4 to 5 side-dish servings

½ cup sun-dried tomatoes
10 medium Yellow Finn potatoes

1 tablespoon plus 2 tablespoons plus 1 tablespoon
    extra-virgin olive oil
4 cloves garlic, peeled and finely chopped
8 ounces shiitake, stems removed and discarded, caps
    thinly sliced
  Salt to taste
2 ears fresh corn, kernels removed
  Pepper to taste
  Olive oil for drizzling

1. Heat the oven to 450°F.
2. Place the sun-dried tomatoes in a bowl, cover them with boiling water, and allow them to macerate for 20 minutes. Drain the tomatoes, finely chop them, and set them aside.
3. Place the potatoes in a large pot, cover them with cold water, and bring the water to a boil. Reduce the heat, and simmer the potatoes until they are tender but not mushy, approximately 20 minutes.
4. While the potatoes are simmering, heat 1 tablespoon of the olive oil in a large skillet over medium heat. Add the garlic, and sauté it, stirring it constantly, until it is fragrant. Add the mushrooms and a pinch of salt, and sauté the mushrooms until they are soft and all of their liquid has evaporated. Add the corn and the sun-dried tomatoes, and sauté them for 1 minute. Remove the skillet from the heat, and set it aside.
5. Drain the potatoes, and return them to the pot. Shake the pot over a high flame for 30 seconds to remove any excess moisture.
6. Coarsely mash the potatoes. They should be lumpy. Add 2 tablespoons of the olive oil to the potatoes, and stir in the mushroom mixture. Season the potatoes with the salt and pepper.
7. Cover the bottom of a small roasting pan with the remaining tablespoon of olive oil. Transfer the potatoes to the pan, spreading them evenly. *Note:* it is important to pack them loosely. Drizzle some olive oil on top of the potatoes.
8. Bake the potatoes for 40 minutes or until the top of the potatoes forms a crust.

Roasted and Chilled Sweet-Potato Salad

*Sweet potatoes, one of the finest sources of vitamin A, also contain significant amounts of carbohydrates, folic acid, calcium, and fiber. Serve this simple, flavorful dish with any meal to enhance the meal's carbohydrate content—especially as your due date draws near. **Tip:** After an overnight chill, the intensity of the spices, tartness of the juices, and sweetness of the potatoes are all evident.*

PREPARATION: 15 minutes
COOKING: 35 minutes
CHILLING: 8 hours
YIELD: 4 to 6 side-dish servings

4 to 5 pounds sweet potatoes, scrubbed, dried, and cut into ⅓-inch cubes
Salt to taste
Pepper to taste
2 tablespoons brown sugar
4 tablespoons peanut oil, divided
1 large red onion, peeled and sliced
2 large red bell peppers, cored, seeded, and diced
½ teaspoon coriander
½ teaspoon cumin
½ teaspoon cinnamon
½ teaspoon nutmeg
Juice 2 limes
2 tablespoons orange-juice concentrate
3 ears fresh corn, kernels removed
½ cup cilantro, chopped

1. Heat the oven to 400°F.
2. Place the potatoes in a large bowl. Sprinkle them with the salt, pepper, and brown sugar, and drizzle them with 1 tablespoon of the peanut oil. Toss the ingredients well. Transfer the potatoes to a large baking sheet, and spread them out in a single layer. Set the potatoes aside.
3. Place the onion and bell peppers in the same bowl, and toss them with 1 tablespoon of the peanut oil. Transfer them to a baking sheet, and spread them out in a single layer.

4. Place both baking sheets in the oven, and roast the vegetables until they are tender, approximately 35 minutes (check the onions and bell peppers after 20 minutes). Remove the baking sheets, and allow the vegetables to cool.

5. While the vegetables are roasting, prepare the dressing. Heat 1 teaspoon of the peanut oil in a small skillet over low heat. Add the coriander, cumin, cinnamon, and nutmeg. Cook the spices, stirring them constantly, for 2 minutes. Transfer them to a mixing bowl. Add the lime juice and orange-juice concentrate to the spices, and mix the ingredients well. Whisk in the remaining peanut oil.

6. Toss the roasted potatoes, onion, bell peppers, and the corn with the cilantro. Add the dressing, and gently mix the ingredients. Season the salad with the salt and pepper, and refrigerate it overnight.

Sweet-Potato Wedges with Coriander

These sweet potato "fries" are a delightful source of complex carbohydrates, the perfect snack or side dish when preparing for labor by carbohydrate loading. The coriander and brown sugar provide a distinctive flavor with a bit of sweetness; the wedges are soft and creamy.

PREPARATION: 10 minutes
BAKING: 35 minutes
YIELD: 4 to 6 side-dish servings

2 tablespoons peanut oil
6 medium sweet potatoes, scrubbed, dried, and cut into 12 lengthwise wedges each
1 tablespoon plus 2 teaspoons coriander
1 teaspoon salt
Pepper to taste
2 tablespoons brown sugar

1. Heat the oven to 400°F.
2. Heat the peanut oil in a large Dutch oven over high heat. Add the potatoes, coriander, salt, pepper, and brown sugar, stirring the in-

gredients well to coat the potatoes with the oil. Sauté the potatoes, stirring them constantly, for 3 minutes.

3. Transfer the potatoes to a large, heavy baking tray, and spread them out in a single layer. Bake the potatoes until they are golden and tender, approximately 35 minutes. Serve them immediately.

Jalapeño-Corn-Cheddar Muffins

Fresh corn and jalapeños are added to a traditional corn-bread recipe to make a unique muffin. These muffins are great with Southwestern White Bean, Bulgur, and Vegetable Stew (page 254) or anytime you feel like a calcium-rich snack.

PREPARATION: 15 minutes
BAKING: 20 minutes
YIELD: 9 to 12 muffins

1¼ cups unbleached, all-purpose flour
1 cup yellow corn meal
2 teaspoons baking powder
1 teaspoon baking soda
1 teaspoon salt
2 tablespoons sugar
1½ cups grated and packed Cheddar
2 jalapeños, seeded and finely chopped
3 scallions, trimmed and finely chopped
2 ears fresh corn, kernels removed, *or* 1½ cups frozen corn kernels, thawed
2 eggs
2 tablespoons unsalted butter, melted, plus extra for buttering the tins
1 cup buttermilk

1. Heat the oven to 400°F.
2. In a large bowl, combine the flour, corn meal, baking powder, baking soda, salt, and sugar, mixing the ingredients well. Add the Ched-

dar, jalapeños, scallions, and corn, thoroughly combining the ingredients.

3. In another large bowl, beat the eggs, and add the butter and buttermilk.

4. Stir the dry ingredients into the wet ingredients until the dry ingredients are just moistened.

5. Lightly butter muffin tins, and fill them two-thirds full with the batter. Bake the muffins for 20 minutes or until the muffins are lightly golden.

Curried Acorn Squash, Red Lentil, and Apple Soup

Sweet, creamy acorn squash and hearty red lentils contribute a powerful nutritional and taste charge to this soup. During the third trimester, when your baby has become large, there is little room left inside your midsection for food. This soup is light enough to keep you from feeling uncomfortable yet is packed with the necessary nutrients for the third trimester. And the lentils will keep you regular. **Tips:** *This soup can be prepared 1 day in advance and gently reheated 20 minutes prior to serving time. Yellow split peas can be substituted for the red lentils.*

PREPARATION: 15 minutes
COOKING: 45 minutes
YIELD: 4 servings

1 cup red lentils, picked over and rinsed
2 cups plus 2 cups plus 2 cups water
1 tablespoon plus 1 tablespoon unsalted butter
1 Spanish onion, peeled and diced
1 medium acorn squash, peeled, seeded, and cubed
    (approximately 4 to 5 cups prepared squash)
    Salt to taste
1 tablespoon peeled and finely chopped gingerroot
2 medium carrots, scrubbed and diced

2 ribs celery, diced
1 red bell pepper, cored, seeded,
   and diced
1 tablespoon curry powder
2 teaspoons coriander
½ teaspoon cinnamon
2 Cortland apples, *unpeeled,*
   cored, and diced
   Pepper to taste

1. Place the lentils in a saucepan, add 2 cups of the water, and bring the water to a boil. Reduce the heat, and simmer the lentils until they are tender but still whole, approximately 5 to 10 minutes. Set the lentils aside.
2. While the lentils are simmering, heat the 1 tablespoon of butter in a Dutch oven over low heat. Add the onion, and sauté it, stirring it often, until it is soft. Add the squash and a dash of salt, cover the pot, and steam-sauté the squash, stirring it often, for 6 minutes. Pour in 2 more cups of the water, and simmer the squash until it is tender, approximately 10 minutes.
3. Puree the onion-squash mixture in a food processor or blender until it is very smooth, and set it aside.
4. Wipe out the Dutch oven, and heat the remaining 1 tablespoon of butter over low heat. Add the gingerroot, and sauté it until it is soft and fragrant.
5. Add the carrots, celery, red bell pepper, and a dash of salt, cover the pot, and steam-sauté the vegetables, stirring them often, for 6 minutes. Add the curry powder, coriander, and cinnamon, and sauté the vegetables 2 minutes longer.
6. Raise the heat, add the remaining 2 cups of water, and bring the mixture to a boil. Reduce the heat, and simmer the mixture until the carrots are tender, approximately 10 minutes. Add the apples, and simmer the mixture 2 minutes longer.
7. Add the pureed squash and the cooked lentils to the vegetable mixture, and stir the soup well. Simmer the soup 5 minutes longer. Season with the salt and pepper.

Chilled Chickpea Salad with Raisins, Pine Nuts, Vegetables, and Yogurt

This salad makes a great light meal during the third trimester, when heavy meals can make you feel uncomfortably full. The chickpeas and yogurt provide a double dose of calcium. Chickpeas are also high in fiber, making them a good cure for constipation. **Tips:** *The beans can be cooked a day in advance. If canned chickpeas are used, skip step 1.*

PREPARATION: 15 minutes
COOKING: 2 hours
CHILLING: 3 hours
YIELD: 6 side-dish or 4 main-course servings

2 cups dried chickpeas, picked over, rinsed, and soaked
    overnight, *or* 4 cups canned chickpeas, drained and rinsed
1 tablespoon peanut oil
3 cloves garlic, peeled and finely chopped
2 tablespoons peeled and finely chopped gingerroot
1 teaspoon cumin
1 teaspoon curry powder
½ teaspoon coriander
¼ teaspoon cinnamon
⅛ teaspoon nutmeg
6 scallions, trimmed and thinly sliced
2 medium tomatoes, diced
1 medium red bell pepper, cored, seeded, and diced
⅓ cup pine nuts, lightly toasted
1 cup raisins
½ cup cilantro, chopped
2 tablespoons fresh mint, chopped
  Juice 1 lemon
2 tablespoons tahini
1½ cups nonfat plain yogurt
  Salt to taste
  Pepper to taste

1. Place the dried chickpeas in a pot, cover them with water, and bring the water to a boil. Reduce the heat, and simmer the chickpeas until

they are tender, approximately 2 hours. If necessary, add more water as the chickpeas are cooking. Drain the chickpeas, and rinse them. Set them aside.

2. While the chickpeas are cooking, heat the peanut oil in a small skillet over low heat. Add the garlic and gingerroot, and sauté them, stirring them often, until they are very soft and fragrant. Add the cumin, curry powder, coriander, cinnamon, and nutmeg, and sauté the ingredients, stirring them constantly, for 2 minutes. Transfer the mixture to a large bowl.

3. Add the scallions, tomatoes, red bell pepper, pine nuts, raisins, cilantro, mint, and the cooked chickpeas.

4. In a medium-sized bowl, whisk together the lemon juice, tahini, and yogurt. Add this mixture to the chickpeas and vegetables, and gently toss the ingredients. Season the salad with the salt and pepper. Tightly cover the bowl, and refrigerate the salad for 3 hours.

Orzo Salad with Spinach, Feta, and Roasted Pumpkinseeds

The variety of ingredients in this pasta salad supply excellent amounts of complex carbohydrates, protein, iron, and folic acid, making it a perfect third-trimester light meal or side dish. **Tips:** *This dish is best prepared 1 day in advance since the flavors will have a chance to mellow and marry. When seasoning the dish, keep in mind that both olives and feta contain salt. Accompany the salad with crusty bread.*

PREPARATION: 15 minutes
COOKING: 8 minutes
CHILLING: 2 hours
YIELD: 6 side-dish or 4 main-course servings

12 ounces orzo (rice-shaped pasta)
¾ pound fresh spinach, finely chopped, washed, and spun dry
½ medium red onion, peeled and finely chopped
3 scallions, trimmed and finely chopped
12 kalamata olives, pitted and finely chopped

½ cup roasted pumpkinseeds

Juice 1 lemon

2 tablespoons olive oil

Salt to taste

Pepper to taste

3 plum tomatoes, diced

4 ounces feta, crumbled

1. Bring a large pot of lightly salted water to a boil. Add the pasta, and cook it until it is tender but still a bit firm. (The lemon juice in the dressing will continue to cook the pasta.) Drain the pasta, and rinse it under cool water.
2. Transfer the pasta to a large mixing bowl. Add the spinach, onion, scallions, olives, and pumpkinseeds, and mix the ingredients well.
3. Add the lemon juice, olive oil, salt, and pepper, and combine the ingredients well.
4. Stir in the tomatoes and feta.
5. Chill the salad for at least 2 hours but preferably 8.

Herb-Garden Haddock

This mild fish is combined with delicate seasonings to make a light, comfortable third-trimester dish with little added fat.

1 medium zucchini, grated and squeezed dry in a towel

1 medium yellow squash, grated and squeezed dry in a towel

1½ cups grated Cheddar

½ cup fresh basil, snipped

3 scallions, trimmed and thinly sliced

Salt to taste

Pepper to taste

1½ pounds haddock fillet, skinned and cut into 4 pieces

PREPARATION: 15 minutes

COOKING: 6 minutes

YIELD: 4 main-course servings

1 medium tomato, cut into 4 slices
¾ cup white wine

1. Heat the oven to 400°F.
2. In a large mixing bowl, combine the zucchini, squash, Cheddar, basil, and scallions, tossing the ingredients well. Season the mixture with the salt and pepper.
3. Place the fish on a heavy-duty baking tray. Place ½ cup of tightly packed vegetable-cheese-herb mixture on the top of each piece of fish (be sure the surface is completely covered). Then place a tomato slice on each piece of fish.
4. Add the wine to the bottom of the tray, and cover the tray loosely with foil.
5. Bake the fish until it is cooked through and flakes when tested with a fork, approximately 6 minutes. Remove the foil carefully (it has a tendency to adhere to the topping).

Gingered Scallops with Summer Vegetables

*This light, fresh-tasting dish will sit well with you during the third trimester. Asparagus is a rich source of folic acid, which you continue to need in large amounts even at this late date in order to manufacture red blood cells in both you and your baby. **Tips:** Shrimp or monkfish can be substituted for the scallops. The shrimp will cook in approximately 1 minute and the monkfish in 5. Cut the monkfish into 2-inch pieces. Steamed rice provides a nice accompaniment to this dish.*

PREPARATION: 10 minutes
COOKING: 12 minutes
YIELD: 4 main-course servings

    1 pound asparagus, tough stems snapped off
    1 tablespoon peanut oil
    1 tablespoon peeled and finely chopped gingerroot

2 cloves garlic, peeled and lightly crushed but in 1 piece

1 medium zucchini, diced

Salt to taste

½ cup white wine

¾ cup fish stock *or* bottled clam juice

4 plum tomatoes, diced

1½ pounds sea scallops, muscle removed and discarded, scallops
cut into uniform sizes, if necessary

1 tablespoon unsalted butter

½ cup fresh basil, snipped

Pepper to taste

1. Loosely tie the asparagus tips together with string. Bring a pot of lightly salted water to a boil. Add the asparagus, and blanch them until they are tender-crisp. Drain them, and submerge them in ice water. When they are cool, drain them again. Untie them, and slice the tips in half on an angle.

2. Heat the peanut oil in a Dutch oven over medium heat. Add the gingerroot and garlic, and sauté them, stirring them constantly, until the garlic is fragrant.

3. Add the zucchini and a pinch of salt, and sauté the zucchini, stirring it constantly, until it begins to soften.

4. Raise the heat, and add the wine. Simmer the mixture until the wine has evaporated. Add the stock or clam juice, and bring the liquid to a boil. Reduce the liquid for 2 minutes.

5. Add the tomatoes, the reserved asparagus, and butter, and simmer the ingredients for 1 minute.

6. Add the scallops, and simmer them until they are just cooked through, approximately 2 minutes.

7. Add the basil, and season the dish with the salt and pepper.

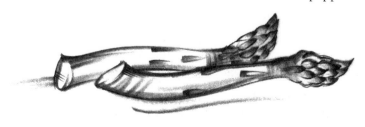

Grilled Sesame-Tamari Pork Tenderloin

*When you are in your third trimester, you may feel hot much of the time because your metabolism has speeded up. The last thing you will want to do is heat your home further by using the oven. So try outdoor grilling—a low-fat cooking technique that is ideal during the hot summer months. We like to skewer the lean pieces of pork, which is high in both protein and thiamine (page 28), with vegetables that have been lightly brushed with sesame oil. By using the marinade tamari or low-sodium soy sauce instead of the usual soy sauce, the meat is less salty and the flavor more well rounded. **Tips:** It is important to plan this dish 1 day in advance since the pork needs to marinate for 24 hours. Chilled Sesame Noodles with Vegetables (see page 165) are an excellent side dish that can also be prepared 1 day ahead.*

PREPARATION: 20 minutes
CHILLING: 24 hours
COOKING: 10 minutes
YIELD: 4 main-course servings

PORK

1½ pounds pork tenderloin, trimmed of all visible fat and cut into
      1½-inch pieces
2 scallions, trimmed and thinly sliced
1 1-inch piece gingerroot, peeled and finely chopped
3 cloves garlic, peeled and finely chopped
5 tablespoons tamari *or* low-sodium soy sauce
2 tablespoons sesame oil
1 teaspoon red-wine vinegar
3 tablespoons rice vinegar
1 tablespoon sugar

VEGETABLES

2 zucchinis, cut
    into 1-inch pieces
12 large white mushrooms,
    wiped clean
2 red bell peppers, cored, seeded, and cut into 1-inch pieces
1 green bell pepper, cored, seeded, and cut into 1-inch pieces
    Sesame oil for brushing

GRILLING

1. Allow the flame to subside before putting food on the grill. Food should be cooked over glowing coals.

2. Build a fire that is hotter on one side than the other. Food can then be seared on the hot side and finished on the cool side.

3. Be patient when grilling. Grilling takes as long as broiling does to cook food.

4. When added to hot coals, fragrant herb stems or wood will give flavor to your food.

1. Combine all the pork ingredients in a large nonmetal bowl, and toss them well. Cover the bowl tightly, and refrigerate the pork for 24 hours.
2. Light a hardwood charcoal fire.
3. Brush the zucchinis, mushrooms, red bell peppers, and green bell pepper with the sesame oil. Thread them and the meat on 8 skewers.
4. Grill the meat and vegetables, turning the skewers often, until the meat is cooked through and the vegetables are soft, approximately 10 minutes.

5. Food should be moist before it is placed on the grill to absorb the heat better.
6. Lift grilled food with tongs. Piercing the food will allow juices to escape.
7. Don't cut food to see if it s done. The juices will escape, causing the fire to flame and the food to overcook. Remove the ifood from the fire, and test it gently. Compare the temperature of the food with the temperature of your head: your forehead temperature would equal medium-well to well-done food; your nose, medium to medium-well food; your chin, medium-rare food.
8. Avoid pressing on the food while it is on the grill. Fat may drip into the fire and cause a flare-up.

Glazed Salmon on Garlicky Greens

Salmon is a fish rich in omega-3 fatty acids, which is heart-healthy. It is high in folic acid, iron, and protein. Blackstrap molasses and spinach are also high in iron. This combination of ingredients makes it an ideal source of iron and the other necessary nutrients for the third trimester. The sweet glaze on the salmon contrasts with the slightly bitter broccoli rabe in this preparation. **Tip:** *If you don't care for the sharp taste of rabe, green or red Swiss chard can be substituted.*

⅓ cup blackstrap molasses
Juice ½ lemon
4 teaspoons honey
1 tablespoon peanut oil
2 teaspoons cumin
1 teaspoon coriander
½ teaspoon cinnamon
1½ pounds salmon fillet, skin intact, cut into 4 pieces
1 tablespoon olive oil

PREPARATION: 10 minutes
COOKING: 20 minutes
YIELD: 4 main-course servings

3 cloves garlic, peeled and finely chopped

1 pound broccoli rabe, trimmed, roughly chopped, and rinsed

Salt to taste

1 pound spinach, trimmed, roughly chopped, washed, and drained

Pepper to taste

1. Heat the broiler.
2. Combine the molasses, lemon, and honey in a bowl, and whisk the ingredients well.
3. Heat the peanut oil in a small skillet over low heat. Add the cumin, coriander, and cinnamon, and cook the spices for 2 minutes, stirring them constantly. Add them to the molasses mixture.
4. Place the salmon on a broiling tray. Broil the salmon 3 inches from the heat for 4 minutes. Remove the salmon, and brush it with the molasses glaze. Return the salmon to the broiler, and broil the salmon 2 minutes longer. Remove the salmon, and again brush it with the glaze. Return the salmon to the broiler to finish cooking, approximately 2 minutes. Remove it from the broiler and brush it one more time. Keep the salmon warm while you prepare the greens.
5. Heat the olive oil in a Dutch oven over medium heat. Add the garlic, and sauté it, stirring it constantly, until it is soft and fragrant.
6. Raise the heat to high. Add the broccoli rabe and a pinch of salt (the water that clings to the vegetable's leaves should be enough to steam it), cover the pot, and steam the broccoli rabe, stirring it occasionally, for 3 minutes.
7. Add the spinach, and stir the ingredients well. Cover the pot, and steam the vegetables until the spinach is wilted and the broccoli rabe is tender, approximately 2 minutes. Season the vegetables with the salt and pepper.
8. Place one-quarter of the greens on each of 4 large plates, and spread the greens evenly around the plate. When removing the fish from the tray, place a spatula between the skin and flesh of the fish, and lift the fish from the pan, leaving the skin behind.

Risotto with White Beans, Spinach, and Shiitake

This flavorful risotto is rich in carbohydrates, fiber, and iron, the perfect combination for the third trimester. **Tip:** *If canned beans are used, skip step 1.*

½ cup dried Great Northern beans, picked over, rinsed, and
    soaked for 8 hours, *or* 1 cup canned Great Northern beans,
    drained and rinsed
1 tablespoon olive oil
4 cloves garlic, peeled and finely chopped
12 ounces shiitake, stems discarded, caps sliced
    Salt to taste
1 pound spinach, trimmed, roughly chopped, washed, and spun
    dry
6 to 8 cups chicken stock (see page 116) *or* low-sodium canned
    chicken broth
2 tablespoon unsalted butter
1 medium Spanish onion, peeled and diced
2 cups Arborio rice
1 cup white wine
½ cup grated Parmesan
    Pepper to taste

PREPARATION: 15 minutes
COOKING: 45 minutes
YIELD: 4 to 6 main-course
    servings

1. Place the beans in a pot, cover them with cold water, and bring the water to a boil. Reduce the heat, and simmer the beans until they are tender, approximately 45 minutes. Drain the beans, and set them aside.

2. While the beans are simmering, heat the olive oil in a Dutch oven over medium heat. Add the garlic, and sauté it, stirring it often, until it is soft. Add the mushrooms and a dash of salt. Sauté the mushrooms until they are soft and all of their liquid has evaporated. Add the spinach, and sauté it, stirring it constantly, until it has wilted.

Set the mushrooms and spinach aside, and clean out the pot.

3. Pour the stock or broth into a large saucepan, bring the stock or broth to a boil, and reduce the heat to a low simmer.

4. Heat the butter in the Dutch oven over low heat. Add the onion, and sauté it until it is soft. Add the rice, combining it well with the onion, and sauté the rice, stirring it constantly, until it is lightly toasted. Raise the heat, add the wine, and simmer the liquid until it has evaporated.

5. Add 1 cup of the hot stock, and combine the ingredients well. Simmer the rice until the liquid is absorbed, stirring the rice often to prevent it from sticking. Add another 1 cup of stock, and repeat the procedure. Continue adding the stock ½ cup at a time, stirring the rice well. It is critical that you only add stock after the previous amount has been almost absorbed. (If you rush, the consistency and texture of the rice will be compromised.) The rice is done when it is creamy and tender but slightly firm. It will take approximately 20 to 25 minutes.

6. Remove the rice from the heat, and stir in the beans and the mushroom-spinach mixture. Add the Parmesan, season with the salt and pepper, and serve the dish immediately.

Tomato and Swiss Chard Bruschetta

PREPARATION: 15 minutes
COOKING: 25 minutes
YIELD: 4 main-course servings

Swiss chard is a leafy dark-green vegetable that is high in iron and folic acid. By combining the chard with vitamin C–rich tomatoes, the absorption of iron is maximized. Bruschetta is an Italian specialty in which thick-crusted bread is brushed with extra-virgin olive oil, rubbed with garlic, and then grilled. The toppings are endless but are often tomato-based. In this recipe, garlic-seasoned tomatoes are topped with green Swiss chard, and the bread is lightly spread with goat cheese—a lot of flavor and few ingredients. (See page 210 for a more elaborate bruschetta.) **Tip:** *Serve the bruschetta with a lightly dressed green salad.*

1 tablespoon plus 1 tablespoon extra-virgin olive oil, plus
    additional for brushing the bread
8 cloves garlic, peeled, 6 finely chopped, 2 left whole
2 28-ounce cans whole tomatoes, drained and roughly chopped
   Salt to taste
   Pepper to taste
1½ pounds green Swiss chard, stems and leaves separated, washed,
    drained, stems julienned, and leaves chopped
4 1-inch-thick slices peasant boule
4 ounces goat cheese

1. Heat 1 tablespoon of the olive oil in a Dutch oven over medium-low heat. Add half of the chopped garlic, and sauté it, stirring it constantly, until it is soft and fragrant. Add the tomatoes, and stir the ingredients well. Simmer the tomatoes, stirring them often, for 15 minutes. Season the tomatoes with the salt and pepper.

2. While the tomatoes are cooking, prepare the chard. Heat 1 table-spoon of the olive oil in a Dutch oven over medium heat. Add the remaining chopped garlic, and sauté it, stirring it constantly, until it is soft and fragrant. Add the chard stems, and sauté them, stirring them constantly, for 3 minutes. Add the chard leaves, and sauté them, stirring them often, for 2 minutes. Cover the pot, and steam the chard until it is tender, approximately 5 minutes. Season the chard with the salt and pepper.

3. Brush the bread slices with the olive oil, and rub them with the two whole cloves of garlic. Broil or grill the bread until it is golden.

4. Remove the slices, and spread them lightly with the goat cheese. Top the bread with, first, the tomatoes and then the chard.

Broiled Kale, Tomato, and Mozzarella Sandwiches

We had these iron-rich sandwiches several times a week for lunch during Hope's pregnancy since iron-deficiency anemia was a problem for her. The kale provides the iron, the tomato the vitamin C to maximize absorption of the iron. In addition, these quickly prepared sandwiches are loaded with folic acid, calcium, and carbohydrates. **Tips:** *Spinach and Swiss chard, both iron-rich vegetables, can be substituted for the kale. If constipation is a problem for you, use whole-grain bagels or whole-grain bread for extra fiber.*

PREPARATION: 10 minutes
COOKING: 20 minutes
YIELD: 4 main-course servings

2 tablespoons extra-virgin olive oil
4 cloves garlic, peeled and
    finely chopped
1 pound kale, roughly chopped,
    washed, and drained
  Salt to taste
  Pepper to taste
4 bagels, each cut in half, *or* 8 ½-inch-thick slices crusty bread,
    preferably cut from a round peasant loaf (boule)
2 medium tomatoes, sliced
6 ounces part-skim mozzarella, sliced or grated

1. Heat the broiler.
2. Heat the olive oil in a Dutch oven over medium heat. Add the garlic, and sauté it, stirring it constantly, until it is soft and fragrant.
3. Add the kale (the water that clings to its leaves should be sufficient to steam it; if necessary, add more water to prevent it from burning), cover the pot, and steam the kale until it is tender, stirring it occasionally. Season it with the salt and pepper.
4. While the kale is steaming, lightly toast the bagels or slices of bread. Place them on a baking sheet.

5. Evenly distribute the kale on each bagel half or slice of bread. Place a slice of tomato and a couple of slices of cheese on each half. Broil the bagels or bread until the cheese is melted and golden.

Shrimp, Scallop, and Squid Risotto

Shellfish are an excellent source of zinc. This lovely shellfish risotto is my version of one that Hope had in a wonderful seafood restaurant near Rome. The broth is light with only a hint of tomato. The basil, added at the end of cooking, provides a burst of flavor that enhances the freshness of the shellfish. **Tips:** *Many fish markets sell frozen fish stock; this is a fine alternative to making your own. Bottled clam juice is also acceptable. The rice is done when it is creamy and tender but still slightly firm—after approximately 20 to 25 minutes of cooking.*

PREPARATION: 15 minutes
COOKING: 30 minutes
YIELD: 4 to 6 main-course servings

    4 to 6 cups fish stock (see page 248) *or* bottled clam juice
 1½ cups crushed tomatoes
    1 tablespoon plus 1 tablespoon unsalted butter
    1 medium Spanish onion, peeled and diced
    2 cups Arborio rice
    1 cup white wine
    ¾ pound sea scallops, muscle removed
    ½ pound large shrimp, peeled and deveined
    ½ pound squid bodies, cut into ⅛-inch-thick rounds
    1 cup fresh basil, snipped
      Salt to taste
      Pepper to taste

1. Combine the stock or clam juice and tomatoes in a large saucepan, and bring the ingredients to a boil. Reduce the heat to a low simmer.

FISH STOCK

Fish stock enhances the flavor of seafood-based risottos, soups, and sauces. If you don't purchase whole fish and fillet them yourself, you may purchase the fish trimmings separately at your local fish market. **Tips:** If you use fish heads, remove the gills since they tend to make the stock bitter. This stock can be refrigerated for 2 days or frozen for 3 months. If you freeze the stock, use several small containers. It will prove convenient when you need only a cup or two.

PREPARATION: 10 minutes
COOKING: 1 hour
YIELD: 2 quarts

2 teaspoons olive oil
1 medium carrot, scrubbed and diced
1 rib celery, diced
1 medium onion, peeled and diced
4 sprigs parsley
3 sprigs fresh thyme
4 black peppercorns
1 cup white wine
3 pounds fish trimmings (heads, tails, and bones)
2 quarts hot water

1. Heat the olive oil in a large Dutch oven over low heat. Add the carrot, celery, onion, parsley, thyme, and peppercorns to the oil, and gently sauté the ingredients, stirring them often, until they are soft, approximately 10 minutes. Raise the heat slightly, add the wine, and simmer the wine for 2 minutes.
2. Spread the fish trimmings evenly over the vegetables. Cover the pot, and steam the ingredients for 10 minutes.
3. Add the water, and raise the heat to high. Bring the ingredients to a boil, reduce the heat, and simmer the ingredients for 10 minutes.
4. Remove the pot from the heat, and allow the stock to rest for 30 minutes.
5. Strain the stock through a fine sieve.

2. Heat 1 tablespoon of the butter in a Dutch oven over low heat. Add the onion, and sauté it, stirring it often, until it is soft.

3. Stir in the rice, combining it well with the onion. Sauté the rice, stirring it constantly, until it is lightly toasted.

4. Raise the heat, and add the wine. Simmer the ingredients until the wine has evaporated.

5. Add 1 cup of the hot stock-tomato mixture, combining the ingredients well, and simmer the rice until the liquid is absorbed, stirring the rice often to prevent it from sticking. Add another 1 cup of stock-tomato mixture, and repeat the procedure. Continue adding the stock-tomato mixture ½ cup at a time, stirring the ingredients well. It is critical that you add stock only after the previous amount has been almost absorbed.

6. Taste the rice after 20 minutes. If it is close to the desired consistency, add the scallops, and cook them for 1 minute. Add the shrimp and squid, and cook them only until the shrimp turn pink.

7. Remove the pot from the heat, and stir in the remaining 1 tablespoon of butter and the basil. Season the risotto with the salt and pepper.

Roasted Chicken with Potatoes and Garlic

Chicken, a good source of low-fat protein, is also an excellent source of heme iron, the most easily absorbed form of iron. And the citrus juice in this dish provides vitamin C, which further enhances the absorption of the iron. This preparation, hardly more difficult than roasting a chicken plain, is a one-dish meal (the potatoes and garlic are roasted in the pan with the chicken)— the recipe simply requires a few more ingredients. The final product has a fresh herb-and-lemon taste; the potatoes are crisp and flavorful; and the roasted garlic is wonderful spread on bread. **Tip:** *It is important to roast*

PREPARATION: 15 minutes
COOKING: 1 hour
YIELD: 4 main-course servings

the chicken on a rack rather than in a pan. When it is roasted on a rack, the fat drips off the bird, keeping its skin crisp and its flesh well basted and moist.

1 3½-pound roasting chicken
3 cloves plus 4 bulbs garlic
¾ cup mixed fresh herbs (parsley, sage, basil, thyme, cilantro, and oregano all work well)
1 tablespoon unsalted butter, cold
½ lemon
1 lime
1 tablespoon plus 1 teaspoon olive oil
8 medium Yukon Gold potatoes, washed and quartered
Salt to taste
Pepper to taste

1. Heat the oven to 450°F.
2. Prepare the chicken by removing its giblets, reserving them for another use, and washing and drying the bird thoroughly.
3. Combine the 3 cloves of garlic and the herbs on a cutting board, chop them very well, and place them in a small bowl. Cut the butter into the garlic-herb mixture.
4. Place three-fourths of the butter-garlic-herb mixture under the skin of the chicken, starting at the neck end, and spread it until the breast is covered with the mixture. Rub the remaining butter-garlic-herb mixture on the skin.
5. Squeeze the lemon over the chicken, and place the lemon half in the cavity. Squeeze the lime over the chicken, and discard the peel.
6. Tuck the wings of the bird behind its shoulders, and tie its legs together.
7. Place the potatoes in a mixing bowl, sprinkle them with the salt, pepper, and the 1 tablespoon of olive oil, and toss the ingredients well. Place them on a heavy-duty roasting pan.
8. Remove the loose skin from the four bulbs of garlic. Cut approximately ¼ inch off the nonstem side of each bulb to expose the raw

garlic. Drizzle the garlic with the remaining 1 teaspoon of olive oil, and place the bulbs on the baking tray with the potatoes.

9. Place the chicken on the middle rack of the oven. The roasting pan containing the garlic and potatoes should be placed on the rack below the bird in order to catch any drippings. Immediately reduce the oven temperature to 350°F.

10. Roast the chicken until the juices run clear when the leg is pierced or until an internal temperature of 180°F is reached, approximately 1 hour.

11. Remove the bird from the oven, and allow it to sit in a warm place for 10 minutes before carving it.

Spinach-Potato Gnocchi with Uncooked Fresh Tomato Sauce

These delicious dumplings are nutritious—they are rich in carbohydrates and iron—perfect for the third trimester. The Parmesan provides the calcium, and the fresh tomatoes, which are cooked only enough to be heated through, are packed with vitamin C.

PREPARATION: Sauce—10 minutes; gnocchi—40 minutes
COOKING: 2 hours
YIELD: 3 to 4 main-course servings

SAUCE

6 medium tomatoes, peeled, seeded, and finely chopped
½ cup fresh basil, snipped
1 tablespoon fresh oregano, chopped
1 tablespoon fresh thyme, chopped
1 tablespoon extra-virgin olive oil
1 clove garlic, peeled and crushed
2 teaspoons balsamic vinegar
Salt to taste
Pepper to taste

GNOCCHI

  3 medium russet potatoes, scrubbed
  1 teaspoon olive oil
  1 pound spinach, finely chopped, washed, and drained
  ¾ teaspoon nutmeg
  ¾ cup unbleached, all-purpose flour
  1 egg yolk
  ¾ cup grated Parmesan plus additional for sprinkling
  ½ teaspoon salt
  ½ teaspoon pepper

1. To prepare the sauce, combine all the sauce ingredients in a large, nonmetal bowl, and mix them well. Cover the bowl tightly, and refrigerate the sauce for 2 hours.
2. While the sauce is chilling, make the gnocchi. Place the potatoes in a large pot, and cover them with cold water. Bring the water to a boil, and cook the potatoes until they are very tender, approximately 20 minutes. Drain the potatoes, and allow them to cool.
3. While the potatoes are cooling, prepare the spinach. Heat the olive oil in a skillet over medium heat. Add the spinach, and sauté it, stirring it constantly, until it is wilted. Add the nutmeg, and set the spinach aside.
4. When the potatoes are cool, slip off their skins. Mash their flesh until it is smooth, or pass it through a food mill. Transfer the mashed potatoes to a large mixing bowl.
5. Stir the flour, egg yolk, Parmesan, reserved cooked spinach, salt, and pepper into the potatoes.
6. Turn the dough out onto a lightly floured work surface. Knead the dough for 3 minutes, and form it into a ball.
7. Slice a 2-inch piece of dough from the ball. On a lightly floured surface, roll the piece into a long cylinder approximately the width of your thumb. Cut the cylinder crosswise into ¾-inch pieces. Set the pieces aside on a lightly floured plate. Repeat the procedure with the remaining dough.
8. Bring a large pot of water to a boil, and add the gnocchi.
9. Heat the fresh tomato sauce in a large Dutch oven over medium heat just until it is warm.

10. When the gnocchi float, drain them, and add them to the sauce. Stir the gnocchi well, and serve them immediately, accompanied by additional Parmesan.

Linguine with Clams, Spinach, and Tomatoes

This dish is perfect for carbohydrate loading in the days preceding labor. The recipe, tailored to meet the extra iron requirement of pregnancy, contains spinach and tomatoes, and it is broth-based, not butter-based like a traditional preparation.

PREPARATION: 20 minutes
COOKING: 15 minutes
YIELD: 4 main-course servings

 2 tablespoons olive oil
 1 small red onion, peeled and diced
 6 cloves garlic, peeled and finely chopped
 1 pound linguine
 ¾ cup dry white wine
40 littleneck clams, lightly scrubbed and rinsed
 ⅓ cup pasta cooking water
 1 pound spinach, finely chopped, washed, and spun dry
 ½ cup flat-leaf (Italian) parsley, finely chopped
 ½ cup fresh basil, snipped
   Salt to taste
   Pepper to taste
 1 large tomato, diced

1. Bring a large pot of lightly salted water to a boil.
2. Heat the olive oil in a Dutch oven over medium heat. Add the onion, and sauté it, stirring it often, until it is soft. Add the garlic, and sauté it until it is fragrant.

CLAMS

The two most common species of clams on the East Coast are the hard-shell and soft-shell. Hard-shell clams range in size from the large chowder clams to the smaller cherrystones and littlenecks. The smaller clams are the choicest to steam open in their shells. Soft-shell clams, or steamers, are most often steamed in water or water and white wine, and are accompanied with their broth and melted butter.

West Coast waters produce hard-shell clams, also known as littlenecks, as well as the long-necked geoducks.

Clams should be purchased alive with uncracked shells. If the shells are slightly ajar, they should close when lightly tapped. Scrub hard-shell clams well, and rinse them under cold running water to remove the sand. Soft-shell clams are more gritty. Soak them in several changes of cold water.

3. Add the pasta to the boiling water.

4. Raise the heat to high under the Dutch oven, add the wine and clams, and cover the pot. Cook the clams for 2 minutes. Add the pasta cooking water and the spinach, and stir the ingredients well. Cook the clams until they open. Add the parsley, basil, salt, and pepper.

5. Drain the pasta, and add it to the clam sauce. Reduce the heat to low, and gently cook the pasta and sauce together, stirring them often, for 2 minutes.

6. Divide the pasta among 4 individual plates. Garnish each portion with the diced tomatoes.

ꟾ

Southwestern White Bean, Bulgur, and Vegetable Stew

Spicy, flavorful, and full of body, this concoction is seasoned like a chili but is significantly lighter, making it perfect for the third trimester, when heavy meals can make you feel uncomfortable. The tomatoes play a supporting role and lend fantastic flavor. With a great deal of fiber, carbohydrates, protein, and vitamin C and a negligible amount of fat, this dish is a powerhouse for the third trimester. To complete the meal with a calcium-rich punch, serve the stew with the Jalapeño-Corn-Cheddar Muffins (see page 232). **Tips:** *To reduce the cooking time by half, prepare the beans and bulgur a day in advance. If canned beans are used, skip step 1.*

PREPARATION: 20 minutes
COOKING: 1¼ hours
YIELD: 4 main-course servings

¾ cup dried Great Northern beans, picked over, rinsed, and soaked overnight, *or* 1½ cups canned Great Northern beans, drained and rinsed

1¼ cups plus 2 cups water

½ teaspoon salt plus additional salt to taste

½ cup bulgur

ꟾ

1 tablespoon plus 2 teaspoons olive oil

1 medium Spanish onion, peeled and finely chopped

4 cloves garlic, peeled and finely chopped

1 large red bell pepper, cored, seeded, and diced

2 jalapeños, seeded and finely chopped (if you prefer less spicy
  food, use only 1)

1 medium zucchini, diced

2 teaspoons chili powder

1 teaspoon cumin

1 teaspoon coriander

12 ounces firm tofu, cut into small cubes

1½ cups canned crushed tomatoes

2 ears fresh corn, kernels removed, *or* 1 cup frozen corn kernels

½ cup cilantro, finely chopped

   Pepper to taste

4 tablespoons nonfat plain yogurt

4 scallions, trimmed and thinly sliced

1. Place the beans in a pot, cover them with water, and bring the water
   to a boil. Reduce the heat, and simmer the beans until they are tender, approximately 45 minutes. Drain the beans, and set them aside.
2. While the beans are simmering, bring the 1¼ cups of water to a boil.
   Add the ½ teaspoon of salt, and then slowly add the bulgur. Remove
   the pot from the heat, and cover it tightly. Allow the bulgur to steam
   for 20 minutes or until it is tender. Set the bulgur aside.
3. Heat all of the olive oil in a large Dutch oven over medium heat. Add
   the onion, and sauté it, stirring it often, until it is soft. Add the garlic, and sauté it, stirring it constantly, until it is fragrant.
4. Add the red bell pepper, jalapeños, and a pinch of salt. Cover the
   pot, and steam-sauté the ingredients, stirring them often, until they
   begin to soften. Add the zucchini, chili powder, cumin, and coriander, and sauté the ingredients, stirring them often, for 5 minutes. Add
   the tofu, and stir the ingredients well.
5. Raise the heat to high, and pour in the remaining 2 cups of water.
   Add the tomatoes, and bring the mixture to a boil. Cover the pot,

and reduce the heat. Simmer the vegetables, stirring them often, for 15 minutes.

6. Add the cooked beans and bulgur, and simmer the stew for 10 minutes.

7. Add the corn and cilantro, and season the stew with the salt and pepper.

8. Divide the stew among 4 individual plates. Garnish each portion with 1 tablespoon of the yogurt and one-quarter of the scallions.

15 POSTPARTUM

Maple-Orange French Toast with Toasted Almonds · Mushroom-Fontina Omelette · Oatmeal with Raisins, Dates, and Wheat Germ · Whole-Grain, Yogurt, and Berry Pancakes · Carons Restaurant's Raisin-Bran Muffins · Buckwheat-Raisin-Pecan Bread · Chickpea, Corn, and Roasted Garlic Soup · Autumn Lentil Soup · Caponata · Penne with Grilled Vegetables and Herbed Ricotta · Spicy Southwestern Omelette · Mussels with Ginger, Tamari, and Herbs · Chicken Marinated in Curried Yogurt · Linguine with Broccoli and Anchovies · Pinto Beans and Tofu · Chickpea and White Bean Ragù with Collard Greens · Linguine with Squid, Tomatoes, Garlic, and Herbs · Eggplant-Mozzarella Grinders with Tomato-Spinach Sauce · Spicy Black Bean Pitas with Vegetables · Creole Red Beans and Brown Rice · Shellfish and Couscous with Fresh Tomatoes

Maple-Orange French Toast with Toasted Almonds

*This dish, an excellent source of fiber, is also rich in calcium, making it a perfect breakfast for lactating women, whose dietary needs include extra calcium. Accompany the French toast with fresh fruit, and the meal is complete. Any leftover bread works well here, but the Buckwheat-Raisin-Pecan Bread on page 264 tastes especially good. **Tip:** To reduce the cooking time, use two skillets.*

PREPARATION: 10 minutes
COOKING: 12 minutes
YIELD: 2 to 3 breakfast
servings

⅓ cup slivered almonds
2 eggs
3 egg whites
3 tablespoons skim milk
2 tablespoons maple syrup plus extra, warmed
1 tablespoon orange rind, finely chopped
6 1-inch-thick slices whole-grain bread, cut from a round peasant loaf (boule)
1 teaspoon unsalted butter

1. Heat a small skillet over low heat. Add the almonds, and toast them, shaking the pan often, until they are golden. Remove the almonds from the heat, and set them aside.
2. In a large mixing bowl, combine the eggs, egg whites, skim milk, the 2 tablespoons of maple syrup, and orange rind. Whisk the mixture thoroughly.
3. Dip 2 slices of bread in the batter. Pierce the bread lightly with a fork 3 or 4 times, and allow the slices to sit in the batter for 1 minute. Turn the bread over, and allow the slices to sit in the batter 1 minute longer.
4. Heat a skillet or griddle over medium heat. Add the butter to the pan, swirling the butter to coat the pan. Add the 2 slices of bread. Cook the bread until one side is golden, flip the slices over, and cook them on the other side until they are golden.

5. While the first 2 slices of bread are cooking, dip 2 more slices in the batter. Repeat steps 3 and 4 until all of the bread is cooked.
6. Garnish the French toast with the almonds, and accompany it with the warm syrup.

Mushroom-Fontina Omelette

An endless variety of ingredients can be folded into an omelette. For a quick meal, any vegetable and cheese you happen to have on hand will turn eggs into a satisfying, calcium-rich dish, perfect for nursing mothers. **Tips:** *To prepare an omelette well, you must use a heavy, heated nonstick skillet, have all your ingredients ready (including the bread, waiting to be toasted), and be quick. An omelette must be served immediately, or it will be tough and dry.*

PREPARATION: 15 minutes
COOKING: 5 minutes
YIELD: 2 breakfast or main-course servings

½ tablespoon plus ½ tablespoon unsalted butter
8 ounces cultivated white mushrooms *or* shiitake, sliced (if you use shiitake, remove and discard the stems)
Salt to taste
3 eggs
4 egg whites
1 tablespoon water
Pepper to taste
½ cup grated fontina

1. Heat a 10-inch omelette pan over medium heat. Add ½ tablespoon of the butter. When the butter has melted, add the mushrooms and a dash of salt. Sauté the mushrooms, stirring them often, until they are soft and all of their liquid has evaporated. Remove the mushrooms from the pan, and set them aside.
2. In a bowl, beat the eggs and the egg whites together very well. Add the water, a dash of salt, and the pepper.
3. Heat the pan again over medium heat. When it is hot, add the re-

maining ½ tablespoon of butter, and swirl it around the pan. Add the eggs, and cover the pan. Allow the eggs to cook until they are almost set but still a bit runny.

4. To one side of the omelette, add the sautéed mushrooms and the cheese. Reduce the heat slightly, and fold the unfilled side of the omelette over the filled side. Cover the pan again, and cook the eggs until they are done and the cheese has melted. Cut the omelette in half, and serve it immediately.

Oatmeal with Raisins, Dates, and Wheat Germ

This may well be the perfect all-round postpartum breakfast. It is carbohydrate-rich and will keep your energy level high and your mind sharp. Cooking the oats in skim milk gives them a creamy texture and adds calcium; since the dish doesn't have any added fat, you can lose those postpartum pounds. **Tip:** *For an even heartier breakfast, substitute steel-cut oats (often called Irish oats) for the rolled oats.*

PREPARATION: 5 minutes
COOKING: 8 minutes
YIELD: 2 to 3 servings

2 cups skim milk plus additional milk for thinning
1 cup water
Dash salt
1½ cups rolled oats (not quick-cooking)
½ teaspoon cinnamon
⅓ cup raisins
⅓ cup pitted dates
½ cup toasted wheat germ
2 to 3 tablespoons warmed maple syrup

1. Add the milk and water to a medium-sized sauce pan, and bring the liquid to a simmer. Add the salt.
2. Slowly stir in the oats and cinnamon, and simmer the oats for 5 min-

utes. Add the raisins. Cook the oats until they are tender, approximately 2 minutes more.

3. Remove the pan from the heat, and stir in the dates, wheat germ, and maple syrup.

4. Divide the oats evenly among two or three bowls. Add additional skim milk until the desired consistency is reached.

Whole-Grain, Yogurt, and Berry Pancakes

Pancakes are a filling and nutritious dish that will help you start your day right. Eating a healthful and well-balanced breakfast is one of the best ways to combat the postpartum blues. High in complex carbohydrates and fiber, this dish will help keep your energy level high and your bowels moving. **Tip:** *To decrease the cooking time, use 2 skillets.*

PREPARATION: 10 minutes
COOKING: 12 minutes
YIELD: 8 large pancakes

PANCAKES

½ cup unbleached, all-purpose flour

½ cup whole-wheat flour

¼ cup toasted wheat germ

¼ cup yellow corn meal

2 teaspoons baking powder

½ teaspoon salt

1 egg

1 tablespoon unsalted butter, melted, plus 1 teaspoon unsalted butter for greasing the skillet

2 tablespoons honey

1¼ cups nonfat vanilla yogurt

⅓ cup skim milk

TOPPING

½ cup fresh blueberries *or* frozen blueberries, defrosted

1 cup fresh strawberries, hulled and sliced, *or* frozen strawberries, defrosted

½ cup fresh raspberries *or* frozen raspberries, defrosted
  Powdered sugar
  Maple syrup, warmed

1. To make the pancakes, in a large bowl combine well the all-purpose flour, whole-wheat flour, wheat germ, corn meal, baking powder, and salt.
2. In another bowl, beat the egg very well. Add the melted butter, honey, yogurt, and skim milk, and mix the ingredients thoroughly.
3. Add the dry ingredients to the wet ones, stirring them until the dry ingredients are just moistened.
4. Preheat a griddle or skillet over medium heat. When it is hot, add ½ teaspoon of the butter, and quickly spread it over the surface of the pan.
5. Add approximately ⅓ cup of the batter to the pan, and cook the pancake until bubbles appear. Flip the pancake over, and cook it on the other side until it is golden and cooked through. Repeat this procedure until all of the batter is used up. Add more butter to the pan as needed.
6. Top each serving of pancakes with some blueberries, strawberries, and raspberries and a sprinkling of the powdered sugar. Accompany the pancakes with the warmed syrup.

Carons Restaurant's Raisin-Bran Muffins

These muffins are the perfect iron- and fiber-rich snack to nibble on post-partem while you are in the hospital. They can be prepared and frozen ahead of time, and then brought to the hospital for you to enjoy. Carons Restaurant, in Hillsboro, New Hampshire, where Lucien and Mary Caron taught me fundamental techniques and the importance of using quality ingredients, provided me with my first restaurant experience. The inspiration for this recipe came from a similar one we made at the restaurant. The iron in the muffins comes from the blackstrap molasses, raisins, and bran cereal.

PREPARATION: 15 minutes
BAKING: 20 minutes
YIELD: 9 to 12 muffins

1¾ cups low-fat, low-sugar raisin-bran cereal
1⅓ cups buttermilk
1 cup unbleached, all-purpose flour
1⅓ cups whole-wheat flour
1 tablespoon baking powder
1 teaspoon baking soda
2 tablespoons brown sugar
¼ teaspoon salt
1 teaspoon cinnamon
2 eggs
2 tablespoons honey
2 tablespoons blackstrap molasses
2 tablespoons unsalted butter plus additional for buttering the tins
1 cup raisins

1. Heat the oven to 400°F.
2. Combine the cereal and buttermilk in a large bowl, and set the mixture aside.
3. In a large mixing bowl, combine the all-purpose flour, whole-wheat flour, baking powder, baking soda, brown sugar, salt, and cinnamon, mixing the ingredients well.
4. In another large bowl, beat the eggs. Add the honey, blackstrap molasses, and the 2 tablespoons of butter, mixing the ingredients well.

Add the wet ingredients to the cereal-buttermilk mixture.

5. Stir the dry ingredients into the wet ingredients until the dry ingredients are just moistened.

6. Stir in the raisins.

7. Lightly butter some muffin tins. Pour the batter in the tins, filling each tin two-thirds full.

8. Bake the muffins for 20 minutes or until they are golden.

Buckwheat-Raisin-Pecan Bread

PREPARATION: 15 minutes
RISING: 3 hours
BAKING: 40 minutes
YIELD: 1 large loaf

*While you are waiting for your baby to arrive, make this dense, nutritious bread and then freeze it. Just defrost it, spread it with reduced-fat cream cheese, and have it brought to you postpartum in the hospital for a quick high-fiber breakfast or snack. The molasses, nuts, and raisins will help keep the bread moist for 2 or 3 days (if the loaf lasts that long) as it continues to develop flavor. **Tip:** The dough can be prepared through the first flour additions (through step 2) 1 day in advance. Cover the bowl tightly with plastic wrap, and leave the dough to rise at room temperature; continue with the recipe the following day. This technique of making bread dough, called a sponge, will give the finished loaf a mildly tangy flavor.*

2½ cups warm water (95°F)
4 tablespoons blackstrap molasses
2 tablespoons active dry yeast
½ cup buckwheat flour
1 cup whole-wheat bread flour
5 cups unbleached, all-purpose flour, divided, plus additional for dusting
1 teaspoon salt
1¼ cups raisins
⅔ cup pecans, roughly chopped

2 teaspoons peanut oil

4 tablespoons corn meal

1. Place the water in a large bowl. Add the molasses, stirring the mixture well. Add the yeast, and stir the ingredients gently until the yeast has dissolved. Allow the yeast to proof at room temperature for 10 minutes.
2. Add the buckwheat flour, whole-wheat bread flour, and 2½ cups of the all-purpose flour. Stir the dough with a wooden spoon for 5 minutes. The dough will be sticky and wet.
3. Add the salt, raisins, pecans, and enough of the remaining all-purpose flour to form a soft dough.
4. Turn the dough out onto a lightly floured work surface. Knead the dough (see page 154) for approximately 10 minutes, adding only enough flour to the work surface to prevent the dough from sticking. The dough will be smooth and somewhat elastic. Form the dough into a ball.
5. Place the oil on the bottom of a large, clean nonmetal bowl. Place the dough in the oil, and turn the dough to coat it all over with the oil. Cover the bowl tightly with plastic wrap, and allow the dough to rise in a warm, draft-free place until it has doubled in bulk, approximately 2 hours.
6. The dough will now be soft and elastic. Pull the sides of the dough toward the center, and deflate the dough by pressing it in the middle to allow the air to escape. Allow the dough to rest for 5 minutes.
7. Turn the dough onto a very lightly floured work surface. Shape the dough into approximately a 10-inch round loaf that is 1-inch high. Sprinkle the corn meal on a heavy baking sheet. Place the dough on the sheet, and return the dough to a warm, draft-free spot to rise until it has doubled in size, approximately 1 hour.
8. Heat the oven to 425°F.
9. With a sharp knife, slash 3 evenly spaced lines approximately ½ inch deep on the top of the loaf. Dust the loaf with the flour.
10. Spray the bottom of the oven with water. Close the oven door, and

wait 1 minute. Spray the oven floor again, and place the bread on the middle rack. Spray the oven at 10-minute intervals for 30 minutes, keeping the oven door open for only as long as is necessary. Bake the bread until its crust is crisp and the bread sounds hollow when tapped, approximately 40 minutes.

11. Carefully remove the hot loaf from the oven, and place it on a rack to cool.

Chickpea, Corn, and Roasted Garlic Soup

If you are trying to lose some of those remaining pregnancy pounds, try this nutrious, filling, low-fat, low-calorie soup. The chickpeas, which provide folic acid, calcium, and fiber, are pureed with roasted garlic to give the soup body without adding the fat calories of cream or a roux. A garlicky tomato broth seasoned with fresh rosemary and basil make this soup a favorite. **Tips:** *The beans and the roasted garlic can be cooked 1 day in advance. If canned chickpeas are used, substitute water for the bean cooking water. If dried basil is used, add it to the onion after the onion has been sautéed. Serve this soup with a crusty bread.*

PREPARATION: 15 minutes
COOKING: 2¼ hours
YIELD: 4 servings

1 cup dried chickpeas, picked over, rinsed, and soaked overnight,
    or 2 cups canned chickpeas, drained and rinsed
1 tablespoon olive oil
1 Spanish onion, peeled and finely chopped
4 cloves garlic, peeled and finely chopped
1 rib celery, diced
1 small carrot, scrubbed and diced
    Salt to taste
2 cups water
1 28-ounce can whole tomatoes, roughly chopped
2 tablespoons fresh rosemary, finely chopped
2 ears fresh corn, kernels removed *or* 1½ cups frozen corn kernels

2 bulbs garlic, roasted (see page 190)
½ cup bean cooking water
½ cup fresh basil, snipped, *or* 2 teaspoons dried basil
   Pepper to taste
   Grated Romano for sprinkling

1. Place the dried chickpeas in a pot, cover them with water, and bring the water to a boil. Reduce the heat, and simmer the chickpeas until they are tender, approximately 2 hours. Drain the chickpeas, and reserve ½ cup of their cooking water. Set the chickpeas aside.
2. While the chickpeas are cooking, heat the olive oil in a Dutch oven over medium heat. Add the onion, and sauté it, stirring it often, until it is soft. Add the chopped garlic, and sauté it until it is fragrant.
3. Add the celery, carrot, and a pinch of salt. Reduce the heat, cover the pot, and steam-sauté the vegetables until they begin to soften.
4. Raise the heat, and add the water. Simmer the vegetables for 3 minutes.
5. Add the rosemary, tomatoes, and half of the cooked beans. Bring the soup to a boil. Reduce the heat, and simmer the soup, stirring it often, for 15 minutes.
6. Add the corn, simmer the soup for 2 minutes, and remove it from the heat.
7. Combine the remaining beans, roasted garlic pulp, and the reserved bean cooking water in the work bowl of a food processor. Puree the ingredients until they are smooth. Add the mixture to the soup, stirring it well.
8. Add the fresh basil, salt, and pepper.
9. Divide the soup among 4 soup plates. Garnish each serving with the grated Romano.

Autumn Lentil Soup

This is a hearty lentil soup that I like to prepare on fall evenings when the air is cool and the harvest is abundant. The lentils are rich in both iron and fiber, making it a wonderful postpartum dish. Prepare this soup while you are still pregnant, then freeze it. Have your partner bring it to you after you have your baby and while you are in the hospital. **Tip:** *This soup can be prepared 1 day in advance and gently reheated 15 minutes before serving.*

PREPARATION: 20 minutes
COOKING: 1 hour
YIELD: 4 servings

1 tablespoon olive oil
1 large onion, peeled and diced
4 cloves garlic, peeled and finely chopped
2 carrots, scrubbed and diced
2 ribs celery, diced
1 medium red bell pepper, cored, seeded, and diced
  Salt to taste
1 cup lentils, picked over and rinsed
6 to 7 cups water
5 plum tomatoes, diced
3 scallions, trimmed and thinly sliced
3 ears fresh corn, kernels removed, *or* 1½ cups frozen corn
    kernels
¼ cup cilantro, roughly chopped
¼ cup flat-leaf (Italian) parsley, roughly chopped
  Juice 1 lemon
  Pepper to taste

1. Heat the olive oil in a Dutch oven over medium heat. Add the onion, and sauté it, stirring it occasionally, until it is soft. Add the garlic, and sauté it until it is fragrant. Add the carrots, celery, red bell pepper, and a pinch of salt, cover the pot, and steam-sauté the vegetables, stirring them often, for 6 minutes.

2. Add the lentils, stirring them to combine them well, and sauté them for 1 minute. Add the water, and bring the ingredients to a boil. Re-

duce the heat, and simmer the soup until the lentils are tender, approximately 40 minutes.

3. Add the tomatoes, scallions, corn, cilantro, parsley, and lemon juice, and simmer the soup 2 minutes longer. Season the soup with the salt and pepper.

Caponata

This version of caponata, a Sicilian eggplant dish, can be used as a dip, as a topping for a bruschetta or pizza, as a filling for a calzone, or it can be tossed with pasta. Try it when you don't much feel like eating—the spiciness will whet your appetite. The roasted eggplant gives texture and an intense flavor to the sauce. **Tips:** *Be certain to peel the eggplant immediately after it is removed from the oven. If the skin is left on, it will discolor the flesh. To peel the hot eggplant, grasp the eggplant by the stem with a kitchen towel, and, with a paring knife in your other hand, carefully remove the skin. Take care not to burn yourself. This dish can be prepared 1 day in advance.*

PREPARATION: 15 minutes

COOKING: 50 minutes

YIELD: 6 appetizer servings or 4 topping, filling, or sauce servings

2 medium eggplants

1 tablespoon olive oil

1 medium red onion, peeled and diced

4 cloves garlic, peeled and finely chopped

1 tablespoon red-wine vinegar

1 medium red bell pepper, cored, seeded, and diced

1 jalapeño, seeded and finely chopped
   Salt to taste

6 large tomatoes, peeled, seeded, and chopped (see page 105), *or*
   1½ cups canned tomatoes plus 1 cup water
   Pepper to taste

1. Heat the oven to 375°F.
2. Place one of the eggplants on the oven rack. Roast the eggplant, turning it occasionally, until it is very soft, approximately 40 minutes. Remove the eggplant from the oven, and peel off the skin. With a spoon, carefully remove the seeds from the flesh. Puree the flesh in a food processor or blender until the flesh is smooth, and set the eggplant aside.
3. While the eggplant is roasting, heat the olive oil in a large Dutch oven over medium heat. Add the onion, and sauté it, stirring it often, until it is soft. Add the garlic, and sauté it, until it is fragrant. Add the vinegar.
4. Add the red bell pepper, jalapeño, and a pinch of salt, and sauté the peppers, stirring them often, until they just begin to soften.
5. Cut the remaining eggplant into ½-inch cubes. Add the cubed eggplant to the pot, and sauté it, stirring it often, until it just begins to soften.
6. Add the tomatoes, raise the heat, and bring the ingredients to a boil. Reduce the heat, and simmer the mixture for 5 minutes.
7. Add the reserved eggplant puree, and simmer the caponata, stirring it often, 5 minutes longer. (It is important that the vegetables remain slightly crunchy.) Season the caponata with the pepper.

Penne with Grilled Vegetables and Herbed Ricotta

PREPARATION: 30 minutes
COOKING: 50 minutes
YIELD: 6 to 8 main-course servings

One-dish entrées are convenient, especially during the busy postpartum period. They can be prepared in advance, there is minimal cleanup, and there are usually leftovers for next day's lunch. The part-skim ricotta and mozzarella are high-calcium cheeses that are relatively low in fat; the asparagus add additional calcium, making this a good choice for nursing mothers.
Tips: *All the elements of this meal can be prepared 1 day in advance: the*

pasta can be cooked, the vegetables grilled, and the sauce made. Twenty-five minutes before serving time, combine the pasta, vegetables, and sauce, stir in the ricotta, sprinkle on the mozzarella, and bake the dish. If fresh herbs are unavailable, use 1 tablespoon of Italian Seasoning or herbes de Provence. Add them after the garlic has been sautéed.

1 pound penne
2 tablespoons plus 1 tablespoon extra-virgin olive oil
1 purple eggplant, sliced into ⅓-inch-thick rounds
2 medium zucchinis, sliced lengthwise into ⅓-inch-thick pieces
½ pound asparagus, tough part of stems snapped off
1 red bell pepper, roasted (see page 161) and sliced into strips
1 yellow bell pepper, roasted (see page 161) and sliced into strips
4 cloves garlic, peeled and finely chopped
1 28-ounce can whole tomatoes, drained and roughly chopped
½ cup fresh basil, snipped
1 tablespoon fresh oregano
2 teaspoons fresh thyme
12 ounces part-skim ricotta
   Salt to taste
   Pepper to taste
4 ounces grated part-skim mozzarella

1. Bring a large pot of lightly salted water to a boil. Add the pasta, and cook it until it is almost tender. Drain the pasta, and run it under cold water until it is cool. Set the pasta aside.
2. While the pasta is cooking, light a charcoal fire, or heat the broiler.
3. Brush the eggplant, zucchinis, and asparagus with the 2 tablespoons of olive oil. Grill or broil the vegetables until they are tender, approximately 4 minutes on each side. Combine the vegetables with the roasted red and yellow bell peppers, and set them aside.
4. Heat the oven to 400°F.
5. Heat the remaining 1 tablespoon of olive oil in a Dutch oven over medium heat. Add the garlic, and sauté it until it is soft. Add the tomatoes, reduce the heat, and simmer the tomatoes, stirring them often, for 15 minutes. Add the basil, oregano, and thyme.

6. Remove the pot from the heat. Add the pasta, grilled vegetables, and ricotta, season the dish with the salt and pepper, and transfer the mixture to a casserole. Sprinkle the mozzarella evenly over the top of the casserole.

7. Bake the casserole until the cheese has melted and the pasta is heated through, approximately 15 minutes.

Spicy Southwestern Omelette

Jalapeño, fresh corn, and cilantro make this an ideal omelette to eat later in the day. Accompany it with Three-Potato Home Fries with Corn, Scallions, and Cheese (see page 157) for an offbeat brunch. Try this dish when you are feeling blue—the spice will give your spirits a lift.

Preparation: 10 minutes
Cooking: 10 minutes
Yield: 2 main-course servings

1½ teaspoons plus 3½ teaspoons unsalted butter
1 jalapeño, peeled, seeded, and finely chopped
   Salt to taste
2 ears fresh corn, kernels removed, *or* 1 cup frozen corn kernels, defrosted
4 tablespoons cilantro, finely chopped
3 eggs
4 egg whites
1 tablespoon water
   Pepper to taste
⅔ cup grated Monterey jack

1. Heat a 10-inch nonstick omelette pan over medium heat. Add the 1½ teaspoons of butter to the pan. When it has melted, add the jalapeño and a dash of salt, and sauté the pepper, stirring it often, until it is soft. Add the corn and cilantro, and sauté the ingredients, stirring them often, 2 minutes longer. Remove the vegetables from the heat, and set them aside.

2. In a bowl, beat the eggs and the egg whites together very well. Add the water, a dash of salt, and the pepper.
3. Heat the pan again over medium heat. When it is hot, add the remaining 3½ teaspoons butter, and swirl it around the pan. Add the eggs, and cover the pan. Allow the eggs to cook until they are almost set but still a bit runny. Lift the sides of the omelette often to allow the eggs to run onto the hot pan.
4. To one side of the omelette, add the sautéed vegetables and the cheese. Reduce the heat slightly, and fold the unfilled side of the omelette over the filled side. Cook the eggs until they are done and the cheese has melted. Cut the omelette in half; serve immediately.

Mussels with Ginger, Tamari, and Herbs

Zinc is a mineral that is commonly lacking in the diet of lactating women. The mussel, a sweet, tender shellfish, is rich in this nutrient. Mussels also contain iron, and the brown rice in this dish adds fiber, making it an excellent postpartum choice. The flavor of the mussels is enhanced by the sweet and spicy sauce in this preparation. The scallions and fresh herbs provide a burst of intense flavor.

PREPARATION: 15 minutes
COOKING: 12 minutes
YIELD: 3 to 4 main-course
    servings

1 tablespoon plus 1 teaspoon peanut oil
1 1-inch piece gingerroot, peeled and finely chopped
4 cloves garlic, peeled and finely chopped
1 medium red bell pepper, cored, seeded, and diced
1 jalapeño, seeded and finely chopped
  Salt to taste
2 tablespoons rice vinegar
1 tablespoon plus 1 teaspoon tamari *or* low-sodium soy sauce
2 teaspoons sugar
4 pounds mussels, thoroughly scrubbed, rinsed, and debearded
5 scallions, trimmed and thinly sliced

MUSSELS

Blue mussels are the most common in America, but the New Zealand species, with their green shell, are becoming more widely available. The flesh of both ranges from cream color to deep orange.

Mussels should be alive when they are purchased. Their shells should be free of cracks and chips, and, if they are open, they should close when tapped or run under cold water. They need to be scrubbed before they are cooked. If they are particularly gritty, soak them in a solution of 1½ teaspoons of salt and 1 gallon of cold water for 20 minutes. Rinse them well. Since debearding mussels kills them, do so only 2 to 3 minutes before cooking them. After the mussels have been cooked, discard any that do not open

¾ cup cilantro, finely chopped
½ cup fresh mint, finely chopped
    Pepper to taste
3 cups cooked brown rice

1. Heat the peanut oil in a large Dutch oven over high heat. Add the gingerroot and garlic, and quickly sauté them, stirring them constantly, until they are fragrant.
2. Add the red bell pepper, jalapeño, and a pinch of salt, and sauté the ingredients, stirring them constantly, for 1 minute.
3. Add the rice vinegar, tamari or soy sauce, and sugar. Gently place the mussels in the pot, and stir the ingredients. Cover the pot tightly, and steam the mussels until they just begin to open.
4. Stir in the scallions, cilantro, and mint, cover the pot, and continue cooking the mussels until they are fully opened. (Discard any that do not open.) Season the mussels with the pepper, and accompany the dish with the brown rice.

Chicken Marinated in Curried Yogurt

*Chicken is a fine source of iron and zinc, while yogurt is high in calcium, making this an excellent postpartum meal for lactating women, who tend to be deficient in both dietary calcium and zinc. A slightly different version of the tandoori chicken prepared in Indian restaurants, this preparation contains a bit of heat, provided by the jalapeño, and is grilled, not cooked in the traditional clay oven. **Tip:** Although I use chicken thighs here, any combination of parts will work well.*

PREPARATION: 15 minutes
MARINATING: 12 hours
COOKING: 15 to 30 minutes
YIELD: 4 to 6 main-course
    servings

    1 1-inch piece gingerroot, peeled and finely chopped
    2 cloves garlic, peeled and finely chopped
    1 jalapeño, seeded and finely chopped
    4 scallions, trimmed and thinly sliced

¼ cup flat-leaf (Italian) parsley, finely chopped

2 cups nonfat plain yogurt

Juice 1 lemon

2 teaspoons peanut oil

1 tablespoon curry powder

½ teaspoon coriander

½ teaspoon cinnamon

Salt to taste

Pepper to taste

10 chicken thighs, skin and visible fat removed

1. In a large nonmetal bowl combine the gingerroot, garlic, jalapeño, scallions, parsley, yogurt, and lemon juice, mixing the ingredients thoroughly.

2. Heat the peanut oil in a small skillet over low heat. Add the curry powder, coriander, and cinnamon. Sauté the spices, stirring them constantly, for 2 minutes. Add the spices to the yogurt mixture. Season the mixture with the salt and pepper.

3. Add the chicken to the yogurt marinade, cover the bowl tightly, and refrigerate the chicken overnight.

4. The following day, light a charcoal fire.

5. Remove the chicken from the marinade. Grill the chicken until it is cooked through, approximately 15 to 20 minutes.

Linguine with Broccoli and Anchovies

Anchovies and broccoli have an affinity for one another. In this preparation, they are paired in an intensely flavored pasta sauce. Broccoli is an excellent nondairy source of calcium that is also well absorbed, making this dish a good choice for nursing mothers who do not eat dairy products. **Tips:** *The sauce of extra-virgin olive oil, garlic, anchovies, red pepper flakes, and dry white wine is versatile. It goes especially well with shellfish such as squid, clams,*

PREPARATION: 10 minutes

COOKING: 12 minutes

YIELD: 4 main-course servings

and shrimp and with vegetables such as spinach, eggplant, and tomatoes. Since anchovies are extremely salty, the dish may not need additional salt.

2 large bunches broccoli, florets and stems (the stems trimmed, peeled, and sliced into ¼-inch-thick disks)
2 tablespoons extra-virgin olive oil
1 pound linguine
6 cloves garlic, peeled and finely chopped
1 2-ounce can anchovy fillets, drained and finely chopped
Dash red pepper flakes
½ cup dry white wine
½ cup pasta cooking water
Salt to taste
Pepper to taste

1. Bring a large pot of lightly salted water to a boil. Add the broccoli stems, and blanch for 1 minute. Add the florets, and blanch until they are tender-crisp, approximately 3 minutes. Drain their blanching water into another large pot, reserving it to cook the pasta. Plunge the broccoli in an ice bath, or rinse it under cold running water until it is cool. Drain the broccoli, and set it aside.
2. Return the cooking water to a boil, adding more water if necessary.
3. Heat the olive oil in a Dutch oven over medium heat.
4. Add the pasta to the boiling water.
5. Add the garlic to the oil, and sauté the garlic, stirring it often, until it is soft and fragrant. Add the anchovies and red pepper flakes, and sauté the ingredients, stirring them constantly, for 2 minutes.
6. Add the wine and the ½ cup of pasta cooking water to the pot, and simmer the ingredients, stirring them constantly, until the anchovies are dissolved. Add the blanched broccoli.
7. When the pasta is tender, drain it, and add it the broccoli and anchovies. Combine the ingredients well, and simmer the mixture, stirring it often, over low heat for 2 minutes. Season the pasta with the salt and pepper.

Pinto Beans and Tofu

Both pinto beans and tofu are excellent nondairy sources of calcium, making this a great low-fat choice for obtaining that nutrient. They are also packed with fiber to combat constipation and complex carbohydrates to provide energy—perfect for the postpartum period. **Tips:** *The dish can also be prepared with red kidney beans, black beans, or cannellini beans. If canned beans are used, you do not have to cook them in step 1. Substitute ½ cup of water for the ½ cup of the bean cooking water.*

PREPARATION: 15 minutes
COOKING: 1½ hours
YIELD: 4 main-course servings

1½ cups dried pinto beans, picked over, rinsed, and soaked
      overnight, *or* 3 cups canned pinto beans, drained and rinsed
 1 tablespoon olive oil
 1 large Spanish onion, peeled and diced
 4 cloves garlic, peeled and finely chopped
 2 teaspoons coriander
 1 teaspoon cumin
 1 teaspoon cinnamon
 1 cup canned crushed tomatoes
2½ cups water
 ½ cup bean cooking water
1¼ pounds firm tofu, cut into ½-inch cubes
  Salt to taste
  Pepper to taste
 4 scallions, trimmed and thinly sliced
 4 to 5 cups cooked brown rice

1. Place the dried beans in a large pot, cover them with water, and bring the water to a boil. Reduce the heat, and simmer the beans until they are tender, approximately 1¼ hours. Drain the beans, and reserve ½ cup of their cooking water. Set the beans aside.
2. While the beans are cooking, heat the olive oil in a large Dutch oven over medium heat. Add the onion, and sauté it, stirring it often, until it is soft. Add the garlic, and sauté it, stirring it constantly, until it is

fragrant. Add the coriander, cumin, and cinnamon, and sauté them, stirring them constantly, 1 minute more.

3. Add the tomatoes, water, and bean cooking water, and bring the ingredients to a boil. Reduce the heat, and simmer the mixture, stirring it often, for 10 minutes. Set the mixture aside while the beans finish cooking.

4. Add the cooked beans and tofu to the tomato-based sauce. Gently stir the ingredients, being careful not to mash the tofu. Reduce the heat, and simmer the mixture for 15 minutes. Season the dish with the salt and pepper, garnish it with the scallions, and accompany it with the brown rice.

Chickpea and White Bean Ragù with Collard Greens

PREPARATION: 15 minutes
COOKING: 2 ¼ hours
YIELD: 4 to 6 main-course servings

Since the three major ingredients in this preparation—chickpeas, white beans, and collard greens—all provide nondairy calcium, nursing mothers get a triple calcium punch. The dish is also high in fiber from the legumes and in iron from the collards, making it a grade A postpartum choice for anyone. This long-simmered recipe is terrific on a cold evening. Traditionally, an Italian ragù is served with pasta. We often accompany it with polenta (we find the combination more interesting and flavorful). With this particular dish, scallion polenta (see page 125) works well. **Tips:** *This meal can be prepared 1 day in advance and gently reheated 15 minutes before serving time. If canned chickpeas and beans are used, skip step 1.*

⅔ cup dried chickpeas, picked over, rinsed, and soaked overnight,
    or 1½ cups canned chickpeas, drained and rinsed
⅔ cup dried navy beans, picked over, rinsed, and soaked

overnight, *or* 1½ cups canned navy beans, drained and
rinsed

1 tablespoon olive oil

1 large Spanish onion, peeled
and finely chopped

6 cloves garlic, peeled and
finely chopped

1 rib celery, finely chopped

1 large carrot, scrubbed and finely chopped

1 jalapeño, seeded and finely chopped

Salt to taste

¾ pound collard greens, trimmed, washed, and thinly sliced

1 28-ounce can crushed tomatoes

1 cup water

¼ cup flat-leaf (Italian) parsley, finely chopped

½ cup fresh basil, snipped

Pepper to taste

1. Place the chickpeas and beans in two separate pots, cover them both
   with water, and bring the water to a boil. Reduce the heat, and simmer them both until they are tender, approximately 1 hour for the
   beans and 2 hours for the chickpeas. Drain them, and set them
   aside.

2. While the chickpeas and beans are cooking, heat the olive oil in a
   large Dutch oven over medium heat. Add the onion, and sauté it until
   it is soft. Add the garlic, and sauté it until it is fragrant.

3. Add the celery, carrot, jalapeño, and a pinch of salt, cover the pot,
   and steam-sauté the ingredients, stirring them often, for 5 minutes.
   Add the collard greens, and sauté them until they are wilted.

4. Add the tomatoes, water, and the cooked chickpeas, and bring the
   mixture to a boil. Reduce the heat, cover the pot, and simmer the
   mixture, stirring it occasionally, for 30 minutes.

5. Add the cooked beans, and, in the uncovered pot, simmer the mixture, stirring it occasionally, 15 minutes longer.

6. Add the parsley, basil, salt, and pepper.

Linguine with Squid, Tomatoes, Garlic, and Herbs

Preparation: 10 minutes
Cooking: 15 minutes
Yield: 4 main-course servings

This pasta meal provides high-quality, low-fat protein (from the squid, which is also a good source of zinc) as well as significant amounts of vitamin C (from the tomatoes), the requirements of which increase the most during lactation. Now that your heartburn is no more, enjoy the spicy addition of the red pepper flakes. A green salad and Italian bread round out the meal. **Tips:** *One tablespoon of Italian Seasoning or herbes de Provence can be substituted for the fresh herbs. Add them after the garlic has been sautéed, and cook them, stirring them constantly, for 30 seconds. Although this summertime dish is particularly enjoyable when garden-ripe tomatoes are at their best and available, during other times of the year or for the sake of convenience, canned tomatoes can be substituted for the fresh.*

    1 tablespoon olive oil
    5 cloves garlic, peeled and finely chopped
    ½ cup dry white wine
    2½ pounds fresh tomatoes, peeled, seeded, and finely chopped, *or* 1
        28-ounce can whole tomatoes, chopped
    1 pound linguine
    ½ cup fresh basil, snipped, *or* ½ cup mixed flat-leaf (Italian)
        parsley, oregano, thyme, and basil
    ⅓ cup pasta cooking water
    1 pound squid, bodies cut into ⅛-inch-thick rounds
        Salt to taste
        Pepper to taste

1. Bring a large pot of lightly salted water to a boil.
2. Meanwhile, heat the olive oil in a Dutch oven over medium heat. Add the garlic, and sauté it until it is soft and fragrant. Add the wine, and reduce it for 1 minute. Add the tomatoes, and bring the mixture to a boil. Reduce the heat, and simmer the mixture, stirring it often, for 10 minutes.

3. Add the pasta to the water.
4. Add the herbs to the tomatoes, and raise the heat to high. Add the pasta cooking water and the squid, and cook the sauce, stirring it often, until the squid is bright white and tender, approximately 1 minute. Season the sauce with the salt and pepper.
5. Drain the pasta, and add it to the sauce. Heat the ingredients, stirring them several times, for 1 minute.

Eggplant-Mozzarella Grinders with Tomato-Spinach Sauce

Often, the eggplant used in restaurants in sandwiches is fried and is, therefore, loaded with unwanted calories. In this recipe, the eggplants are lightly brushed with olive oil and then baked until they are soft and golden. The resulting dish is light, flavorful, and low in fat and calories. When I tested this recipe for the first time, the spinach was added to the tomato sauce as an afterthought (I had some leftover from a previous recipe and didn't want to waste it). It not only added character and flavor to a basic sauce, but extra iron as well. This dish can be prepared in a casserole and then frozen. Have your partner bring it to you in the hospital postpartum along with some fresh crusty bread. The dish contains all the carbohydrates your body craves. **Tips:** *Salting eggplant and allowing it to sit for ½ hour before cooking draws out the moisture, which prevents it from absorbing large amounts of oil in the cooking process. This keeps the fat content low. Some believe that the salting process also decreases the bitterness of the skin, but I have not found this to be true. Bitterness comes from eggplants that are old, that are too large, or that contain many seeds. Choose smaller eggplants—the Japanese or Italian variety, or small white eggplants—since these are generally sweeter. Instead of serving the eggplant in baguettes, serve it with pasta or polenta (see page 125). Accompany the grinders with a green salad.*

PREPARATION: 15 minutes
COOKING: 45 minutes
YIELD: 4 main-course servings

1 tablespoon plus 2 tablespoons olive oil

1 medium Spanish onion, peeled and diced

4 cloves garlic, peeled and finely chopped

½ cup water

1 35-ounce can crushed tomatoes

¾ pound fresh spinach, finely chopped, washed, and dried

⅓ cup fresh basil, snipped

   Salt to taste

   Pepper to taste

2 medium purple eggplants, cut into ⅓-inch-thick rounds, lightly salted, and placed in a large colander to drain for 35 minutes.

6 ounces part-skim mozzarella, sliced or grated

2 medium baguettes, cut in half and sliced open horizontally

1. Heat the oven to 400°F.
2. Heat the 1 tablespoon of olive oil in a Dutch oven over medium heat. Add the onion, and sauté it, stirring it often, until it is soft. Add the garlic, and sauté it until it is fragrant.
3. Raise the heat, add the water, and simmer the ingredients for 2 minutes. Add the tomatoes, and bring the sauce to a boil. Reduce the heat, and simmer the sauce for 15 minutes.
4. Add the spinach and basil, stirring the sauce until the spinach is wilted. Season the sauce with the salt and pepper, and set the sauce aside.
5. While the sauce is simmering, prepare the eggplants. Rinse the eggplant rounds very well, pat them dry, and place them on 2 large baking sheets. Brush both sides of the eggplant rounds with the remaining 2 tablespoons of olive oil. Bake the rounds until they are soft and golden, approximately 20 minutes.
6. Cover the bottom of a medium-sized casserole with sauce. Place a layer of eggplant over the sauce, then a layer of cheese, and another layer of sauce. Repeat with the remaining eggplant and sauce, finishing with a layer of cheese. Bake the casserole in the hot oven until it is bubbly, approximately 15 minutes.

7. Remove the casserole from the oven, and allow it to rest for 5 minutes. Cut the casserole into four equal portions. Carefully place one portion into half a baguette. Repeat this procedure with the remaining eggplant and bread.

Spicy Black Bean Pitas with Vegetables

Black beans are the Cadillac of dried beans. Not only are they versatile and loaded with flavor and texture, but they are a nutritional star as well. They provide significant amounts of protein, folic acid, fiber, iron, and potassium. Try this meal if you do not have much of an appetite postpartum; the spice may just coax it to life. **Tips:** *This black-bean spread is equally good hot or cold and can be served as a dip. The beans can also be rolled into flour tortillas, topped with Cheddar or Monterey jack, and baked. Tomato-Avacodo Salsa (see page 133) is a fine accompaniment. The best plan for this recipe is to put the beans up to cook and then proceed with the remainder of the recipe. When the beans are tender, all you will have to do is puree them with the seasonings. You can then build the sandwiches. If desired, both the beans and yogurt-tahini sauce can be prepared 1 day in advance. If canned beans are used, skip step 1; add ¾ cup of water and salt to taste.*

PREPARATION: 30 minutes
COOKING: 1¼ hours
YIELD: 4 main-course servings

BEANS

1½ cups dried black beans, picked over, rinsed, and soaked
    overnight, *or* 3 cups canned black beans, drained and rinsed
  Salt to taste
1 tablespoon olive oil
1 medium Spanish onion, peeled and diced
1 Scotch bonnet *or* jalapeño *or* serrano, finely chopped
3 cloves garlic, peeled and finely chopped
1 teaspoon coriander

1 teaspoon cumin

1 teaspoon chili powder

½ cup water

Juice 1 lemon

½ cup cilantro, finely chopped

Pepper to taste

SAUCE

1 cup nonfat plain yogurt

2 tablespoons tahini

Juice ½ lemon

2 tablespoons cilantro, finely chopped

Salt to taste

Pepper to taste

SANDWICH

4 medium pitas

2 medium tomatoes, diced

1 medium cucumber, peeled, seeded, and diced

½ cup alfalfa sprouts

4 ounces feta, crumbled

1. To make the beans, place them in a Dutch oven, and cover them with cold water. Bring the water to a boil, reduce the heat, and simmer the beans until they are tender, approximately 1 hour. Sprinkle them with the salt.

2. While the beans are simmering, heat the olive oil in a sauté pan over medium heat. Add the onion and hot pepper, and sauté the ingredients, stirring them often, until they are soft. Add the garlic, and sauté it until it is fragrant.

3. Add the coriander, cumin, and chili powder, and sauté them for 1 minute. Add the water, and simmer the ingredients for 2 minutes.

4. Add the sautéed seasonings to the cooked beans and their liquid. Transfer the mixture to the work bowl of a food processor, and blend the mixture until it is smooth.

5. Transfer the bean puree to a nonmetal container. Add the lemon juice, cilantro, salt, and pepper.

6. To make the sauce, combine all the sauce ingredients in a nonmetal bowl, and chill the sauce for 1 hour.

7. To make the sandwiches, spread the pitas with the black beans. Fill them with the tomatoes, cucumber, alfalfa sprouts, and feta, and drizzle the sauce over the filling.

Creole Red Beans and Brown Rice

Here is another terrific-tasting and healthful rice-and-bean combination. Fresh okra, hearty red kidney beans, fiery hot pepper, and a multitude of other vegetables characterize this southern favorite. Try this zesty dish if you do not have much of an appetite postpartum—the spiciness will surely wake it up. This dish can be prepared ahead of time and frozen; have your partner bring it to the hospital postpartum for you to eat instead of hospital food. The fiber will give your bowels a jump start. **Tip:** *If canned kidney beans are used, decrease the water to 1 cup and add it after the tomatoes.*

PREPARATION: 20 minutes
COOKING: 2 hours
YIELD: 4 main-course servings

2 cups dried red kidney beans, picked over, rinsed, and soaked for 8 hours, *or* 4 cups canned beans, drained and rinsed
6 cups water
2 tablespoons olive oil
1 Spanish onion, peeled and diced
6 cloves garlic, peeled and finely chopped
3 ribs celery, diced
2 medium carrots, scrubbed and diced
2 sweet potatoes, peeled and cut into ½-inch chunks
1 Scotch bonnet, seeded and finely chopped

1 large green bell pepper, cored, seeded, and diced

1 tablespoon dried oregano

2 teaspoons dried thyme

2 teaspoons coriander

1 teaspoon cumin

   Salt to taste

½ pound fresh okra, wiped with a dry towel, trimmed, and diced

1 cup dry sherry

1 cup canned crushed tomatoes

1 tablespoon brown sugar

   Pepper to taste

4 cups cooked brown rice

4 tablespoons nonfat plain yogurt

4 scallions, trimmed and thinly sliced

1. Place the dried beans in a large pot, add the water, and bring the water to a boil. Reduce the heat, and simmer the beans until they are tender, approximately 1½ hours. While they are cooking, prepare the rice and vegetables.

2. Heat the olive oil in a large Dutch oven over medium heat. Add the onion, and sauté it until it is soft. Add the garlic, and sauté it until it is fragrant.

3. Add the celery, carrots, potatoes, Scotch bonnet, bell pepper, oregano, thyme, coriander, cumin, and salt, cover the pot, and steam-sauté the ingredients, stirring them often, for 6 minutes. Add the okra, and steam-sauté the ingredients 3 minutes longer.

4. Add the sherry, and simmer the ingredients until the sherry has evaporated. Add the tomatoes and brown sugar, stir the ingredients well, and simmer the vegetables for 10 minutes.

5. Add the cooked beans to the vegetables, cover the pot, and simmer the mixture, stirring it often, for 20 minutes.

6. Season the bean mixture with the salt and pepper.

7. Divide the rice among 4 individual shallow bowls, and place the beans on top of the rice. Garnish each portion with 1 tablespoon of the yogurt and a sprinkling of the scallions.

Shellfish and Couscous with Fresh Tomatoes

This extremely light and delectable dish, rich in zinc, is a favorite in the summer, when tomatoes are at their best. The straightforward technique, short list of ingredients, and emphasis on freshness makes this recipe the standard for all of the others in this collection. **Tips:** *As with all dishes that contain a variety of seafood, timing is critical for success. Carefully monitor the cooking of the shellfish so that each variety is added at the appropriate moment. Serve this dish with a crusty bread.*

PREPARATION: 15 minutes
COOKING: 15 minutes
YIELD: 4 main-course servings

2½ cups water
    Salt to taste
1¼ cups couscous
  2 tablespoons extra-virgin olive oil
  5 cloves garlic, peeled and finely chopped
½ cup white wine
2½ cups fresh tomatoes, peeled, seeded, and pureed
  1 pound mussels, scrubbed and rinsed
24 littleneck clams, lightly scrubbed
    and rinsed
⅔ pound medium shrimp,
    peeled and deveined
⅔ pound squid, cut into
    ¼-inch-thick rounds
  1 cup fresh basil, snipped
    Pepper to taste

1. Bring the water to a boil in a large pot. Add a dash of salt, and stir in the couscous. Turn off the heat, and cover the pot tightly.
2. Heat the olive oil in a large Dutch oven over medium heat. Add the garlic, and sauté it, stirring it often, until it is fragrant. Raise the heat, add the wine, and reduce it for 1 minute. Add the tomatoes, and

bring the sauce to a boil. Reduce the heat, and simmer the sauce for 5 minutes.

3. While the sauce is simmering, debeard the mussels.

4. Raise the heat under the sauce, and gently add the clams (their shells tend to crack easily). Cover the pot, and steam the clams until they begin to open.

5. Add the mussels, and gently stir the ingredients. Cover the pot, and steam the mussels until they begin to open. Add the shrimp and the squid, and cook the shellfish only until the shrimp turns pink.

6. Remove the pot from the heat, and stir in the basil, salt, and pepper.

7. Fluff the couscous with a fork.

8. To serve, put the couscous in a large shallow bowl, and spoon the shellfish and tomato broth over the couscous.

16 SNACKS AND DESSERTS

Orange Baked Apples with Pecans · Fresh Berry Cheesecake · Chocolate-Almond Biscotti · Sinful Chocolate Chip Cookies · Tofu Chocolate Mousse · Apple-Date Crisp · Bread Pudding with Dates and Pecans · Oatmeal-Apricot-Walnut Cookies · Strawberries, Peaches, and Balsamic Vinegar

Orange Baked Apples with Pecans

Slow-baked apples are a sweet yet nutritious dessert or snack. Apples are an excellent source of fiber.

PREPARATION: 10 minutes
COOKING: 40 minutes
YIELD: 4 servings

4 large Cortland apples *or* other baking apples
½ cup pecans, chopped and lightly toasted
4 tablespoons brown sugar
½ teaspoon cinnamon
2 tablespoons unsalted butter
¾ cup orange juice

1. Heat the oven to 350°F.
2. Wash and core the apples. Place them in a baking dish.
3. In a medium-sized bowl, stir together the pecans, brown sugar, and cinnamon. Cut in the butter with a fork.
4. Fill the cavity of each apple with one-quarter of the pecan mixture. Pour the orange juice on the bottom of the baking dish.
5. Cover the baking dish, and bake the apples, basting them two or three times, for 30 minutes. Uncover the baking dish, and bake the apples until they are very soft, approximately 10 minutes more.
6. Before you serve the baked apples, spoon some pan juices over each serving.

Fresh Berry Cheesecake

Cheesecakes are irresistible. Unfortunately, a traditional cheesecake is laden with fat and calories. This version uses reduced-fat cream cheese (Neufchâtel) and light sour cream to lower the fat and calorie content. Fresh strawberries and blueberries add fantastic color and flavor to the cake. **Tip:** *To* *prevent any lumps in your cheesecake batter, be certain that the cream cheese is whipped until it is light and fluffy.*

1½ cups graham-cracker crumbs
  2 tablespoons plus 1 tablespoon unsalted butter, melted
  1 pound Neufchâtel
  ½ cup sugar
  1 teaspoon vanilla
1½ cups light sour cream
  1 teaspoon grated lemon zest
  3 eggs
  2 cups strawberries, hulled and sliced
  1 cup blueberries

PREPARATION: 10 minutes
COOKING: 35 minutes
CHILLING: 2 hours
YIELD: 8 servings

1. To prepare the crust, combine the graham-cracker crumbs and the 2 tablespoons of butter in a bowl. Lightly butter a 10-inch pie plate. Press the crumbs into the plate.
2. Heat the oven to 325°F.
3. To prepare the filling, beat the Neufchâtel until it is smooth. Add the remaining 1 tablespoon of butter, sugar, vanilla, sour cream, and lemon zest, and blend the ingredients until they are smooth. Beat in the eggs, and whip the filling until it is smooth.
4. Pour the filling into the pie plate. Bake the cake in the center of the oven for 35 minutes or until the filling is just set in the center.
5. Allow the cake to cool on a wire rack, and then place the cake in the refrigerator. Chill the cake until it is set, approximately 2 hours. Arrange the berries over the surface of the cake.

Chocolate-Almond Biscotti

*Biscotti, the traditional twice-baked Italian cookies found in many restaurants, grocery and specialty stores, and cafés, are the ideal cookies for dipping in coffee and cappuccino. (Caffeine in pregnancy is fine for most women—just keep it to no more than 2 cups of coffee per day or 1 cup of cappuccino.) Made without butter and with less sugar than other cookies, biscotti are the perfect snack or dessert. The ingredients vary, but the technique never does: the cookies must first be baked, then cooled and cut, and, finally, baked again. The second baking draws out the moisture, resulting in a hard cookie. **Tips:** To make plain almond biscotti, eliminate the chocolate chips and the cocoa powder and increase the sugar to 1 cup. This cookie is especially good dipped in melted chocolate and cooled until the chocolate has hardened.*

PREPARATION: 15 minutes
BAKING AND COOLING: 1 hour 20 minutes
YIELD: 24 biscotti

2 cups unbleached, all-purpose flour
¾ cup sugar
1 teaspoon baking soda
¼ teaspoon salt
2 tablespoons good-quality cocoa
2 eggs
1 egg yolk
1 tablespoon ouzo
1 teaspoon vanilla
¾ cup whole almonds, lightly toasted and coarsely chopped
⅔ cup semisweet chocolate morsels
    Egg wash made by beating 1 egg with 2 teaspoons water

1. Heat the oven to 300°F.
2. Lightly butter and flour a large baking sheet.
3. In a large bowl, combine the flour, sugar, baking soda, salt, and cocoa, and stir the ingredients well.
4. In another bowl, beat the eggs and egg yolk. Add the ouzo and vanilla.

5. Add the liquid ingredients to the dry ingredients, and stir the mixture with a wooden spoon.

6. Add the almonds and chocolate chips, and stir the mixture until a dough is formed.

7. Turn the dough out onto a lightly floured surface, and knead it for 1 minute. Divide the dough in half. Form each half into a log 10 inches long and 3 inches wide, approximately the size of a loaf of French bread. Transfer the loaves to the prepared baking sheet, separating them by 3 inches, and brush the loaves with the egg wash.

8. Bake the loaves in the center of the oven for 50 minutes. Remove the tray, and place it on a rack for 15 minutes to cool.

9. Carefully transfer the logs to a cutting board. Cut the logs on the diagonal into ¾-inch-thick slices. Place the biscotti back on the tray with the cut side down.

10. Bake the biscotti for 7 minutes. Turn the biscotti over, and bake them 7 minutes longer. Transfer the biscotti to a rack to cool. Store the cookies in airtight containers.

Sinful Chocolate Chip Cookies

There is a reason why these cookies are called sinful: the other dessert recipes in this book are lower in fat and calories than many traditional treats; this recipe is not. A cup of butter, chocolate chips, and a chocolate bar make these cookies rich and satisfying. They are perfect when you feel like indulging.

PREPARATION: 15 minutes
CHILLING: 45 minutes
COOKING: 8 minutes per batch
YIELD: about 52 cookies

¾ cup (1½ sticks) unsalted butter
2 tablespoons freshly ground peanut butter
1 cup sugar
¾ cup brown sugar
2 eggs
1½ teaspoons vanilla
1⅔ cups of unbleached, all-purpose flour

¼ cup whole-wheat flour

2 cups oatmeal, pulverized in a blender or food processor until it has the consistency of flour

½ teaspoon salt

2 teaspoons baking soda

1½ cups semisweet chocolate morsels

1 4-ounce bar white chocolate, grated

1. In a large mixing bowl, cream together the butter, peanut butter, sugar, and brown sugar. Stir in the eggs and vanilla.
2. In a separate bowl, mix together the all-purpose flour, whole-wheat flour, oatmeal, salt, and baking soda.
3. Stir the dry ingredients into the butter mixture. Fold in the chocolate morsels and chocolate bar. Cover the bowl tightly, and chill the dough for 45 minutes.
4. Heat the oven to 375°F.
5. Lightly grease 3 baking sheets. Shape the dough into 1-inch balls, and place them on the prepared trays 2 inches apart, flattening each cookie lightly.
6. Bake the cookies until they are lightly browned around the edges, about 7 to 9 minutes. Allow the cookies to cool for 5 minutes before transferring them to wire racks to cool completely.

Tofu Chocolate Mousse

PREPARATION: 15 minutes
CHILLING: 12 hours
YIELD: 6 servings

Chocolate mousse is a dessert we love but, since it is so rich, rarely eat. Here is a lean version that will fool you. It contains many of the ingredients found in traditional recipes such as semisweet chocolate, vanilla, and strong coffee; but instead of whipping cream and eggs, silken tofu (a good source of calcium) is used. The result: a decadent-tasting dessert that is actually healthful. **Tips:** *Silken tofu, also called aseptic tofu, makes an excellent base for desserts because of its creamy texture. Other methods of melting chocolate* are in a heavy saucepan over very low heat or in a glass bowl over boiling water. An alternative way to serve the mousse is to pour it into a pie shell and slice it as you would a pie.

    5 ounces semisweet chocolate morsels
    ⅓ cup strong coffee such as espresso or French roast
    ½ teaspoon vanilla
    ⅔ cup sugar
    2 pounds silken tofu
    3 tablespoons cocoa powder

1. Melt the chocolate in a double boiler. Add the coffee, and allow the mixture to cool to room temperature.
2. Transfer the mixture to a blender or food processor. Add the remaining ingredients, and puree them until the mixture is smooth.
3. Spoon the mousse into individual desert cups or champagne glasses. Cover the cups or glasses tightly, and chill the mousse overnight.

Apple-Date Crisp

The dates in this recipe add the sweetness to the apples instead of a large amount of refined sugar. **Tip:** *Top this light, fiber-rich dessert with frozen nonfat vanilla yogurt.*

PREPARATION: 15 minutes
BAKING: 30 minutes
YIELD: 4 to 6 servings

    6 medium Cortland apples, *unpeeled,* cored, and thinly sliced
   10 Medjool dates, pitted and snipped
      Juice 1 lemon
    2 teaspoons cinnamon
    ¼ teaspoon nutmeg
    4 tablespoons sugar
    2 tablespoons unsalted butter
    ¼ cup honey

⅓ cup toasted wheat germ

1⅓ cups rolled oats

¾ cup unbleached, all-purpose flour

¼ teaspoon salt

1. Heat the oven to 350°F.
2. Combine the apples, dates, lemon juice, cinnamon, nutmeg, and sugar in a large bowl, and toss the ingredients well. Set the bowl aside.
3. Place the butter and honey in a small saucepan over low heat, and cook the ingredients until they are melted.
4. In another bowl, mix together the wheat germ, oats, flour, and salt. Add the honey mixture to the dry ingredients, and mix the ingredients well.
5. Spread half of the apple mixture on the bottom of a 12-inch oval casserole. Scatter half of the oat topping over the apples. Cover this with the remaining apples and topping.
6. Bake the dessert until the apples are tender and the top is crisp, approximately 30 minutes.

Bread Pudding with Dates and Pecans

This dish may help you sleep when it is consumed at bedtime with a glass of warm milk. Many bread-puddings are laden with fat and calories from butter, eggs, and cream. This one contains only 1 teaspoon of butter and 2 eggs, and substitutes skim milk for cream. **Tip:** *Stale bread works best in bread puddings. Since its moisture has evaporated, the stale bread will act like a sponge and soak up all of the liquid.*

PREPARATION: 20 minutes

BAKING: 45 minutes

YIELD: 6 servings

1 teaspoon butter

2 cups skim milk

2 tablespoons brown sugar

1 teaspoon vanilla

1 teaspoon cinnamon

½ teaspoon nutmeg

2 eggs

4 egg whites

¼ cup honey

4 cups stale peasant bread, cut into ½-inch cubes

1 cup pitted dates, roughly chopped

⅓ cup pecans, roughly chopped

1. Heat the oven to 375°F.
2. Lightly grease an 8-inch baking pan with the butter.
3. In a large bowl, whisk together the skim milk, brown sugar, vanilla, cinnamon, and nutmeg.
4. In another bowl, whisk together the eggs, egg whites, and honey. Add this mixture to the milk mixture.
5. Place the bread in the prepared baking pan. Pour the milk-egg mixture over it, and gently mix in the dates and pecans. Allow the mixture to sit for 15 minutes.
6. Place the pan in the center of a larger, deeper pan. Pour boiling water into the larger pan until it reaches one-third of the way up the sides of the smaller pudding pan.
7. Bake the pudding until it is set and is no longer runny, approximately 45 minutes.

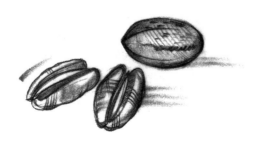

Oatmeal-Apricot-Walnut Cookies

PREPARATION: 15 minutes
BAKING: 10 minutes
YIELD: about 36 cookies

These slightly sweet, low-fat cookies are perfect with a glass of milk or a hot cup of decaffeinated coffee or tea at bedtime (avoid herbal teas in pregnancy since some of them contain potentially dangerous herbs). The cookies offer a nutrition boost as well since they are high in fiber, iron, and protein. **Tip:** *The recipe can be doubled and the extra dough frozen for a future batch of cookies.*

1 cup unbleached, all-purpose flour

⅓ cup whole-wheat flour

½ cup toasted wheat germ

½ teaspoon salt

2 teaspoons baking powder

2 teaspoons baking soda

1 teaspoon cinnamon

½ cup honey

2 tablespoons peanut butter (preferably freshly ground)

2 eggs

2 tablespoons skim milk

1 teaspoon vanilla

1 cup rolled oats

1 cup dried apricots, roughly chopped

⅓ cup walnuts, finely chopped

1. Heat the oven to 350°F.
2. Lightly grease 2 baking sheets.
3. In a large bowl, combine the all-purpose flour, whole-wheat flour, wheat germ, salt, baking powder, baking soda, and cinnamon, mixing the ingredients well.
4. In another bowl, cream the honey and peanut butter together until the mixture is light and fluffy. Beat in the eggs, milk, and vanilla. Stir in the oats, apricots, and walnuts.
5. Roll the dough into balls, using approximately 1 tablespoon for each

ball. Place the balls of dough 2 inches apart on the baking sheets, and flatten the dough slightly. Bake the cookies until they are golden, approximately 10 minutes.

Strawberries, Peaches, and Balsamic Vinegar

Here is a simple, delicious, and healthful dessert.

3 pints fresh strawberries, hulled and halved
2 medium peaches, diced
3 tablespoons plus 1 teaspoon sugar
1 tablespoon plus 2 teaspoons balsamic vinegar

PREPARATION: 10 minutes
RESTING: 3$\frac{1}{2}$ hours
YIELD: 6 servings

1. Place the strawberries and peaches in a large, shallow nonmetal bowl. Sprinkle the berries and peaches with the sugar, tossing them well. Cover the bowl with plastic wrap, and allow the berries and peaches to sit at room temperature for 3 hours, gently stirring the fruit every hour.
2. Thirty minutes before serving the berries and peaches, drizzle them with the balsamic vinegar, tossing them well.

APPENDICES

1 Iron-Rich Dishes

Spinach-Potato Gnocchi with Uncooked Fresh Tomato Sauce (*main course, p. 251*)

Linguine with Clams, Spinach, and Tomatoes (*main course, p. 253*)

Carons Restaurant's Raisin-Bran Muffins (*breakfast or snack, p. 263*)

Autumn Lentil Soup (*soup, p. 268*)

Mussels with Ginger, Tamari, and Herbs (*main course, p. 273*)

Chicken Marinated in Curried Yogurt (*main course, p. 274*)

Linguine with Broccoli and Anchovies (*main course, p. 275*)

Chickpea and White Bean Ragù with Collard Greens (*main course, p. 278*)

Spicy Black Bean Pita with Vegetables (*main course, p. 283*)

2 FOLIC ACID–RICH DISHES

3 CALCIUM-RICH DISHES

Cashew and Black Bean Chili (*main course, p. 196*)

Chickpeas with Kale, Sun-Dried Tomatoes, and Pine Nuts (*main course, p. 202*)

Potato Gnocchi with Butter and Parmesan (*main course, p. 204*)

Classic Risotto (*main course, p. 205*)

Pappardelle with Spinach-Mushroom Sauce (*main course, p. 206*)

Brown Rice, Tofu, and Eggs (*breakfast, p. 222*)

Jalapeño-Corn-Cheddar Muffins (*side dish or snack, p. 232*)

Chilled Chickpea Salad with Raisins, Pine Nuts, Vegetables, and Yogurt (*side dish or main course, p. 235*)

Broiled Kale, Tomato, and Mozzarella Sandwiches (*main course, p. 246*)

Spinach-Potato Gnocchi with Uncooked Fresh Tomato Sauce (*main course, p. 251*)

Southwestern White Bean, Bulgur, and Vegetable Stew (*main course, p. 254*)

Maple-Orange French Toast with Toasted Almonds (*breakfast, p. 258*)

Mushroom-Fontina Omelette (*breakfast or main course, p. 259*)

Oatmeal with Raisins, Dates, and Wheat Germ (*breakfast, p. 260*)

Chickpea, Corn, and Roasted Garlic Soup (*soup, p. 266*)

Penne with Grilled Vegetables and Herbed Ricotta (*main course, p. 270*)

Chicken Marinated in Curried Yogurt (*main course, p. 274*)

Linguine with Broccoli and Anchovies (*main course, p. 275*)

Pinto Beans and Tofu (*main course, p. 277*)

Chickpea and White Bean Ragù with Collard Greens (*main course, p. 278*)

Eggplant-Mozzarella Grinders with Tomato-Spinach Sauce (*main course, p. 281*)

Fresh Berry Cheesecake (*dessert, p. 290*)

Tofu Chocolate Mousse (*dessert, p. 294*)

Bread Pudding with Dates and Pecans (*dessert, p. 296*)

4 FIBER-RICH DISHES

Cashew and Black Bean Chili (*main course, p. 196*)

Curried Basmati Rice and Chicken (*main course, p. 198*)

Turkey Sausage with White Beans, Tomatoes, and Sage (*main course, p. 200*)

Red Lentil and Bulgur Salad with Cashews and Corn (*main course, p. 201*)

Chickpeas with Kale, Sun-Dried Tomatoes, and Pine Nuts (*main course, p. 202*)

Gravid Granola (*breakfast or snack, p. 220*)

Brown Rice, Tofu, and Eggs (*breakfast, p. 222*)

Oatmeal-Prune-Walnut Muffins (*breakfast or snack, p. 223*)

Chilled Couscous Salad (*side dish or main course, p. 227*)

Curried Acorn Squash, Red Lentil, and Apple Soup (*soup, p. 233*)

Chilled Chickpea Salad with Raisins, Pine Nuts, Vegetables, and Yogurt (*side dish or main course, p. 235*)

Risotto with White Beans, Spinach, and Shiitake (*main course, p. 243*)

Southwestern White Bean, Bulgur, and Vegetable Stew (*main course, p. 254*)

Oatmeal with Raisins, Dates, and Wheat Germ (*breakfast, p. 260*)

Whole-Grain, Yogurt, and Berry Pancakes (*breakfast, p. 261*)

Carons Restaurant's Raisin-Bran Muffins (*breakfast or snack, p. 263*)

Buckwheat-Raisin-Pecan Bread (*breakfast or snack, p. 264*)

Chickpea, Corn, and Roasted Garlic Soup (*soup, p. 266*)

Autumn Lentil Soup (*soup, p. 268*)

Mussels with Ginger, Tamari, and Herbs (*main course, p. 273*)

Pinto Beans and Tofu (*main course, p. 277*)

Chickpea and White Bean Ragù with Collard Greens (*main course, p. 278*)

Spicy Black Bean Pitas with Vegetables (*main course, p. 283*)

Creole Red Beans and Brown Rice (*main course, p. 285*)

Apple-Date Crisp (*snack or dessert, p. 295*)

Oatmeal-Apricot-Walnut Cookies (*snack or dessert, p. 298*)

INDEX

Page numbers in **bold type** refer to recipes.

steak, with mushrooms, garlic, and
Gorgonzola, strip, **189–90**
steak restaurants, 83
Steve and Julie's Cape Cod scallops and
pasta, **151–52**
stock:
chicken, **116–17**
fish, **248**
strawberries:
fresh berry cheesecake, **290–91**
peaches, and balsamic vinegar, **299**
whole-grain, yogurt, and berry pancakes,
261–62
strip steak with mushrooms, garlic, and
Gorgonzola, **189–90**
stroke, 8
sudden infant death syndrome (crib death),
17, 71
sugar snap peas with mint and butter, **99–100**
sweeteners, artificial, 30
sweet potato(es):
root-vegetable puree, **115–16**
salad, roasted and chilled, **230–31**
three-potato home fries with corn,
scallions, and cheese, **157–58**
wedges with coriander, **231–32**
swelling, 29, 56, 61
Swiss chard:
penne with pine nuts and, **191–92**
stuffed with gnocchi, **108–9**
and tomato bruschetta, **244–45**
Swiss cheese, and turkey on whole-grain
bread with mustard, lettuce, and
tomato, 79
swordfish:
broiled, with mango-kiwi salsa, **185–86**
lime-ginger, with tomato-avocado salsa,
133–34

tabbouleh, quinoa-basil, **140–41**
tamari:
mussels with ginger, herbs and, **273–74**
-sesame pork tenderloin, grilled, **240–41**
tarragon:
-mustard chicken, **162–63**
penne with chicken, asparagus, lemon
and, **146–47**
teratogens, 17
thiamine (vitamin B$_1$), 27–28
third trimester, 59–64
fetal development in, 59
weight gain in, 60
swelling in, 61
thyme:
linguine with monkfish, pecans, raspberry
vinegar and, **192–93**
linguine with squid, tomatoes, garlic and
herbs, **280–81**
roasted new potatoes with red bell
peppers, fennel and, **183–84**

tofu:
brown rice, and eggs, **222–23**
chocolate mousse, **294–95**
pinto beans and, **277–78**
tomato(es):
-avocado salsa, lime-ginger swordfish with,
133–34
bean, and bread soup (ribollita), **120–22**
-bread salad, **182–83**
caponata, **269–70**
and corn salad, **98**
farfalle with eggplant, zucchini,
mushrooms and, **216–17**
farfalle with spicy sausage, squid, and
onions, **213–14**
feta, olives, and olive oil in pita, **81**
herbed basmati rice with, **122–23**
kale, and mozzarella sandwiches, broiled,
246–47
linguine with clams, spinach and, **253–54**
linguine with squid, garlic, herbs and,
280–81
Mexican black bean "lasagna," **128–31**
paella with salt cod, **194–95**
peeling, seeding, and chopping of, 105
potato and egg medley, **177–78**
pot roast pomodoro, **131–33**
rigatoni with wild mushroom ragú,
167–69
sauce, fresh uncooked, spinach-potato
gnocchi with, **251–53**
sauce, tricolor farfalle with, **148–49**
shellfish and couscous with fresh,
287–88
spaghetti with turkey sausage, red bell
peppers, onions and, **136–37**
-spinach sauce, eggplant-mozzarella
grinders with, **281–83**
stuffed roasted bell peppers, **160–62**
sun-dried, chickpeas with kale, pine nuts
and, **202–4**
sun-dried, twice-cooked potatoes with
corn, shiitake and, **228–29**
and Swiss chard bruschetta, **244–45**
Swiss chard stuffed with gnocchi, **108–9**
turkey sausage with white beans, sage and,
200–201
Tuscan pork chops, **209–10**
white bean, and escarole soup, **164–65**
tortilla(s):
Mexican black bean "lasagna," **128–31**
Spanish, **225–26**
toxoplasmosis, 89–90
trans fatty acids, 9
tricolor farfalle with tomato sauce,
148–49
tuna:
grilled, with navy bean ragú, **141–43**
rotelle, and summer vegetables in a
balsamic vinaigrette, **124–25**

Credit: Melinda Bruno

Hope Ricciotti, M.D., is an obstetrician/gynecologist at Beth Israel Hospital in Boston. Vincent Connelly has worked as a chef for numerous years. They live in Brookline, Massachusetts, with their son, Joey.